Department of Economic and Social Affairs
Population Division

Abortion Policies
A Global Review

Volume III
Oman to Zimbabwe

United Nations
New York, 2002

NOTE

The designations employed and the presentation of the material in this publication do not imply the expression of any opinion whatsoever on the part of the Secretariat of the United Nations concerning the legal status of any country, city or area or of its authorities, or concerning the delimitation of its frontiers or boundaries.

The designations "developed" and "developing" countries and "more developed" and "less developed" regions are intended for statistical convenience and do not necessarily express a judgement about the stage reached by a particular country or area in the development process.

The term "country" as used in the text of this publication also refers, as appropriate, to territories or areas.

Mention of the names of firms and products does not imply the endorsement of the United Nations.

ST/ESA/SER.A/196

UNITED NATIONS PUBLICATION

Sales No. E.02.XIII.5
ISBN 92-1-151365-0

Printed in United Nations, New York

PREFACE

Abortion Policies: A Global Review presents, in three volumes, a country-by-country examination of national policies concerning induced abortion and the context within which abortion takes place. Comparable information is presented for all States Members of the United Nations and non-member States. The countries are arranged in alphabetical order: volume I covers Afghanistan to France; volume II covers Gabon to Norway; and volume III covers Oman to Zimbabwe. In volume I, the country names are those in use as of 31 December 1999.

This report was prepared by the Population Division of the United Nations Secretariat. The assessment was facilitated to a great extent by close cooperation among the United Nations bodies. The financial support of the United Nations Population Fund (UNFPA) is also gratefully acknowledged. Acknowledgement is also due to Reed Boland, who assisted the Population Division in the preparation of this report.

The availability of information on abortion policies varies widely from one country to another. As a result, data for some countries may be incomplete or almost entirely absent. Readers are therefore invited to send any information, comments or corrections they deem useful to the Director, Population Division, Department of Economic and Social Affairs, United Nations Secretariat, New York, NY 10017, United States of America.

CONTENTS

Explanatory notes

Symbols of United Nations documents are composed of capital letters combined with figures.

Various symbols have been used in the tables throughout this report, as follows:

Two dots (..) indicate that data are not available or are not separately reported.

An em dash (—) indicates that the population is less than 500 persons.

A hyphen (-) indicates that the item is not applicable.

A minus sign (-) before a figure indicates a decrease.

A full stop (.) is used to indicate decimals.

Use of a hyphen (-) between years, for example, 1995-2000, signifies the full period involved, from 1 July of the beginning year to 1 July of the end year.

Details and percentages in tables do not necessarily add to totals because of rounding.

Countries and areas are grouped geographically into six major areas: Africa, Asia, Europe, Latin America and the Caribbean, Northern America and Oceania. Those major areas are further divided geographically into 21 regions. In addition, for statistical convenience, the regions are classified as belonging to either of two general groups: more developed or less developed regions. The less developed regions include all regions of Africa, Asia (excluding Japan), Latin America and the Caribbean, Melanesia, Micronesia and Polynesia. The more developed regions comprise Northern America, Japan, Europe and Australia/New Zealand.

The group of least developed countries currently comprises 48 countries: Afghanistan, Angola, Bangladesh, Benin, Bhutan, Burkina Faso, Burundi, Cambodia, Cape Verde, the Central African Republic, Chad, the Comoros, the Democratic Republic of the Congo, Djibouti, Equatorial Guinea, Eritrea, Ethiopia, the Gambia, Guinea, Guinea-Bissau, Haiti, Kiribati, the Lao People's Democratic Republic, Lesotho, Liberia, Madagascar, Malawi, Maldives, Mali, Mauritania, Mozambique, Myanmar, Nepal, the Niger, Rwanda, Samoa, Sao Tome and Principe, Sierra Leone, Solomon Islands, Somalia, the Sudan, Togo, Tuvalu, Uganda, the United Republic of Tanzania, Vanuatu, Yemen and Zambia.

The following abbreviations are used in this volume:

AIDS	acquired immunodeficiency syndrome
ASFR	age-specific fertility rate
CDC	United States Centres for Disease Control and Prevention
CFA	Communauté financière africaine
HIV	human immunodeficiency virus
ICPD	International Conference on Population and Development
IPPF	International Planned Parenthood Foundation
IUD	intrauterine device
KAP	Knowledge, attitude and practice
MCH	Maternal and child health
NHS	National Health Service
PAHO	Pan American Health Organization
TFR	total fertility rate
UNFPA	United Nations Population Fund
UNICEF	United Nations Children's Fund
USAID	United States Agency for International Development
USSR	the former Union of Soviet Socialist Republics
WHO	World Health Organization

INTRODUCTION

Although abortion is commonly practised throughout most of the world and has been practised since long before the beginning of historical records, it is a subject that arouses passion and controversy. Abortion raises fundamental questions about human existence, such as when life begins and what it is that makes us human. Abortion is at the heart of such contentious issues as the right of women to control their own bodies, the nature of the State's duty to protect the unborn, the tension between secular and religious views of human life and the individual and society, the rights of spouses and parents to be involved in the abortion decision, and the conflicting rights of the mother and the foetus. Also central to a consideration of abortion is one of the most highly controversial social issues of all, sexuality. Any discussion of abortion almost inevitably leads to a consideration of how a pregnancy came about and ways that the pregnancy could have been prevented by the use of contraceptive methods. As the new century begins, these questions and issues continue to occupy a significant place in public discourse around the world.

This study does not attempt to answer any of these questions or resolve these controversies. Rather, it aims at providing objective information about the nature of laws and policies relating to abortion. It consists of an analysis of abortion law and policy in all countries, both developed and developing. Included in this analysis is information on the social and political settings of these developments, the ways in which these laws and policies have been formulated, and how they have evolved over time. Where possible, data on the incidence of abortion have been cited. Although information on the incidence of abortion and the setting within which abortion takes place are not the focus of the study, these data are provided to enrich the policy picture.

I. MAJOR DIMENSIONS OF ABORTION POLICY

A. Practical challenges

Preparing a worldwide overview of abortion law and policy and an analysis of recent developments involves a number of major challenges. Some are largely practical in nature. Legal materials in many countries, particularly in the developing countries, are difficult to obtain. The legal infrastructure of some countries is not well developed, laws in force have not been collected or brought up to date and information about laws is not widely disseminated even within the country. Other more pressing social and economic problems often consume scarce resources that otherwise might be devoted to the publication and consolidation of legislation and court decisions. Wars, civil disturbances, dramatic changes in Governments and even legal systems also contribute to this problem, making it difficult in a few countries even to ascertain what laws are in effect. In some countries language is also a barrier, as legislation is published in a vernacular that is not widely known outside the country or is not accurately translated. A further complication arises from the federal nature of certain countries. As the individual sub-jurisdictions—usually states—of these countries have their own separate laws, more than one abortion law may be in effect within a country. When the inevitable delays in the communication of legal and policy changes are taken into consideration, the challenge of compiling accurate information can be formidable.

Moreover, the legal provisions governing abortion in many countries are not always conveniently located within one text. The most common place in which such provisions appear is a country's criminal code or criminal laws relating to offences against persons, for abortion has, at least in the last two centuries, been considered a criminal offence of a highly serious nature. However, with the movement during the last half of the twentieth century to liberalize abortion laws, this is no longer invariably the case; consequently, legal provisions on abortion can be found in a variety of places. Some countries have incorporated liberalized abortion provisions into their criminal codes. Others have enacted special abortion laws that are separate from criminal codes. Thus it is possible for a criminal code to prohibit abortions, while a law on abortion will describe the circumstances under which abortions are allowed. In still other countries, public health codes or medical ethics codes may contain special provisions that clarify how to interpret an abortion law. For example, a medical ethics code may specify the circumstances under which it is ethically acceptable for a physician to perform an abortion. In a final group of countries, mostly common-law countries (see below), abortion may not be governed by a specific law, but by a court decision. In a few cases, the existence of multiple texts, each with conflicting provisions, can make it difficult to determine the exact nature of the law and policy concerning abortion in a specific country.

B. Conceptual challenges

1. World legal systems

Even when specific legal materials are available, other challenges abound. One major problem relates to the wide variations in the sources of abortion law. Although in recent years tentative efforts have been made to internationalize or standardize some aspects of law, most notably through international and regional bodies, abortion law, like most law in the countries of the world, is governed by widely differing legal systems. These systems are based on varying sets of principles; they formulate issues and define terms in dissimilar ways. Comparing the treatment of a specific topic under these systems is, of necessity, a hazardous undertaking.

In general, the majority of countries at the beginning of the twenty-first century adhere to one of three major legal systems: civil law, including what was once denominated "socialist law"; common law; and Islamic law. Civil law, which derives ultimately from Roman law, and more recently from the Napoleonic Code enacted by the Government of France at the beginning of the nineteenth century, is a system based primarily on codified laws, such as civil codes, penal codes, family codes and commercial codes, each devoted to a specific topic. These codes have been designed by Governments to serve as a general guide to proper conduct for individuals, with the goal of protecting justice and morality in society as a whole. Civil law places an emphasis on social responsibility, and the rights of the person are viewed within a social context rather than as a separate and inalienable characteristic of individuals. Interpretation of the laws by judges plays a relatively minor role in shaping law under civil systems.

One major branch of civil law is socialist law, which was enacted in the twentieth century, after the First and Second World Wars, by the newly created Marxist States in Eastern Europe and parts of Asia. Like civil law, socialist law is based on codification, largely of Marxist and socialist principles, and allows judges little room for interpretation of laws, except to conform to those principles. It emphasizes primarily the good of society as a whole, not the rights of individuals, and establishes a sort of guide for conduct. It differs from the civil law model in that it was initially imposed as a means of radically transforming the economic and social bases of society, as well as the behaviour and attitudes of its people. It was only after this transformation occurred that it came to function as a means of preserving the order of society.

In contrast, common law has its origins not in codes, but in court determinations made by judges within the lands governed by the English crown. Law was viewed primarily not as a guide for conduct, but as a means of resolving disputes by individuals. It emphasized principles of self-reliance and individual rights such as property rights and freedom of contract more than the order and welfare of society. Under a common law system, law changes and progresses not primarily by means of enactment by the Government, but through the development of a body of court decisions containing the changing interpretations of judges as social conditions change. Although statutes are enacted under the common law system, judges are given much greater leeway than under the civil law system to interpret these statutes in novel ways. Hence, under the common law system, law is more fluid and less static than under the civil law system.

Islamic law, known as Shariah, which can be viewed as an example of a larger category of religious law, differs in important ways from both civil law and common law. The primary difference is in its conception of law as inseparable from religion, so that no distinctions exist between the secular and the religious, as there are under the civil and common law systems. Law under Islam is based primarily on the text of the Qu'ran, the holy book of Islam, and the *sunnah*, the collection of acts and statements made by the prophet Mohammed, and is considered a guide for human conduct. Owing to its reliance on these texts, Islamic law is for the most part fixed and viewed as unchanging, except with respect to issues and situations not specifically encountered within the Qu'ran and *sunnah*. In these cases, Islamic jurists engage in interpretation and employ deductive or analogical reasoning leading to consensus.

In practice, only in very few cases does the law of any individual country conform exactly to one of the above models. Most legal systems contain elements of more than one model, drawing as well on local indigenous legal traditions. Two recent trends tending to break down these distinctions between the systems are of particular significance. One is the tendency of common law and civil law systems to merge; countries that initially followed a common law tradition have engaged in greater efforts to codify laws, while countries that relied mainly on a civil law tradition have given greater interpretive powers to courts. This was especially evident at the end of the twentieth century as numerous civil law countries established new constitutional courts with wide authority to rule on the validity of legislative enactments. The second is the collapse of the socialist Governments of the former Union of Soviet Socialist Republics and Eastern Europe since 1990 and the withering away of the particularly socialist elements of their law. Naturally, some countries have not followed these trends. For example, China, Cuba, Viet Nam and the Democratic People's Republic of Korea still maintain socialist legal systems. Yet, even in a number of these countries, the law, at least in commercial areas, is moving away from socialist principles as their Governments increasingly turn to capitalist models of economic development.

Moreover, laws in many countries, although based on one of the above models, have been strongly influenced by local legal and cultural traditions. Religions play or have played an important role in shaping legislation in a number of countries, particularly law relating to personal relationships, such as marriage, family interactions, children and inheritance. Although not accepted as official law, canon law as developed by the Roman Catholic Church has been a significant force in countries with large Catholic populations such as Portugal, Spain and the countries of Latin America, as have Shintoism and Buddhism in Japan. Local customary law, as practised by indigenous populations before the advent of European colonialism, has played a similar role in many developing countries of Africa and Oceania. There, much of the law dealing with personal relationships—mostly family law—is based on the traditions of various ethnic groups.

One of the most challenging and complex problems that has faced many developing countries since their independence, with the exception of those in Latin America, is how to integrate and harmonize the various legal traditions in operation within their boundaries, including religious-based law, customary law, and the common law and civil law imposed by or imported from Western countries. Different strategies have been tried. Some have preserved religious and customary law within the sphere of personal relationships while relying on colonial-based law in other areas of life. Some, such as Indonesia, have tried to blend the two to form a unique national system. Some, including Turkey and Japan, have almost entirely adopted Western models similar to those of France, Germany and Switzerland. Owing to civil unrest and economic hardship, a few countries have not yet begun the process and have left colonial laws intact. Most recently, some countries, such as Afghanistan, Iran, The Sudan and, increasingly, Pakistan, have moved to Islamic models.

Despite the hybrid nature of law in many countries, their legal systems can still be broadly categorized under the three major systems, resulting in great part from the phenomenon of colonialism, which was experienced by almost all developing countries from the sixteenth to the twentieth centuries. The United Kingdom of Great Britain and Northern Ireland and most of the countries once under its colonial rule have followed a common law path. Thus, Australia, Bangladesh, Canada, India, Ireland, Malaysia, New Zealand, Pakistan, Singapore and the United States of America as well as the anglophone countries of Africa, the Caribbean and Oceania have adopted common law. Most of the remaining countries of Europe, including Belgium, France, Portugal and Spain and the developing countries formerly under their control, adhere to a civil law system. Among these countries are those of Latin America, non-anglophone sub-Saharan Africa, the former Soviet republics of Central and Western Asia, and various other developing countries. In addition, the law of a number of countries of Northern Africa and the Middle East has been significantly influenced by French civil law and, as noted above, Turkey and Japan have adopted civil law models. Islamic law is of greatest importance in the countries of Northern Africa and Western Asia, regions with predominantly Muslim populations, and strongly influences personal law in other countries such as Bangladesh, Indonesia, Malaysia and Pakistan.

2. *Abortion laws within legal systems*

The above differences in legal systems and in sources of laws have left a strong imprint on the abortion law of various countries. Most common law countries, other than the United States, have abortion laws that are based on various English laws and court decisions. Some take as their model the

Offences Against the Person Act of 1861. Under this Act it was prohibited "unlawfully" to use any means to procure an abortion either for oneself or for another person or unlawfully to supply means for that end, and the prescribed punishment was imprisonment. Originally, this Act was interpreted as prohibiting all abortions, except those performed on the grounds of necessity, in order to save the life of the pregnant woman. Other countries follow the English court decision, *Rex* v. *Bourne*, in which it was held that abortions performed for serious physical or mental health reasons would not be considered "unlawful" under the 1861 Act. Still other countries have looked to the British Abortion Act of 1967, which sets forth broad health, foetal impairment and socio-economic indications for abortions, in general until the twenty-fourth week of pregnancy.

The abortion laws of many civil law countries are based on the abortion provisions of the French Napoleonic Code of 1810, the 1939 French version of that Code or the 1979 abortion law of France. Under the 1810 Napoleonic Code, any person who by any means procured the abortion of a pregnant woman was punished with imprisonment, as was a pregnant woman who procured her own abortion, although it was understood that an abortion could be performed when necessary to save the life of the pregnant woman. To the provisions of the 1810 Code, the 1939 French Penal Code added language specifically allowing an abortion to be performed to save the life of the pregnant woman. The 1979 Law allows a woman who is in a state of distress to have an abortion performed on request during the first ten weeks of pregnancy after she undergoes counselling and waits a week, and later in pregnancy on other serious grounds. In contrast to the common law system, court interpretations of these laws play a minor role.

Unlike the situation in either the common law or civil law countries, no single abortion text or court case can be identified as the model for most modern Islamic abortion laws. The Qu'ran and the *sunnah*, the two primary sources of Islamic law, do not deal specifically with abortion. Moreover, until recently, Islamic criminal laws were not always codified. Consequently, Islamic law adopts a number of approaches towards abortion, depending upon which of the five major schools of Islamic law is followed. In general, the attitude of Islamic law towards abortion is dependent upon whether the abortion is performed before ensoulment, the time at which a foetus gains a soul. This is most often viewed as occurring 120 days into a pregnancy, but is also interpreted as occurring at 40 days. Some schools permit abortion for justifiable reasons before ensoulment, while others generally prohibit it at all points of pregnancy. All schools, however, allow abortion at any time during pregnancy in order to save the life of the pregnant woman. In contrast to the situation under both common law and civil law, the punishment for abortion under classic Islamic law is payment of a sum of money to the relatives of the foetus. The amount of payment depends upon the stage of pregnancy reached at the time of the abortion. Before ensoulment, the foetus or embryo passes through a number of developmental stages; these are variously described in Arabic as "the lump" or "something that clings."

Owing to the different treatments of abortion in these three legal systems, a number of ambiguities arise in interpreting specific indications for abortion, making any comparison challenging. The most widely accepted indication for abortion—to save the life of the pregnant woman—provides a good example. Broadly speaking, this indication is valid in two categories of countries: those with abortion laws that specifically mention it and those with laws in which it is not mentioned but is inferred from the general criminal law principles of necessity. In the latter, an abortion, although considered illegal, can be performed on the rationale that it is necessary to preserve a greater good, the life of the pregnant woman.

In practical terms, these two situations differ substantially. In the first, a physician contemplating the performance of an abortion is able to point to a specific legal provision authorizing such an act and be reasonably certain that he or she was acting within the law. In the second, no such certainty exists, only a general principle that could be raised as a defence if the physician were prosecuted for performing an illegal abortion. It would then be a matter for a court to determine after a trial. The result is that in the latter case, a physician would in general exercise much more caution in determining whether to perform an abortion to save the life of the pregnant woman.

A similar situation arises with respect to laws that permit an abortion to be performed to preserve the health of a pregnant woman. An important distinction holds between countries with laws that specifically state that an abortion is allowed to preserve the health of a pregnant woman and countries in which a court or courts have, through their interpretation of a law that lacks specific provisions, allowed such an abortion to take place. In the former, a physician can be reasonably certain of acting within the law; again, in the latter, he or she might have to rely on a court decision as a defence in criminal proceedings. Moreover, unless the court whose decision is being relied on is the highest court in the country, its ruling may not be definitive. Even in common law countries, lower courts are not bound by the decision of another lower court, although they may pay it great heed. Indeed, one reason that the United Kingdom enacted the 1967 Abortion Act was to give statutory expression to *Rex* v. *Bourne* and ensure that it would be considered the law of the land. By means of this legislation, it hoped to provide physicians with greater guidance and legal security in the performance of legal abortions.

Additional ambiguities are connected with the health indication for abortion. One is that a number of countries use the term "health" in their abortion laws without specifying what it encompasses. Thus it is unclear whether they intend abortions to be allowed in cases of a threat to mental and physical health or only physical health. If one followed the definition of health accepted by the World Health Organization, for which health is a very broad term—"a state of complete physical, mental, and social well-being and not merely the absence of disease or infirmity"—then abortion for health reasons would be very common (WHO, 1994b). It is doubtful, however, that such an expansive definition of health was intended by many of the abortion laws enacted so long ago. The question arises as to whether health should be interpreted as historically understood or in the light of current thinking. Similarly, unless a country specifies that the threat must be serious or grave or permanently disabling, it is unclear what degree of threat to health is intended.

Other terms referring to health are even more ambiguous. Some countries allow abortions for "therapeutic" purposes or permit abortions for the purpose of "medical or surgical treatment". Others provide that the threat to health by continuation of the pregnancy must be greater than the threat posed by its termination. Statistically, during the first trimester, a pregnancy is always a greater threat to health than its termination; it is therefore difficult to determine how to interpret this phrase. A literal interpretation would allow abortion under most circumstances. Given such a lack of clarity in the laws, the designation of a country as allowing abortions for health purposes can cover a wide variety of situations. These range from allowing abortion only in cases that threaten permanent and serious damage to physical health, to cases that threaten mental health owing to socio-economic distress, to the case of "medical or surgical treatment", which is essentially abortion on request. Unless the issue has been the subject of litigation in the courts, or a target of significant legal analysis of the nature of the threat in legal commentaries, it is difficult to ascertain exactly what the circumstances must be to justify an abortion.

Procedural requirements to establish the presence of an indication for abortion are also a factor in determining the exact nature of an indication for abortion. In the context of the indication of health, it may be necessary for two or three physicians to attest to the threat to health. A great deal of difference exists between this and the situation in which the physician who is willing to perform the abortion is the only judge of whether the indication is present. In the context of abortions performed in cases of pregnancy due to rape or incest, a variety of mandated procedures also prevail. In some countries, the incident of rape or incest must be reported to police or judicial authorities, while in others the pregnant woman must only reasonably believe that the pregnancy was the result of rape or incest. Some specify no procedural requirements or, conversely, require a judicial determination that the pregnancy was the result of rape or incest. Such differences again produce a significant variation in the nature of the indication of pregnancy due to rape or incest in various countries.

The terminology employed under Islamic law presents another formidable challenge in comparing abortion laws. The principles underlying Islamic law differ fundamentally from those of common and civil law, which have at the most basic level a Western orientation; it is therefore difficult to compare laws under the two systems. An example of this problem involves the notion under Islamic law that the crime of abortion is punished not by imprisonment and government-imposed fines, but by the payment of compensation by the perpetrator of the crime to the relatives of the victim of the crime. In the context of abortion, this is entirely foreign to Western law. The problem is also illustrated in the definition of the stages of pregnancy. While Western law does recognize different stages of pregnancy, in present-day law they are almost exclusively defined by weeks of gestation; under Islamic law they can be defined in more descriptive terms such as "the lump," "something that clings," "ensoulment," or "the forming of organs and limbs".

C. Law and policy versus practice

Beyond these conceptual challenges, determining whether the written law or policy of a country conforms to the practice observed or inferred remains a major problem. In many countries where the performance of abortions is generally illegal, statistics indicate that large numbers are being carried out, most of them illegally, with few prosecutions. Of the approximately 50 million abortions carried out every year in the world, estimates place the number performed illegally at 40 per cent (WHO, 1994a). In these countries, law enforcement authorities ignore or tolerate the performance of illegal abortions or even unofficially license clinics for that purpose. A number of factors are responsible for this situation. Among these are the ease with which abortions can be performed, the lack of will or resources to prosecute, particularly in the light of more pressing social needs, and the clandestine nature of the procedure. In some countries where abortion is technically legal, access to authorized facilities and personnel may be limited, or resources to pay for the abortion may be lacking, resulting in more illegal abortions. In a few cases, although abortion is authorized, the Government may not have issued regulations allowing the law to be effectively implemented. In all of these situations, legal action is rarely taken except in the most egregious cases, usually involving the death of a pregnant woman. In some countries, the indifference to abortion is so great that most of those performing abortions or enforcing laws do not know what the provisions of the law actually are. The advent of new scientific developments such as RU-486, the so-called "abortion pill", which makes abortion even easier to perform without the need for special facilities, will in all probability only increase the gap between law and practice.

II. COUNTRY PROFILES: DESCRIPTION AND REVIEW OF VARIABLES

This chapter contains a detailed description of the variables identified on the first page of each country profile. An attempt was made to provide comparable information for each country. Abortion laws can be complex and diverse; consequently, considerable space is dedicated to the description of the coding of the legal grounds for abortion. The section on abortion policy addresses the grounds on which abortion is permitted, and it is followed by a short section describing any additional conditions required by the law. The causes and consequences of induced abortion differ from one country to another. In order to capture some of these differences, explanations of a number of reproductive health indicators are given below. In the background section that follows each country profile, abortion policies and their national context are described in further detail.

A. ABORTION POLICY

1. Grounds on which abortion is permitted

The most commonly cited instances in which abortion is permitted include the following:

a) Intervention to save the life of the woman (life grounds);
b) Preservation of the physical health of the woman (narrow health grounds);
c) Preservation of the mental health of the woman (broad health grounds);
d) Termination of pregnancy resulting from rape or incest (juridical grounds);
e) Suspicion of foetal impairment (foetal defect);
f) Termination of pregnancy for economic or social reasons (social grounds).

These are the grounds for abortion that are coded in the first section of each country profile. A few countries may recognize additional grounds for abortion, including the presence in the mother of the human immunodeficiency virus (HIV); the age of the mother, when the pregnant woman is a minor; or contraceptive failure. These categories have only limited applicability, and they are not coded in this variable. However, detailed descriptions are provided in the background section for the relevant country profiles. The exact wording of many laws differs significantly; therefore, variations in the language and interpretation of each of the grounds are also reviewed in detail on the second page. When it is evident that policy deviates from the exact wording of the law, an asterisk is placed next to the relevant item indicating that the legal or official interpretation usually allows the abortion to be performed on those particular grounds. For example, in countries where the performance of an abortion is specifically prohibited under all circumstances, but where performing an abortion to save the life of the pregnant woman is permitted under the general criminal law principle of "necessity", "saving the life of the woman" is coded as permitted but is followed by an asterisk.

In the limited number of countries where abortion law is determined at the local level rather than at the national level, the coded law is marked with an asterisk and an explanation is given below. Where local laws apply, a detailed description of this situation follows in the "Background" section of the text.

(a) Intervention to save the life of the woman

The performance of abortions is most commonly permitted on the grounds of saving the life of the pregnant woman. Although some countries provide detailed lists of what they consider life-threatening situations, in general, these situations are not specified but left to the judgement of the physician or physicians performing and/or approving the performance of the abortion. Almost all countries allow abortions to be performed to save the life of the pregnant woman either explicitly or under the general criminal law principle of necessity. Exceptions may include Chile, El Salvador and Malta, all of which have amended their abortion laws to eliminate provisions permitting the performance of abortions on certain grounds. Nonetheless, even in these countries, it is unclear whether a defence of necessity would be rejected by a court in the most serious cases of a threat to the life of a pregnant woman.

(b) Preservation of the physical health of the woman

In the majority of countries, abortion is permitted when it is necessary to preserve the physical health of the pregnant woman. The term "physical health", however, has been defined in a number of different ways. In some countries, the definition is narrow, often encompassing lists of conditions that are considered to fall under this category; in other countries, the term "physical health" is broadly defined, allowing much room for interpretation. When possible, the permissible range of interpretations is reviewed in the text. In general, the countries of the British Commonwealth permit a broader definition of health than do the African or Latin American countries adhering to civil law.

In a number of countries, the abortion law does not specify whether the term "health" encompasses both physical and mental health, but merely provides that an abortion is permitted when it averts a risk of injury to the pregnant woman's health. As a rule, the interpretation of health tends to be narrow, referring only to physical health. However, since the law does not make such a distinction, both physical and mental health have been coded as permitted, with an asterisk referring the reader to a footnote explaining this situation. Any distinctions in terms of actual practice are reviewed in the text.

(c) Preservation of the mental health of the woman

Many abortion laws specifically provide for the legal performance of abortions in cases involving a threat to the mental health of the pregnant woman. What constitutes a threat to "mental health," however, varies significantly. In some countries, no definition exists, while in others, most of them Commonwealth countries, mental health is defined to include emotional distress caused to children of the marriage or emotional distress caused to the pregnant woman as a result of her environment. In these cases, the country has been coded as permitting abortions for socio-economic reasons (see below).

Countries coded as permitting abortions to be performed on mental health grounds also include those British Commonwealth countries that have followed the ruling of the landmark British decision, *Rex v. Bourne*, in which it was held that, although the law may not specifically allow abortions to be performed for physical or mental health reasons, such abortions are considered lawful (see above). The extent to which an abortion is permitted on mental health grounds varies from country to country.

(d) Termination of a pregnancy resulting from rape or incest

Permitting abortions to be performed in cases of rape or incest is a common provision of the world's abortion laws. Even in countries with restrictive abortion legislation, such as the Latin American countries, abortion is often allowed on these grounds. Such justifications for the performance of abortions take several forms. Some countries specifically mention rape and incest in their legislation. Other countries refer to these as cases in which the pregnancy is the result of a "criminal offence", with no specification of the nature of the offence. This phrasing of the law is somewhat broader, encompassing statutory rape (consensual sex with a minor) as well as forced rape and incest. Procedural requirements also vary. Some countries require the case to be brought to court or reported to the authorities before permission for an abortion can be granted, thus discouraging many women from seeking to obtain an abortion on these grounds.

(e) *Suspicion of foetal impairment*

As is the case with the juridical grounds for abortion, abortions are often permitted on the grounds of foetal impairment in countries with restrictive abortion laws. Several countries specify the type and level of impairment necessary to justify this ground.

(f) *Termination of pregnancy for economic or social reasons*

The phrasing of laws permitting abortion on socio-medical, social or economic grounds varies widely. Some specifically mention social or economic conditions while others only imply them. For example, in Barbados, the abortion law specifies that, in determining whether the continuation of the pregnancy would involve a risk of injury to the health of the pregnant woman, the medical practitioner must take into account the "pregnant woman's social and economic environment, whether actual or foreseeable". In New South Wales, Australia, where similar wording is employed, reference is made to social and economic stresses. In other cases, as in South Australia and Belize, social and economic grounds are strongly implied: the determination of risk of injury to the health of the pregnant woman must take into account "the woman's actual or reasonably foreseeable environment". Other countries, such as Burundi and Ethiopia, do not permit abortions to be performed on social and economic grounds, but allow such grounds to be taken into consideration in sentencing. Most laws that permit abortions to be performed on social and economic grounds are interpreted quite liberally and, in practice, differ very little from laws that allow abortions on request.

(g) *Availability upon request: abortion permitted on all grounds*

In countries that allow abortions to be performed on request, a pregnant woman seeking an abortion is not required to justify her desire to have an abortion under the law. She needs only to find a physician who is willing to perform the abortion. In a number of countries, such as Albania, Belgium and France, she may be required to state that she is in a situation of crisis or distress. This requirement, however, is purely a formality and the decision to have the abortion is still completely her own so long as she finds a physician who agrees to perform the abortion. These countries have been coded with an asterisk. Even in countries where abortion is allowed on request, time limits are usually set for the performance of the abortion, often within the first trimester. After this stage of pregnancy, the woman must present a valid ground for the abortion to be permitted.

2. *Additional requirements*

This section concerns the additional procedural requirements that must be met before an abortion may be legally performed. It includes requirements relating to consent, personnel permitted to perform abortions, places where abortions may be performed, and the time limits within which abortions may be performed.

B. Reproductive health context

1. *Government view of fertility level*

This variable identifies the Government's perception of the overall acceptability of aggregate national fertility; it is divided into three categories: not satisfactory because too low; satisfactory; and not satisfactory because too high.

2. *Government intervention concerning fertility level*

Governmental intervention concerning the level of fertility is classified as four types: (*a*) to raise the fertility level; (*b*) to maintain the fertility level; (*c*) to lower the fertility level; and (*d*) no intervention or no policy formulated.

3. *Government policies on effective use of modern methods of contraception*

Four categories of governmental policy concerning individual fertility behaviour were adopted to categorize countries according to their level of support for modern methods of contraception:

(*a*) The Government limits access to information, guidance and materials in respect of modern methods of contraception that would enable persons to regulate their fertility more effectively and would help them achieve the desired timing of births and completed family size;

(*b*) The Government does not limit access to information, guidance and materials but provides no support direct or indirect for their dissemination;

(*c*) The Government provides indirect support for the dissemination of information, guidance and materials by subsidizing the operating costs of organizations supporting such activities outside the Government's own services. The indirect support may take various forms, such as direct grants, tax reductions or rebates, or assignment of special status;

(*d*) The Government provides direct support for the dissemination of information, guidance and materials within government facilities.

4. *Percentage of currently married woman using modern contraception*

The percentage of currently married women aged 15-49 years that use modern contraception provides an indication of the actual availability of contraceptives. Use of contraception is inversely associated with abortion at the aggregate level. A low availability of modern contraceptives tends to be correlated with high abortion rates. Conversely, when modern contraceptive methods are widely available and are used effectively, abortion rates tend to be relatively lower. At the individual level, the use of contraception is positively associated with the practice of abortion. Women that have used a contraceptive method are at some time, on average, more likely to resort to abortion than those that have never used any contraceptive method. However, women that have had an abortion are more likely to use contraception than women that have never done so. It has been suggested that contraceptive use increases after an abortion because of the provision of contraceptives and counselling in abortion clinics.

Information on contraceptive use was obtained primarily from representative national sample surveys of women of reproductive age conducted by various governmental and non-governmental agencies. The data pertain to women currently married or in a consensual union.

5. *Total fertility rate*

The total fertility rate (TFR) measures the number of children a woman would have during her lifetime if she were to follow current age-specific fertility rates. For most countries, the rates presented here are medium-variant estimates for the period 1995-2000 and are based on available data that have been adjusted to reflect rates for the same five-year period.

6. Age-specific fertility rate for women aged 15-19

The age-specific fertility rate (ASFR) for women aged 15-19 is an indicator of current rates of adolescent fertility. Specifically, the rate is the number of births to women aged 15-19 per 1,000 women in that age group. In general, adolescent fertility has been increasing in a number of countries in recent years. Many of these young mothers are unmarried, have no means of financial support and may face social disgrace as a result of the pregnancy. Consequently, many resort to abortion.

7. Government concern about morbidity and mortality resulting from induced abortion

This variable indicates government views of existing health complications resulting from induced abortion and notes any expression of special concern. The information was obtained from government replies to the Eighth United Nations Inquiry among Governments on Population and Development in 1998, or from the Seventh Inquiry in 1992. If a Government did not respond to the Inquiry, statements made in official government documents and publications were reviewed in order to determine that Government's concern about morbidity and mortality resulting from induced abortion.

8. Government concern about complications of childbearing and childbirth

This variable indicates whether the Government views existing health complications resulting from childbearing and childbirth with special concern. The information was obtained from the government reply to the Eighth and Seventh United Nations Population Inquiries among Governments, conducted by the Population Division. If a Government did not respond to the Inquiry, statements made in official government documents and publications were reviewed in order to determine that Government's concern about complications of childbearing and childbirth.

9. Maternal mortality ratio

Induced abortion accounts for a large percentage of maternal mortality in developing countries, particularly in those with very restrictive abortion laws. According to the World Health Organization (WHO), a maternal death is defined as "the death of a woman while pregnant or within 42 days of termination of pregnancy regardless of the duration and site of the pregnancy, from any cause related to or aggravated by the pregnancy or its management, but not from accidental or incidental causes" (WHO, 1974, p. 764, cited in PAHO, 1990). Thus, the maternal mortality ratio measures the number of maternal deaths occurring in a given year per 100,000 live births during that year. Ideally, both that ratio and the proportion of deaths attributable to abortion should be included. Because induced abortion is frequently performed illegally, however, only deaths occurring in hospitals are reported, and even then the cause of death is often omitted. This practice greatly underestimates the number of deaths caused by abortion. Given these additional reasons for unreliability of data, the proportion of deaths attributable to abortion was not included.

Caution should be exercised when examining maternal mortality ratios and making comparisons across countries. Under-registration of maternal deaths varies by country, as does under-registration of the cause of death. Even in developed countries, such as the United States of America, maternal mortality has been found to be under-registered by as much as 27 per cent (PAHO, 1990). Under-registration of births is also significant, and when the degree of under-reporting of births and deaths differs, the direction of the bias will also differ. Limiting the puerperal period to 42 days also introduces a downward bias. Studies conducted in the United States have shown that 16 per cent of the "deaths associated with pregnancy, delivery and the puerperium occur between 42 days and one year afterwards" (PAHO, 1990, p. 119). Given the unreliability of data on maternal mortality and the lack of information for many countries, ratios for both the country and the region are included with each country profile. Where both figures are available and it is thought that the country in question might have very deficient vital statistics, the regional figure provides an idea of the extent of possible bias of the national figures.

10. Female life expectancy at birth

Female life expectancy at birth is included as a measure of women's overall health. The figure represents the number of years that a newborn female child would live, on average, if she were subjected during her lifetime to the risk of dying observed for each age group in the current year. For most countries, all the measures are medium-variant estimates for the period 1995-2000 unless otherwise specified and therefore permit cross-country comparisons.

III. COUNTRY PROFILES

Oman

ABORTION POLICY

Grounds on which abortion is permitted:

To save the life of the woman	Yes
To preserve physical health	No
To preserve mental health	No
Rape or incest	No
Foetal impairment	No
Economic or social reasons	No
Available on request	No

Additional requirements:

Information is not readily available.

REPRODUCTIVE HEALTH CONTEXT

Government view on fertility level:	Too high
Government intervention concerning fertility level:	To lower
Government policy on contraceptive use:	No support provided
Percentage of currently married women using modern contraception (under age 50,[a,b] 1995):	18[c]
Total fertility rate (1995-2000):	5.9
Age-specific fertility rate (per 1,000 women aged 15-19, 1995-2000):	80
Government has expressed particular concern about:	
Morbidity and mortality resulting from induced abortion	..
Complications of childbearing and childbirth	..
Maternal mortality ratio (per 100,000 live births, 1990):	
National	190
Western Asia	320
Female life expectancy at birth (1995-2000):	73.3

[a] Adjusted from source to exclude breast-feeding.
[b] Households of nationals of the country.
[c] Preliminary or provisional.

Source: Population Policy Data Bank maintained by the Population Division of the Department of Economic and Social Affairs of the United Nations Secretariat. For additional sources, see list of references.

BACKGROUND

Abortion in Oman is governed by the provisions of the Penal Code of 16 February 1974 (Law No. 7/1974). Under the Code, the performance of abortions is prohibited unless there exists a situation of necessity and the abortion is carried out by a physician in the sincere conviction that it is the only means of saving the life of the pregnant woman. The woman must consent to the abortion.

A person who intentionally performs an illegal abortion without the consent of the woman is subject to at least five years' imprisonment. If the woman consents, the person performing the abortion is subject to six months' to six years' imprisonment. A woman who performs her own abortion or lets another person do so is subject to three months' to three years' imprisonment. If the abortion results in the death of the woman, the person performing it is subject to at least seven years' imprisonment.

The Government seeks to maintain the population growth rate but lower the total fertility rate, which is estimated at 5.9 children per woman for the period 1995-2000. The 1995 modern contraceptive prevalence rate is estimated at 18 per cent. Contraceptives are available through private hospitals, dispensaries and commercial outlets.

Government policy has focused mainly on improving the economic, social and health conditions of the Omani population. Whereas progress in achieving economic and social development goals was impressive during the 1970s and early 1980s, the steep fall of oil prices in 1986 resulted in a decline in per capita income, a large budget deficit and a slowdown in the implementation of many of the development programmes. At current rates of extraction, the oil reserves of Oman will be depleted in another 20-25 years. In addition, population growth is expected to result in increasing pressure on the already scarce water resources. In December 1993, the Government conducted the first comprehensive census of Oman and used the data to formulate its fifth five-year economic plan for the period 1996-2000.

Source: Population Policy Data Bank maintained by the Population Division of the Department of Economic and Social Affairs of the United Nations Secretariat. For additional sources, see list of references.

ABORTION POLICY

Grounds on which abortion is permitted:

To save the life of the woman	Yes
To preserve physical health	Yes
To preserve mental health	Yes
Rape or incest	No
Foetal impairment	No
Economic or social reasons	No
Available on request	No

Additional requirements:

Information is not readily available.

REPRODUCTIVE HEALTH CONTEXT

Government view on fertility level:	Too high
Government intervention concerning fertility level:	To lower
Government policy on contraceptive use:	Direct support provided
Percentage of currently married women using modern contraception (aged 15-49, 1996/97):	17
Total fertility rate (1995-2000):	5.0
Age-specific fertility rate (per 1,000 women aged 15-19, 1995-2000):	90
Government has expressed particular concern about:	
Morbidity and mortality resulting from induced abortion	No
Complications of childbearing and childbirth	Yes
Maternal mortality ratio (per 100,000 live births, 1990):	
National	340
South-central Asia	560
Female life expectancy at birth (1995-2000):	65.1

Source: Population Policy Data Bank maintained by the Population Division of the Department of Economic and Social Affairs of the United Nations Secretariat. For additional sources, see list of references.

Pakistan

BACKGROUND

Until 1990, abortion in Pakistan was regulated by century-old provisions of the Penal Code of 1860 which had been developed for India by the British colonial government and remained in force in Pakistan following independence. Under this Code, abortion was a crime unless performed in good faith in order to save the pregnant woman's life. Article 312 of the Penal Code provided that any person performing an illegal abortion was subject to imprisonment for three years and/or a fine; if the woman was "quick with child", the penalty was imprisonment for up to seven years and payment of a fine. The same penalty applied to a woman who caused herself to miscarry.

Following a 1989 decision of the Pakistani Supreme Court, which held that part of the Penal Code of 1860 dealing with offences against the human body was invalid because it was repugnant to the injunctions of Islam, Pakistan revised its law in this area, reformulating a number of its provisions to conform to the principles of Islamic law. The revised law came into effect provisionally in 1990 and became permanent law in 1997.

Under the new law, abortion offences are divided into two categories depending on the stage of pregnancy during which the abortion is performed. Abortions carried out before the unborn child's organs have been formed are prohibited except when performed in good faith for the purpose of saving the life of the woman or providing necessary treatment. The punishment is the imposition of the penalty for a *ta'zir* crime—that is penalties other than the traditional Islamic penalties of retaliation and compensation—in this case, imprisonment for up to three years if the woman consented and up to ten years if she did not. Abortions carried out after some of the unborn child's organs or limbs have formed are prohibited except for the first of the above reasons. The penalty is, in general, the imposition of *diyah*, or compensation to the heirs of the victim by the offender. If the child is born dead, the amount of *diyah* is one twentieth of that for a full person; if the child is born alive but dies as a result of an act of the offender, a full *diyah* is payable; if the child is born alive, but dies for any other reason, *ta'zir* shall be imposed consisting of up to seven years' imprisonment. Under Islamic law, organs and limbs are usually deemed to be formed in a foetus by the fourth month of pregnancy.

There are a number of interesting features of the law. One is that it appears to represent an expansion of indications for abortion in early pregnancy. Abortions are allowed not only to save the life of the pregnant woman, but also to provide "necessary treatment," a phrase that, although not defined, is likely to encompass threat to health of some sort. Another is the law's hybrid nature. On the one hand, the law retains features of the old law. Penalties for the crime are still dependent upon which of two stages of development the pregnancy has reached and on whether the woman consents or not. In some cases, they also include imprisonment, now denominated a *ta'zir* penalty. On the other hand, the law defines the stages of pregnancy in terms of the formation of organs or limbs according to Islamic law principles and it introduces the distinctive Islamic law penalty of compensation or *diyah* in the case of late-term pregnancies. Finally, the new law is somewhat ambiguous: there is no clear demarcation of the two stages of pregnancy or definition of what constitutes "necessary treatment". Indeed, the law has been criticized for just this reason.

In part because of the lack of data on the incidence of induced abortion, illegal abortion has not been an area of major governmental concern in Pakistan. However, illegal abortion does take place and complications from septic abortions are believed to be a major cause of maternal mortality. Only 5-10 per cent of births occur in hospitals. According to a study conducted in a hospital at Karachi in 1985, about 300 maternal deaths per 100,000 live births were due to complications from abortion. Multiple unspaced pregnancies

---

Source: Population Policy Data Bank maintained by the Population Division of the Department of Economic and Social Affairs of the United Nations Secretariat. For additional sources, see list of references.

combined with poor maternal nutrition and scarce maternity services have resulted in high (though declining) maternal mortality rates, estimated at 340 deaths per 100,000 live births (1990).

Family planning in Pakistan has a long history. A family planning association was established in 1953, the National Population Programme was begun in 1955 and the Population Welfare Programme has been part of the National Five-Year Plans since 1960. Despite these early efforts in family planning in Pakistan, modern contraceptive prevalence remains low. It was estimated in a Demographic and Health Survey at 11 per cent in 1991 and 17 per cent in 1994-1995. Under 5 per cent of the population is estimated to have easy access to family planning services. However, although contraceptive use remains low, demand is increasing and the Programme has succeeded in creating awareness and demand for family planning services.

The total fertility rate has hovered since the late 1960s at about 6.0 children per woman and is currently (1995-2000) at 5.0 children per woman. Greatly concerned by the rapid population growth, the Government of Pakistan formulated a new population policy in 1991 that included an improved family planning programme. The Population Welfare Division's 1993-1998 comprehensive programme sought to reduce the average annual rate of population growth from 2.9 to 2.6 per cent, mainly by increasing coverage of the family planning programme from 5 to 70 per cent in rural areas and from 54 to 100 per cent in urban areas. The 1996 population growth rate was 2.8 per cent. Following the International Conference on Population and Development (ICPD), held in Cairo in 1994, Pakistan has gradually integrated family planning with reproductive health services and adopted a voluntary and target-free approach to family planning services. The Government continues to focus on improved delivery of health care to an overwhelmingly rural population.

Source: Population Policy Data Bank maintained by the Population Division of the Department of Economic and Social Affairs of the United Nations Secretariat. For additional sources, see list of references.

ABORTION POLICY

Grounds on which abortion is permitted:

To save the life of the woman	Yes
To preserve physical health	No
To preserve mental health	No
Rape or incest	No
Foetal impairment	No
Economic or social reasons	No
Available on request	No

Additional requirements:

Not applicable.

REPRODUCTIVE HEALTH CONTEXT

Government's view on fertility level:	Satisfactory
Government's intervention concerning fertility level:	No intervention
Government's policy on contraceptive use:	Indirect support provided
Percentage of currently married women using modern contraception (aged 15-49):	..
Total fertility rate (1995-2000):	..
Age-specific fertility rate (per 1,000 women aged 15-19, 1995-2000):	..
Government has expressed particular concern about:	
Morbidity and mortality resulting from induced abortion	..
Complications of child-bearing and childbirth	..
Maternal mortality ratio (per 100,000 live births, 1990):	
National	..
Oceania	680
Female life expectancy at birth (1995-2000):	..

Source: Population Policy Data Bank maintained by the Population Division of the Department of Economic and Social Affairs of the United Nations Secretariat. For additional sources, see list of references.

Palau

BACKGROUND

The status of abortion law in Palau is not entirely clear. Prior to its independence in 1994, Palau was one component of the Trust Territory of the Pacific Islands. Though nominally under the control of the United Nations, the Trust Territory's day-to-day administration, legislation, and adjudication were the responsibility of the United States of America. As such, the legal system of the Territory was based on the Code of the Trust Territory, imposed by the United States after the Second World War, and its development through court decisions interpreting the common law as generally understood and applied in the United States.

The Trust Territory Code provided that every person who unlawfully caused the miscarriage or premature delivery of a woman, with intent to do so, was guilty of the crime of abortion. Although the Code prohibited all abortions, general criminal law principles of necessity could have been relied upon as a defence in the case of an abortion performed to save the life of a pregnant woman. In 1971, however, the Appellate Division of the High Court of the Trust Territory ruled that these abortion provisions were invalid because they were so vague and indefinite as to constitute a denial of due process of law (*Trust Territory v. Tarkong*, 1971). The Court objected to the fact that the provisions did not set forth any circumstances under which abortions were legal. No replacement abortion provision was ever enacted. Since the United States Supreme Court decision in *Roe v. Wade* established the right of a woman to obtain an abortion in the first two trimesters of pregnancy only two years later, perhaps none was thought necessary as Trust Territory courts were required to follow United States common law.

The above case suggests that up until independence, no valid abortion law was in effect in Palau and that the holding of *Roe v. Wade* was applicable after 1973. Palau became independent in 1994 and entered into a Compact of Free Association with the United States, with two attendant developments. First, independence allowed courts in Palau to apply the common law of jurisdictions other than the United States, including common law developed locally. Second, it gave a prominent place to local customary law in court deliberations. Consequently, the exact status of the law on abortion remains unclear at this date. It may be that the 1971 Appellate Court decision is applicable and that there is no abortion law, or that customary law of some sort prevails. The Republic of Palau National Code, which is based on the Trust Territory Code, implies that the former is the case. Although the Code defines abortion as a crime, reproducing the exact language of the Trust Territory Code, the editor's annotations to the Code still refer to the Appellate Court's 1971 ruling that these abortion provisions are invalid.

No reliable figures on abortion are readily available in Palau, which has a population of 18,000. The United Nations Children's Fund (UNICEF) reports a contraceptive prevalence rate of 38 per cent.

Source: Population Policy Data Bank maintained by the Population Division of the Department of Economic and Social Affairs of the United Nations Secretariat. For additional sources, see list of references.

ABORTION POLICY

Grounds on which abortion is permitted:

To save the life of the woman	Yes
To preserve physical health	Yes
To preserve mental health	No
Rape or incest	Yes
Foetal impairment	No
Economic or social reasons	No
Available on request	No

Additional requirements:

A multidisciplinary commission appointed by the Ministry of Health must authorize an abortion on the grounds of averting a health risk that would endanger the life of the mother or the foetus; in the case of rape, the authorities must be aware of the crime and the abortion must be performed within the first two months of pregnancy. An abortion must be performed by a physician in a government health-care centre.

REPRODUCTIVE HEALTH CONTEXT

Government view on fertility level:	Satisfactory
Government intervention concerning fertility level:	To maintain
Government policy on contraceptive use:	Direct support provided
Percentage of currently married women using modern contraception (aged 15-44, 1984):	54
Total fertility rate (1995-2000):	2.6
Age-specific fertility rate (per 1,000 women aged 15-19, 1995-2000):	82
Government has expressed particular concern about:	
Morbidity and mortality resulting from induced abortion	Yes
Complications of childbearing and childbirth	Yes
Maternal mortality ratio (per 100,000 live births, 1990):	
National	55
Central America	140
Female life expectancy at birth (1995-2000):	76.4

Source: Population Policy Data Bank maintained by the Population Division of the Department of Economic and Social Affairs of the United Nations Secretariat. For additional sources, see list of references.

Panama

BACKGROUND

Until 1982, abortion was generally illegal in Panama under the Criminal Code of 17 November 1922. Anyone who performed an abortion was subject to imprisonment for 20 months to 3 years. A woman who induced her own abortion was subject to imprisonment for 8-30 months. Harsher penalties were prescribed for medical personnel who performed abortions. Under general criminal law principles of necessity, however, abortion was permitted to save the life of the pregnant woman.

On 22 September 1982, a new Penal Code was enacted that liberalized Panama's abortion law and set new penalties for abortions performed illegally. Under the Code, a woman who causes her own abortion or consents to another person carrying it out is subject to one to three years' imprisonment. Anyone inducing an abortion with the woman's consent is subject to three to six years' imprisonment. The penalty for inducing an abortion without the woman's consent or against her will is four to six years' imprisonment. If the woman dies as a result of the abortion or the means used to induce it, the penalty is 5-10 years' imprisonment. These penalties are increased by one sixth if the person guilty of inducing the abortion is the woman's husband.

There is no penalty if an abortion is performed, with the consent of the woman, in order to destroy the product of conception resulting from rape, provided that the rape has been evidenced in a court proceeding. In such cases, the competent authorities must be aware of the crime and the abortion must be performed within the first two months of pregnancy. There is also no penalty if the abortion is performed, with the consent of the woman, for serious health reasons that endanger the life of the mother or the product of conception. In such cases, a multidisciplinary commission appointed by the Ministry of Health is to determine the serious health reasons and authorize the abortion. Under Ministry of Health Resolution No. 02007 of 2 August 1988, the multidisciplinary commission is composed of representatives from various health professions as well as a lawyer from the legal department of the Ministry of Health. The Resolution authorizes the commission to seek aid from other health professions and to establish rules approving therapeutic abortions.

On 21 April 1989, the Ministry of Health (Resolution No. 1) approved the rules of the multidisciplinary commission established to authorize therapeutic abortions. In order for a petition for a therapeutic abortion to be considered, a written request must be submitted by the pregnant woman. This request must be accompanied by a medical record which specifies and supports the diagnosis motivating the petition and by laboratory tests and/or supplementary information confirming the request. Women who are minors or who are incapacitated for legal reasons must have the consent of a legal representative. If necessary, the multidisciplinary commission may request the written opinion of other health professionals, who must cooperate with its members. In each region, the chief of gynaecology and obstetrics of each hospital must analyse the requests of patients in that region and verify the fulfilment of the requirements. The documents must be sent to the national commission, which must meet within the shortest possible time for review and a final decision. Once authorized by the commission, the abortion must be performed by a medical specialist in the state hospital of the health region where it is requested. A therapeutic abortion can never be performed without the written consent of the multidisciplinary commission.

The Government of Panama has strongly supported family planning and has been providing subsidized services since 1973. The Government promotes natural and modern methods of family planning through the Ministry of Health and a private family planning organization of the country, the Asociación Panameña para

Source: Population Policy Data Bank maintained by the Population Division of the Department of Economic and Social Affairs of the United Nations Secretariat. For additional sources, see list of references.

el Planeamiento de la Familia (APLAFA), which was founded in 1965. The modern contraceptive prevalence rate was estimated at 54 per cent in 1984. Adolescent fertility is a major concern of the Government and a programme of sex education in the schools has been implemented. Parental participation and the dissemination of information on sex education through the press also encouraged. Despite these efforts, it is estimated that more than 20 per cent of declared abortions in Panama involve adolescents.

APLAFA is confronting the problem of adolescent pregnancy with a wide range of activities that focus not only on the prevention of unwanted pregnancies but also on the provision of prenatal and postnatal care for those choosing to carry an unwanted pregnancy to term. Sterilization is legal in Panama. The programme also includes an educational component offering employment services, vocational training, and social and recreational activities, as well as extensive reproductive health services.

Efforts to promote family planning in Panama have been generally successful. Between 1965 and 1985, for example, the total fertility rate decreased from 6.0 to 3.0 children per woman. The total fertility rate is currently (1995-2000) at 2.6 children per woman while the population growth rate has slowed to an estimated 1.8 per cent.

Source: Population Policy Data Bank maintained by the Population Division of the Department of Economic and Social Affairs of the United Nations Secretariat. For additional sources, see list of references.

Papua New Guinea

ABORTION POLICY

Grounds on which abortion is permitted:

To save the life of the woman	Yes
To preserve physical health	Yes
To preserve mental health	Yes
Rape or incest	No
Foetal impairment	No
Economic or social reasons	No
Available on request	No

Additional requirements:

A legal abortion is permitted within 12 weeks of gestation. It should be performed by a registered physician in a government health-care institution.

REPRODUCTIVE HEALTH CONTEXT

Government view on fertility level:	Too high
Government intervention concerning fertility level:	To lower
Government policy on contraceptive use:	Direct support provided
Percentage of currently married women using modern contraception (aged 15-49, 1996):	20
Total fertility rate (1995-2000):	4.6
Age-specific fertility rate (per 1,000 women aged 15-19, 1995-2000):	24
Government has expressed particular concern about:	
Morbidity and mortality resulting from induced abortion	Yes
Complications of childbearing and childbirth	Yes
Maternal mortality ratio (per 100,000 live births, 1990):	
National	930
Oceania	680
Female life expectancy at birth (1995-2000):	

Source: Population Policy Data Bank maintained by the Population Division of the Department of Economic and Social Affairs of the United Nations Secretariat. For additional sources, see list of references.

BACKGROUND

The Criminal Code (Ordinance No. 7 of 1902), which reproduces the 1899 Criminal Code Act of Queensland and was adopted as the law of then British New Guinea, is still in effect. Under this Code, the performance of abortions is generally illegal. A person who unlawfully administers any means to a woman with intent to procure her miscarriage is subject to up to fourteen years' imprisonment. A woman who undertakes the same activity or consents to it is subject to up to seven years' imprisonment.

The Code however, allows an abortion to be performed to save the life of a pregnant woman. It provides that a person is not criminally responsible for performing in good faith and with reasonable care and skill a surgical operation on an unborn child for the preservation of the mother's life if the performance of the operation is reasonable, having regard to the patient's state at the time and to all the circumstances of the case. Moreover, in 1974 the Justice Department of the Government of Papua New Guinea expressed the opinion that preservation of life includes preservation of the physical and mental health of the pregnant woman.

Abortion in Papua New Guinea is also regulated to some extent by customary law; indeed, the Constitution of the country requires that courts take custom into account in reaching their decision. In some parts of the country, abortion may not be regarded as wrong if the mother is unmarried or if the pregnancy is a result of an adulterous or incestuous relationship. Accordingly, if abortion is acceptable according to local custom, the person accused of performing an illegal abortion may be exonerated.

Induced abortion is practised in most of Papua New Guinea. It frequently has been done by such methods as ingestion of plant substances, binding of the abdomen and heavy massage. Although the number of illegal abortions is unknown, the available evidence suggests that the practice is common and possibly increasing. There has been a relatively high incidence of septic and haemorrhagic complications from "spontaneous abortions", a high incidence of pelvic inflammatory disease and large numbers of patients with septic abortion and premature labour following unsuccessful illegal attempts at pregnancy termination.

As a result the demand for legal and safe medical termination of pregnancy is increasing. In 1990 the maternal mortality ratio was a high 930 deaths per 100,000 live births. Major causes included puerperal sepsis, post-partum haemorrhage, associated medical and surgical complications and prolonged or obstructed labour and ruptured uterus. By 1996, the modern contraceptive prevalence rate was 20 per cent, the total fertility rate for the 1995-2000 period was estimated at 4.6 children per woman.

Community-based family planning distribution programmes have been in operation for 25 years. The Government has been receiving international assistance to improve the health status of women and children through adequate maternal and child health and family planning care by focusing on the proper timing and spacing of births. Under the ICPD Programme of Action, Papua New Guinea began reforming its delivery of health services and promoting further training and awareness in reproductive health and family planning.

Source: Population Policy Data Bank maintained by the Population Division of the Department of Economic and Social Affairs of the United Nations Secretariat. For additional sources, see list of references.

Paraguay

ABORTION POLICY

Grounds on which abortion is permitted:

To save the life of the woman	Yes
To preserve physical health	No
To preserve mental health	No
Rape or incest	No
Foetal impairment	No
Economic or social reasons	No
Available on request	No

Additional requirements:

Information is not readily available.

REPRODUCTIVE HEALTH CONTEXT

Government view on fertility level:	Too high
Government intervention concerning fertility level:	No intervention
Government policy on contraceptive use:	Direct support provided
Percentage of currently married women using modern contraception (aged 15-44, 1998):	49*
Total fertility rate (1995-2000):	4.2
Age-specific fertility rate (per 1,000 women aged 15-19, 1995-2000):	76
Government has expressed particular concern about:	
Morbidity and mortality resulting from induced abortion	Yes
Complications of childbearing and childbirth	Yes
Maternal mortality ratio (per 100,000 live births, 1995):	
National	190
South America	260
Female life expectancy at birth (1995-2000):	72.0

* Preliminary or provisional.

Source: Population Policy Data Bank maintained by the Population Division of Department of Economic and Social Affairs of the United Nations Secretariat. For additional sources, see list of references.

BACKGROUND

The Paraguayan Penal Code (Law No. 1160/97) of 26 November 1997 in general prohibits the performance of abortions. Anyone who performs an abortion, including a woman who causes her own abortion or consents to it, is subject to fifteen to thirty months' imprisonment. If the abortion is performed without the consent of the woman, the penalty is increased to two to five years' imprisonment. If the abortion results in the death of the woman, the penalty is increased to four to six years' imprisonment if the woman consented and to five to ten years' imprisonment if she did not consent. Penalties are increased by 50 per cent if the abortion is performed by the husband of the woman or by a member of a health profession. A woman who causes her own abortion to preserve her honour is subject to six to twelve months' imprisonment, and the penalties imposed on a person who performs an illegal abortion are decreased by one half if the abortion is performed to preserve the honour of that person' spouse, daughter, or sister.

Nonetheless, the Penal Code explicitly allows an abortion to be performed to save the life of a woman. It provides that a member of the health professions shall be exempt from punishment if he or she justifies having indirectly caused an abortion for the purpose of saving the life of a woman endangered by pregnancy or childbirth. Moreover, article 109 of the Code provides that a person who indirectly causes the death of a foetus during acts relating to childbirth does not act illegally if, taking into consideration the knowledge and experiences of the medical profession, this is necessary and inevitable to prevent serious danger to the life or health of the mother.

Clandestine abortion is common in Paraguay. It is estimated that approximately 26,000 illegal abortions are performed annually and that 35 per cent of Paraguayan women have had at least one abortion. Illegal abortion, together with a lack of adequate prenatal and obstetric care, has contributed to a high maternal mortality rate. The maternal mortality ratio has, however, been declining, from 300 deaths per 100,000 live births in 1986 to the most recent 1995 government estimate of 190 deaths per 100,000 live births. Surveys in 1979 and 1984 estimated the abortion rate at around 145 abortions per 1,000 pregnancies.

Family planning services were illegal or discouraged for decades in Paraguay but started expanding in the late 1980s, and the right to family planning was guaranteed under the 1992 Constitution of Paraguay. The expansion of family planning services occurred primarily through the efforts of the national family planning association, the Centro Paraguayo de Estudios de Población (CEPEP), founded in 1966, which provides subsidized family planning services and operates clinics that offer gynaecological services, prenatal and postnatal care, and contraceptives. The association sponsors campaigns to involve rural community leaders in family planning and provides training to physicians in remote frontier regions. In an effort to increase public knowledge and to improve the image of family planning, CEPEP disseminates information in magazines and on radio and television programmes.

The use of modern contraceptives has increased steadily from an estimated 35 per cent in 1990 to 41 per cent in 1995/1996 and a provisional 49 per cent in 1998. The 1990 Demographic and Health Survey found that 93 per cent of women knew of at least one modern family planning method. The most frequently used contraceptive methods were the pill (14 per cent), female sterilization (7 per cent), the intrauterine device (6 per cent) and contraceptive injections (5 per cent). Thirteen per cent used a traditional method.

The Government of Paraguay considers the current rates of population growth and fertility (estimated at 4.2 children per woman in 1995-2000) to be too high but pursues a general policy of non-intervention on

Source: Population Policy Data Bank maintained by the Population Division of the Department of Economic and Social Affairs of the United Nations Secretariat. For additional sources, see list of references.

fertility levels. The public sector has provided natural family planning services as a health measure and as part of maternal and child health care, while other modern methods of contraception are available on the commercial market. In 1988, the Government decided to expand the provision of family planning to include other methods. Although there are no specific legal provisions in regard to sterilization, it is believed that the law prohibiting corporal injury applies.

The Government has formulated policies to improve population welfare through improved health services and family planning activities. It has implemented programmes to promote responsible parenthood and to improve the provision of family planning services as an integral part of maternal and child health (MCH) care, primarily to promote child spacing and maternal health. Family life education has been introduced into the school curricula, and information, education and communication programmes have been implemented. In 1994, following the International Conference on Population and Development, the Government established a National Council for Reproductive Health, responsible for formulating a national reproductive health plan.

Source: Population Policy Data Bank maintained by the Population Division of Department of Economic and Social Affairs of the United Nations Secretariat. For additional sources, see list of references.

ABORTION POLICY

Grounds on which abortion is permitted:

To save the life of the woman	Yes
To preserve physical health	Yes
To preserve mental health	Yes
Rape or incest	No
Foetal impairment	No
Economic or social reasons	No
Available on request	No

Additional requirements:

An abortion must be performed by a physician, with the consent of the pregnant woman and after consultation with two physicians.

REPRODUCTIVE HEALTH CONTEXT

Government view on fertility level:	Too high
Government intervention concerning fertility level:	To lower
Government policy on contraceptive use:	Direct support provided
Percentage of currently married women using modern contraception (aged 15-49, 1996):	41
Total fertility rate (1995-2000):	3.0
Age-specific fertility rate (per 1,000 women aged 15-19, 1995-2000):	58
Government has expressed particular concern about:	
Morbidity and mortality resulting from induced abortion	Yes
Complications of childbearing and childbirth	Yes
Maternal mortality ratio (per 100,000 live births, 1990):	
National	280
South America	260
Female life expectancy at birth (1995-2000):	70.9

Source: Population Policy Data Bank maintained by the Population Division of the Department of Economic and Social Affairs of the United Nations Secretariat. For additional sources, see list of references.

BACKGROUND

Abortion in Peru is governed by the provisions of the Criminal Code of 11 January 1924, as amended in 1991, and the Health Code of 1969, as amended in 1981. Under the Criminal Code, the performance of abortions is generally illegal. A woman who causes her own abortion or consents to its performance by another person is subject to not more than two years' imprisonment or to the provision of community service for 52 to 104 days. A person who causes the abortion of a pregnant woman with her consent is subject to one to four years' imprisonment, and to three to five years' imprisonment if she does not consent. Harsher penalties are applied if the pregnant woman dies, and health personnel who perform abortions are subject to suspension from practising their profession. The performance of abortions is not punishable if carried out by a physician with the consent of the pregnant woman when it is the only means of saving her life or preventing serious and permanent injury to her health.

The Health Code provides that human life and the right to health begin with conception. Thus, the process of pregnancy is to terminate in birth, except in the case of an unavoidable natural occurrence or a danger to the life or health of the mother, and abortions performed on moral, social, or economic grounds or as a means of birth control are prohibited. Like the Criminal Code, the Health Code allows the performance of abortions when carried out by a physician with the consent of the pregnant woman as the only means of saving the life of the pregnant woman or preventing serious and lasting injury to her health. Moreover, the Code requires two physicians to approve the abortion before it is performed.

Abortion is also mentioned to in Peru's National Population Policy, Legislative Decree No. 346 of 6 July 1995. The Policy guarantees the individual the right to life from the time of conception and excludes abortion as a method of family planning.

In recent years there have been minor changes to the abortion law. The 1991 amendment of the Criminal Code reduced the penalties imposed on a woman who performed her own abortion or consented to its performance from up to four years' imprisonment to not more than two years' imprisonment or to the provision of community service for 52 to 104 days, as noted above. In addition, it greatly reduced the maximum sentence (three months) for the performance of an illegal abortion when the pregnancy is the result of rape or "involuntary artificial insemination" outside of marriage reported to the police; or when a medical diagnosis points to a probable risk of serious physical or mental defects in the child if it were born.

The Government of Peru considers the current rates of population growth and fertility to be too high and seeks to lower them through direct support of contraception. The National Population Policy Law of 1985 outlined a government plan of action concerning population, focused on promoting a balanced relation between population and socio-economic development and encouraging responsible parenthood. During the 1990s, the Government increasingly emphasized the crucial role of family planning in the development process. The modern contraceptive prevalence rate increased from 33 per cent in 1992 to 41 per cent in 1996. The government's target fertility rate of 3.0 births per woman for the period 1995-2000 and target rate of population growth of about 2 per cent per by the year 2000 have both been met according to current estimates.

The Directorate-General of Family Planning within the Ministry of Health oversees the national programme and the coordination of all activities in the public and private sectors. The main targets of family planning services are the poor living in the suburbs of Lima and in other urban areas. Although adolescent fertility is a major concern, access to contraception is forbidden to unmarried adolescents. Female sterilization was legalized as a method of family planning in August 1995. The maternal mortality ratio, though in decline, continues to be one of the highest in South America. 1990 estimates place it at 280 deaths per 100,000 live births.

Source: Population Policy Data Bank maintained by the Population Division of the Department of Economic and Social Affairs of the United Nations Secretariat. For additional sources, see list of references.

Philippines

ABORTION POLICY

Grounds on which abortion is permitted:

To save the life of the woman	Yes
To preserve physical health	No
To preserve mental health	No
Rape or incest	No
Foetal impairment	No
Economic or social reasons	No
Available on request	No

Additional requirements:

Authorization of an abortion requires consultation with a panel of professionals.

REPRODUCTIVE HEALTH CONTEXT

Government view on fertility level:	Too high
Government intervention concerning fertility level:	To lower
Government policy on contraceptive use:	Direct support provided
Percentage of currently married women using modern contraception (aged 15-44, 1998):	28
Total fertility rate (1995-2000):	3.6
Age-specific fertility rate (per 1,000 women aged 15-19, 1995-2000):	43
Government has expressed particular concern about:	
Morbidity and mortality resulting from induced abortion	Yes
Complications of childbearing and childbirth	Yes
Maternal mortality ratio (per 100,000 live births, 1990):	
National	280
South-eastern Asia	440
Female life expectancy at birth (1995-2000):	70.2

Source: Population Policy Data Bank maintained by the Population Division of the Department of Economic and Social Affairs of the United Nations Secretariat. For additional sources, see list of references.

BACKGROUND

Abortion in the Philippines is generally illegal. Under the abortion provisions of the Revised Penal Code of 1930, as amended, a person who intentionally causes an abortion with the consent of the pregnant woman is subject to a penalty of *prison correccional* (i.e., imprisonment for from six months to six years) in its medium or maximum period. A physician or midwife who causes or assists in the performance of an abortion is subject to the maximum period of this penalty, as well as suspension from the right to follow a profession. A woman performing an abortion on herself to conceal her dishonour is subject to the minimum or medium period of this penalty. A person performing an abortion without the consent of the pregnant woman is subject to a penalty of *prison major* (i.e., 6-12 years' imprisonment).

Although the Penal Code does not list specific exceptions to the general prohibition on abortion, under the general criminal law principles of necessity as set forth in article 11(4) of the Code, an abortion may be legally performed to save the pregnant woman's life.

In addition to these provisions, the Constitution of 1987 provides that the State "shall equally protect the life of the mother and the life of the unborn from conception". This provision reinforces the provision contained in a Presidential Decree of 1975 establishing the Child and Youth Welfare Code, which stipulates that a child has the dignity and worth of a human being from the moment of conception and has the right to be born well.

Despite the severity of the law, abortion appears to be widely practised in the Philippines as a means of birth control and is rarely prosecuted. The International Planned Parenthood Federation reports estimates ranging from 155,000 to 750,000 induced abortions per year. However, illegal abortion is performed in a climate of fear and shame resulting from strong cultural, religious and legal prohibitions. Surveys indicate that women resorting to abortion are often from economically disadvantaged groups and take this step because they are unable to provide for another child. Surveys also indicate a high incidence of repeat abortion. In a context of poor health conditions and widespread malnutrition, and where some 76 per cent of deliveries occur at home and only 21 per cent are attended by a physician, induced abortions are poorly performed and result in high maternal mortality and morbidity. The maternal mortality ratio was estimated at 280 deaths per 100,000 live births in 1990. Hospital surveys have found that about one third of maternal deaths occurring in hospitals can be attributed to induced abortion.

The Government of the Philippines is greatly concerned about the high incidence of induced abortion and hopes to reduce illegal abortion through an expansion of family planning activities and through information, education and communication services. As early as 1972, the Revised Population Act referred to abortion as an unacceptable method of birth control, which should be discouraged and prevented. In 1988, a Presidential Proclamation on the Respect and Care for Life Week emphasized the constitutional provision that the State has an obligation to protect the life of the unborn from conception.

The Philippines' total fertility rate has declined in the last ten years, from a 1985-1990 rate of 4.3 children per woman to a 1995-2000 rate of 3.6. The Government seeks to lower the fertility level on an ongoing basis. The national family planning programme in the Philippines has encountered many obstacles.

Source: Population Policy Data Bank maintained by the Population Division of the Department of Economic and Social Affairs of the United Nations Secretariat. For additional sources, see list of references.

Philippines

Contraceptive use is relatively low and has grown slowly. The modern contraceptive prevalence rate was estimated to be 22 per cent in 1988 and 28 per cent a decade later, in 1998. Access to family planning services is limited and adequate services are often unavailable. Indeed, after a first phase of expansion in the 1970s, the national family planning programme was largely neglected; and as of 1992, only about 2 per cent of field personnel in the Department of Health had been trained to provide family planning services. Moreover, according to the Republic Act of 1966, contraceptives can be sold only in licensed pharmacies and can only be purchased with a prescription from a qualified physician. Many women cannot afford contraceptives, and many encounter difficulties in obtaining access to Government-dispensed supplies.

In 1990, the Government launched a new family planning programme and established a number of incentives, including tax exemptions for couples that limited their family size to two children. However, the family planning programme encountered strong opposition from the Catholic Church. Following a series of negotiations, the Catholic Bishops Conference of the Philippines sanctioned in 1990 the government policy of providing support for artificial methods of contraception (the condom, the pill and the intrauterine device, as well as sterilization) in exchange for the Government's commitment to promote natural methods of family planning. However, in 1993, the Church denounced the new Government's plan to expand the national family planning programme. Following some government concessions, the programme was launched, but the Catholic Bishops Conference once again voiced its opposition and called for a boycott by health practitioners.

In implementation of the ICPD Programme of Action, the Government created the Philippine Reproductive Health Programme in 1998 to deliver ten different services as part of a comprehensive reproductive health service package, including family planning, maternal and child health, and prevention and management of abortion complications. The accessibility and delivery of health services continues to be the main challenge in this nation of 880 inhabited islands.

Source: Population Policy Data Bank maintained by the Population Division of the Department of Economic and Social Affairs of the United Nations Secretariat. For additional sources, see list of references.

ABORTION POLICY

Grounds on which abortion is permitted:

To save the life of the woman	Yes
To preserve physical health	Yes
To preserve mental health	Yes
Rape or incest	Yes
Foetal impairment	Yes
Economic or social reasons	No
Available on request	No

Additional requirements:

An abortion must be performed by an obstetrician or gynaecologist who has passed the national proficiency tests. The abortion must be performed in a hospital or clinic with the consent of the pregnant woman or her parents or guardian if she is a minor. The procedure must be performed within the first 12 weeks of pregnancy, unless continued pregnancy would endanger the life or health of the pregnant woman.

REPRODUCTIVE HEALTH CONTEXT

Government view on fertility level:	Too low
Government intervention concerning fertility level:	To raise
Government policy on contraceptive use:	Direct support provided
Percentage of currently married women using modern contraception (aged 20-49, 1991):	19[a,b]
Total fertility rate (1995-2000):	1.5
Age-specific fertility rate (per 1,000 women aged 15-19, 1995-2000):	23
Government has expressed particular concern about:	
Morbidity and mortality resulting from induced abortion	Yes
Complications of childbearing and childbirth	No
Maternal mortality ratio (per 100,000 live births, 1990):	
National	19
Developed countries	27
Female life expectancy at birth (1995-2000):	76.9

[a] Including consensual unions, where possible.
[b] Excluding sterilization.

Source: Population Policy Data Bank maintained by the Population Division of the Department of Economic and Social Affairs of the United Nations Secretariat. For additional sources, see list of references.

Poland

BACKGROUND

Until 1932, abortion was generally prohibited in Poland. On 11 July 1932, the restrictive legislation was modified to allow abortion when a pregnancy endangered the life or health of the woman or resulted from a crime (rape or incest). The law required a legal abortion to be performed by a physician with the consent of two other physicians.

A law adopted by the Polish Parliament (Sejm) on 27 April 1956 (Law No. 61) further liberalized the abortion laws by permitting abortion on medical grounds, if the pregnancy resulted from a criminal act or because of "difficult living conditions". Although abortion was not explicitly permitted on grounds of foetal impairment, serious defects of the unborn child often constituted "difficult living conditions" for the pregnant woman. The great majority of abortions were performed on the ground of "difficult living conditions", which, under regulations issued subsequent to the law, left the decision essentially to the pregnant woman as long as she could find a physician willing to perform the operation.

Although the procedural requirements to be observed in order for a lawful abortion to be performed were amended repeatedly over the years (1956, 1959, 1969, 1981 and 1990), access to abortion after the passage of the 1956 legislation remained largely constant until 1990 with the election of the first non-Communist Government in Poland since the end of the Second World War. Under regulations issued by the Ministry of Health and Social Welfare (Ordinance of 30 April 1990), a request for an abortion on the grounds of difficult living conditions had to be approved by two gynecologists and a general practitioner. The pregnant woman was also required to obtain the counselling of a State-approved psychologist. The Ministry also set a fee for the performance of abortions on non-therapeutic grounds.

In 1993, Parliament enacted further restrictions on access to abortion by eliminating entirely "difficult living conditions" as a ground for the performance of legal abortions. Henceforth, abortions could be performed legally only in cases of serious threat to the life or health of the pregnant woman, as attested by two physicians, cases of rape or incest confirmed by a prosecutor, and cases in which prenatal tests, confirmed by two physicians, demonstrated that the foetus was seriously and irreversibly damaged. A ban was also placed on the performance of abortions in private clinics. A physician who performed an abortion in violation of the law was subject to up to two years' imprisonment, although the pregnant woman herself was exempt from punishment. The law also amended the abortion law to provide that "Every human being shall have a natural right to life from the time of his conception" and gave a person who was damaged before birth a right to seek compensation. The Law set no time limits on the performance of abortions.

In addition, the law contained provisions obligating the Government to guarantee "free access to methods and means of birth control", to provide social, medical and legal assistance during pregnancy and after childbirth, including material support and information on the rights, benefits and services available to families and unmarried mothers; to allow pregnant students maternity leave; and to introduce into schools classes on human sexuality, including information on birth control, responsible procreation, and the value of the family and the life of the unborn child. The provisions were designed to address the problem of abortion in ways other than restricting the performance of the procedure.

These amendments to Poland's abortion law did not end the controversy. Because the Law had eliminated socio-economic grounds for abortion, woman's groups and left-leaning political parties, including the successor to the Communist party, began working to modify its effects. Conversely, some of the strongest opponents of the former law sought to restrict abortion even further, believing abortion to be immoral under

Source: Population Policy Data Bank maintained by the Population Division of the Department of Economic and Social Affairs of the United Nations Secretariat. For additional sources, see list of references.

all circumstances. The former groups were aided in their cause by the results of the next set of elections held in 1993. Owing in part to the hardships faced by much of the Polish population by the abrupt shift from a socialist economy to a capitalist one and the loss of many social benefits that had been taken for granted, a new Government made up of left-leaning parties, including the former Communists, gained control of Parliament.

One year after the elections, this Parliament, despite considerable opposition, approved a bill to allow abortions for socio-economic reasons. The bill, however never went into effect. To become law, it needed the approval of Poland's President who is separately elected from Parliament. Because the President was opposed to abortion, he refused to sign the law, thus leaving in place the 1993 restrictive legislation.

Two years later, however, after another election resulted in a new president who was favourable to abortion law reform, the Government again introduced liberalized legislation. Parliament voted to amend the recent law to allow abortions to be performed on the grounds of difficult living conditions or a precarious personal situation up until the twelfth week of pregnancy. The pregnant woman would be required to undergo counselling, give written consent to the operation, and wait three days after the counselling until the abortion took place. The law once again allowed abortions to be performed in private clinics. It also set a 12-week limit for abortions performed on the grounds of health, foetal impairment or as a result of a criminal act (rape or incest), and provided for sex education in schools and cheaper contraceptives.

Enactment of the new law heightened the hostility of pro-life groups to the performance of abortions. Many legislators, religious leaders and health personnel opposed to abortion pledged themselves to counter its effect. At the same time, growing numbers of physicians and hospitals refused to perform abortions, as they were allowed to do under a conscience clause contained in the law. In some cities, there were no public institutions willing to perform abortions, leaving private clinics with much higher fees as the only resort for women seeking abortions. Some estimates were that almost half of all public hospitals in Poland had adopted this approach to the issue.

In addition, shortly after the passage of the amendments, a number of legislators moved to challenge the law's constitutional validity before Poland's Constitutional Tribunal. They argued that, because the law allowed the performance of abortions, it violated provisions of the Constitution guaranteeing the rule of democratic law and social justice and the Constitution's implied guarantee of the right to life. In its ruling later in the case in mid 1997, the Court essentially agreed with this argument. It pointed specifically to the part of the Law that allowed abortions on socio-economic grounds. It found this to be defective because of a lack of precise justified criteria as to what constituted difficult living conditions or a precarious personal situation and to constitute abortion on request. It reasoned that, without such criteria, the law did not sufficiently protect human life from the moment at which it arises, which it stated was a value protected under the Constitution, even though not so expressed. It concluded that the law amounted to authorization of abortion on request.

The effect of the decision was to give the Government six months' time to enact new legislation conforming to the decision or to override it by a two thirds majority vote in Parliament. During this time, the provisions of the law were to remain in effect. The Government, however, was unable to override the Court's decision by the required majority, and after elections that brought a pro-life majority to Parliament, Parliament voted to endorse the court's decision and reinstate the former law of 1993.

Source: Population Policy Data Bank maintained by the Population Division of the Department of Economic and Social Affairs of the United Nations Secretariat. For additional sources, see list of references.

Poland

It is difficult to determine the number of abortions being carried out in Poland. Official abortion statistics are believed to underestimate the true extent of abortion because it is not known how many abortions are performed in private out-patient clinics. For example, although there were 123,000 officially reported abortions in 1987, some estimates suggest that the actual number of abortions performed may have been from three to four times the official number. Underground private abortion services are robust in Poland, as is "tourism" abortion by Polish women who travel to neighbouring countries including, Austria, Belarus, Belgium, the Czech Republic, Germany, Holland, Lithuania, the Russian Federation, Slovakia and Ukraine. Rough 1996 estimates suggest there may be 50,000 underground abortions a year.

The suspected high incidence of abortion is due to a number of factors, including shortages of low-cost, high-quality modern contraceptives, reliance upon less reliable natural methods of fertility control and a lack of comprehensive sex education programmes. The Polish Government is concerned about the high level of induced abortions and the lack of popularity of contraceptives. The modern contraceptive prevalence rate was estimated in 1991 to be 19 per cent.

The Government of Poland considers the current total fertility rate to be too low. Government policy is to encourage the well-being of the family as a whole. Towards this end, the Government has created an extensive system of social benefits, including maternity leave, a three-year leave for child-rearing, an annual leave of up to 60 days for taking care of sick children, birth grants, family allowances for low-income families, and loans and scholarships to assist student marriages. An alimony fund provides a minimum income to divorced mothers not receiving alimony. Moreover, family life education courses have been established in schools.

Source: Population Policy Data Bank maintained by the Population Division of the Department of Economic and Social Affairs of the United Nations Secretariat. For additional sources, see list of references.

ABORTION POLICY

Grounds on which abortion is permitted:

To save the life of the woman	Yes
To preserve physical health	Yes
To preserve mental health	Yes
Rape or incest	Yes
Foetal impairment	Yes
Economic or social reasons	No
Available on request	No

Additional requirements:

An abortion must be performed by, or under the direction of, a physician within the first 12 weeks of gestation on the grounds of preserving the woman's physical or mental health or in the case of rape; or within 16 weeks if there is a risk that the child will be born with an incurable disease or malformation. The existence of these circumstances must be certified in writing by a physician other than the one performing the procedure. This certification must be accompanied by the written consent of the woman requesting the abortion, not less than three days prior to the date of the procedure; women under age 16 must have the consent of the husband, parents or, in their absence, any relative. Abortions must be performed in an official or officially approved health-care establishment.

REPRODUCTIVE HEALTH CONTEXT

Government view on fertility level:	Too low
Government intervention concerning fertility level:	No intervention
Government policy on contraceptive use:	Direct support provided
Percentage of currently married women using modern contraception (aged 15-49, 1979/80):	33
Total fertility rate (1995-2000):	1.4
Age-specific fertility rate (per 1,000 women aged 15-19, 1995-2000):	20
Government has expressed particular concern about:	
Morbidity and mortality resulting from induced abortion	No
Complications of childbearing and childbirth	No
Maternal mortality ratio (per 100,000 live births, 1990):	
National	15
Developed countries	27
Female life expectancy at birth (1995-2000):	78.8

Source: Population Policy Data Bank maintained by the Population Division of the Department of Economic and Social Affairs of the United Nations Secretariat. For additional sources, see list of references.

BACKGROUND

The Portuguese Criminal Code of 16 September 1886 prohibited abortion. Any person that terminated a pregnancy, including the pregnant woman, was subject to imprisonment for from two to eight years. According to section 358 of the Code, the woman was subject to imprisonment under a less severe regimen if she committed the offence to conceal her dishonour.

Termination of pregnancy was permitted to save the life of the mother, despite the fact that there was no specific provision for such cases in the Criminal Code. Decree Law No. 40,651 of 21 June 1956, which approved the statutes of the Order of Physicians, stated that the physician should observe absolute respect for human life from the moment of conception and expressly prohibited abortion. However, even prior to the subsequent constitutional changes in Portugal, medical indication to save the life of the mother was recognized in legal doctrine. Portuguese Law No. 6/84 of 11 May 1984 liberalized abortion in Portugal, permitting the termination of pregnancy executed by, or under the direction of, a physician in an official or officially approved health-care establishment, and with the consent of the pregnant woman. Abortion could be performed provided that, based on the current state of medical knowledge and experience: (a) it was the only means of eliminating a risk of death or serious permanent damage to the physical or mental health of the mother; (b) it would avert a risk of death or serious damage to the physical or mental health of the mother, and the procedure was performed during the first 12 weeks of gestation; (c) there were substantial grounds for believing that the child would be born with a serious or incurable disease or malformation, and the procedure was performed during the first 16 weeks of gestation; or (d) there were significant indications that the pregnancy resulted from rape, and the procedure was performed during the first 12 weeks of gestation. Prior to the abortion, a physician other than the one performing the procedure must sign a medical certificate attesting to the existence of circumstances that render an abortion permissible. In cases of rape, the verification of circumstances depends upon evidence of criminal involvement. The abortion must be performed with the consent of the pregnant woman; the woman, or someone on her behalf, must sign a document to this effect not less than three days prior to the date of the procedure.

In case of emergency, if it is imperative that the abortion be performed immediately to save the life of the mother or to avert a serious threat to her life or lasting damage to her physical or mental health, the prescribed time limit may be waived, as well as the required consent of the woman if she is unable to express her consent and if it may reasonably be assumed that she would normally have granted it. In such cases, the circumstances must be recorded on the medical certificate. If the pregnant woman is under age 16 or is incompetent, the written consent may be provided, in order of priority, by her competent and non-separated husband, her legal representative, a competent ascendant or descendant or, in their absence, by any relative. If no such person can be found to consent to the woman's abortion and if the procedure must be performed as a matter of urgency, the physician may decide how to proceed, according to his own conscience, while, if possible, consulting one or more other physicians. The circumstances must be recorded on the medical certificate.

Physicians that fail to obtain the required documents justifying the legal voluntary termination of pregnancy, prior to or after the procedure, may be subject to imprisonment for a maximum of one year.

Any person procuring an abortion by any means without the consent of the pregnant woman may be subject to imprisonment for two to eight years. A person procuring an abortion by any means with the consent of the pregnant woman, other than in cases permitted by law, may be subject to a maximum of three years in

Source: Population Policy Data Bank maintained by the Population Division of the Department of Economic and Social Affairs of the United Nations Secretariat. For additional sources, see list of references.

prison. A pregnant woman that consents to the inducement of an abortion by a third party or induces her own miscarriage, with or without the help of a third party, other than on the grounds permitted by law, also may be subject to a maximum of three years in prison. If an abortion is induced by a third party or by the pregnant woman herself, other than in cases permitted by law, but is performed to avoid the social reprobation of the woman or on grounds constituting significant mitigating circumstances in favour of the person responsible, the penalty may not exceed one year. The maximum penalty applicable may be increased by one third if an abortion performed or the methods employed, on grounds other than those permitted by law, result in the death of the pregnant woman or in serious injury to her body or her physical or mental health, and the person that procured the abortion was in a position to have foreseen the inevitable consequences of his or her conduct. The increased penalty is also applicable to any person habitually engaging in the illicit practice of abortion or inducing illicit abortion for profit.

In June 1996 the Communist Party introduced legislation to liberalize abortion. The proposed law made abortion legal up to 12 weeks on demand. The proposed law also made abortion legal up to 16 weeks (a) if the mother was found to be using illegal drugs; (b) if the mother's physical or psychological health was at risk; (c) if the pregnancy resulted from rape; d) if the mother was less than 16 years old; or (e) if the mother was mentally ill. The proposed law made abortion legal up to 22 weeks for eugenic (deformation) reasons, including testing positive for the human immunodeficiency virus/acquired immune deficiency syndrome (HIV/AIDS). The proposed law was narrowly defeated in February 1997.

There are an estimated 16,000 illegal abortions each year in Portugal.

In 1976, the law forbidding the advertising of contraceptives was repealed and the Secretary of State for Health officially pledged that family planning services would be made available in all health centres throughout the country. The subsequent rapid development of family planning programmes in Portugal has contributed to the decline in infant and maternal mortality. Contraceptives are widely available and prescriptive methods are free of charge.

Although the Government considers the fertility rate to be too low, it does not intervene with respect to this variable; however, various indirect measures have been implemented within the sphere of family policy. These measures, which are intended to protect maternity and paternity and to strengthen the family unit, include a maternity benefit of 100 per cent of earnings payable during 30 days before and 60 days after confinement, a marriage grant, a birth grant, a nursing allowance for up to 10 months and a family allowance for each child. The Government provides direct support for contraceptives and permits sterilization for women over age 25.

Source: Population Policy Data Bank maintained by the Population Division of the Department for Economic and Social Affairs of the United Nations Secretariat. For additional sources, see list of references.

Qatar

ABORTION POLICY

Grounds on which abortion is permitted:

To save the life of the woman	Yes
To preserve physical health	Yes
To preserve mental health	Yes
Rape or incest	No
Foetal impairment	Yes
Economic or social reasons	No
Available on request	No

Additional requirements:

A medical commission consisting of three medical specialists, one of whom must be a specialist in gynaecology and the others in obstetrics, are required by law to recommend the procedure before any induced abortion can be performed. All induced abortions must be performed in a government hospital. The consent of both spouses is required for an abortion on eugenic grounds.

REPRODUCTIVE HEALTH CONTEXT

Government view on fertility level:	Satisfactory
Government intervention concerning fertility level:	To maintain
Government policy on contraceptive use:	Direct support provided
Percentage of currently married women using modern contraception (under age 50,* 1987):	29
Total fertility rate (1995-2000):	3.7
Age-specific fertility rate (per 1,000 women aged 15-19, 1995-2000):	66
Government has expressed particular concern about:	
Morbidity and mortality resulting from induced abortion	..
Complications of childbearing and childbirth	..
Maternal mortality ratio (per 100,000 live births, 1990):	
National	..
Western Asia	320
Female life expectancy at birth (1995-2000):	75.4

* Adjusted from source to exclude breastfeeding.

Source: Population Policy Data Bank maintained by the Population Division of the Department of Economic and Social Affairs of the United Nations Secretariat. For additional sources, see list of references.

BACKGROUND

Under the Penal Code of Qatar of 28 August 1971, abortion is generally illegal. A pregnant woman who performs an abortion on herself or consents to its performance is subject to up to five years' imprisonment. A person who intentionally performs an abortion on a pregnant woman is subject to the same penalty if she consents, or to up to ten years' imprisonment if she does not consent.

The Code also provides, however, that the performance of an abortion to save the life of the pregnant woman is legal. Law No.2/1983 of 22 February 1983 governing the practice of the professions of physician, surgeon and dentist, contains a similar provision. Moreover, it provides that if the pregnancy is of less than four months' duration an abortion may be legally performed: a) if continuation of the pregnancy would cause certain and serious harm to the mother's health; or b) if there is evidence that the child would be born with serious and incurable physical malformations or mental deficiency, and both spouses consent to the abortion.

Under Law No. 3/1983, a medical commission consisting of three medical specialists, one of whom must be a specialist in gynaecology and another a specialist in obstetrics, must recommend the procedure before an abortion can be performed. All abortions must be performed in a government hospital.

The Government of Qatar considers the overall rate of population growth (1995-2000 estimates place it at 1.8 per cent) to be satisfactory but considers the growth rate of its nationals to be too low. A rapidly increasing native-born population is considered a means of helping reduce future dependency upon foreign workers, who currently constitute an estimated 70 per cent of the total population of 560,000. The Government of Qatar has one of the most advanced and extensive welfare systems in the Persian Gulf region. The provision of family allowances for each child, which are granted to male heads of households employed in the public sector, and of free schooling and health services is consistent with the Government's desire to increase the size of the native-born population. The modern contraceptive prevalence rate was estimated at 29 per cent in 1987. The Government actively supports contraceptive use by providing them through government services.

Source: Population Policy Data Bank maintained by the Population Division of the Department of Economic and Social Affairs of the United Nations Secretariat. For additional sources, see list of references.

Republic of Korea

ABORTION POLICY

Grounds on which abortion is permitted:

To save the life of the woman	Yes
To preserve physical health	Yes
To preserve mental health	Yes
Rape or incest	Yes
Foetal impairment	Yes
Economic or social reasons	Yes
Available on request	Yes

Additional requirements:

An abortion can be performed by a physician within 28 weeks of pregnancy. The consent of the pregnant woman is required, as well as that of her spouse if she is married.

REPRODUCTIVE HEALTH CONTEXT

Government view on fertility level:	Satisfactory
Government intervention concerning fertility level:	No intervention
Government policy on contraceptive use:	Direct support provided
Percentage of currently married women using modern contraception (aged 15-44, 1991):	70
Total fertility rate (1995-2000):	1.7
Age-specific fertility rate (per 1,000 women aged 15-19, 1995-2000):	4
Government has expressed particular concern about:	
Morbidity and mortality resulting from induced abortion	Yes
Complications of childbearing and childbirth	Yes
Maternal mortality ratio (per 100,000 live births, 1990):	
National	70
Eastern Asia	95
Female life expectancy at birth (1995-2000):	76.0

Source: Population Policy Data Bank maintained by the Population Division of the Department of Economic and Social Affairs of the Nations Secretariat. For additional sources, see list of references.

BACKGROUND

Sections 269 and 270 of the Criminal Code of the Republic of Korea of 1953 strictly prohibited abortion on any grounds. In 1973, however, the Maternal and Child Health Law established exemptions from this prohibition. According to this law, a physician may perform an abortion if the pregnant woman or her spouse suffers from an eugenic or hereditary mental or physical disease specified by Presidential Decree, if the woman or her spouse suffers from a communicable disease specified by Presidential Decree, if the pregnancy results from rape or incest or if continuation of the pregnancy is likely to jeopardize the mother's health. In all other circumstances, a pregnant woman inducing her own miscarriage or any person performing an abortion is subject to imprisonment for one year or a fine. The penalties for medical personnel are increased to imprisonment for up to two years.

The legal situation of abortion in the Republic of Korea is the result of a long process of evolution. After the Government established a national family planning programme in 1962 as part of its socio-economic development strategy, abortion became a common practice despite the legal prohibition, mainly because a large number of physicians were willing to perform abortions and the officials were reluctant to enforce the law. A majority of women strongly supported abortion, as indicated by a 1971 national survey, in which 81 per cent of the women reported a strong preference for legalizing abortion. Moreover, since 1962, the medical profession has favoured legalizing induced abortion. However, the Government's attempts to liberalize the abortion law in order to reduce the gap between law and practice encountered opposition. After various failed attempts, on 30 January 1973, the Government enacted the Maternal and Child Health Law, which still appears to be in effect.

The passage of the 1973 law had only a limited effect because prior to its enactment, most women in the Republic of Korea did not realize that abortion was illegal and abortions were widely performed. The estimated abortion rate (based on surveys of ever-married women aged 20-44) rose as high as 64 abortions per 1,000 women but has declined to 36 in 1990 and 20 in 1996. However, statistics on the actual number of abortions performed may be underestimated, as reporting is not mandatory, and most abortions are performed in private clinics. The recent trend towards a decline in the incidence of abortion is counterbalanced by an increase in the age-specific abortion rate for women in their twenties; most of these women use abortion as a means of contraception.

Many women in the Republic of Korea use abortion not as a backup for contraceptive failure but as a primary method of birth control, as is shown by the high rates of repeat abortion. The overall behavioural pattern is for couples to achieve the desired number of children (usually two) and then to practise contraception—including resorting to abortion—to prevent subsequent births. Although the induced abortion rate has been declining mainly as a result of increased contraceptive usage, the principal reason women reported in the National Fertility and Family Health Survey of 1985, for having an abortion was to prevent subsequent births (61.3 per cent), followed by birth-spacing (15.1), mother's health and foetal impairment (7.3), unwanted pregnancy (5.7) and other reasons (10.6).

In the 1970s, 84 per cent of induced abortions in the Republic of Korea were performed in clinics by private physicians. Costs are subsidized for indigent women, as well as in cases when sterilization is also performed at the time of abortion or when the pregnancy was due to failure of an intrauterine device.

Source: Population Policy Data Bank maintained by the Population Division of the Department of Economic and Social Affairs of the Nations Secretariat. For additional sources, see list of references.

Republic of Korea

The total fertility rate in the Republic of Korea has declined over the period 1970-2000 from 4.3 children per woman to 1.7, while the population growth rate has similarly fallen from 2.0 to 0.8 per cent over the same period, well below replacement level. As a result, the population programme shifted emphasis from a policy of modifying fertility levels to maintaining the level and improving the quality of family planning programmes, improving maternal and child health care through prevention of unwanted pregnancies and induced abortions, and sex education for adolescents. The Republic of Korea recorded a modern contraceptive prevalence rate of 70 per cent in 1991. Female sterilization accounted for almost half of the total. Until recently, the Government offered family planning services free of charge. The Government has now decided to impose user fees for family planning services, to eliminate the incentive schemes for the one-child family and to support instead a two-child policy.

Source: Population Policy Data Bank maintained by the Population Division of the Department for Economic and Social Affairs of the United Nations Secretariat. For additional sources, see list of references.

ABORTION POLICY

Grounds on which abortion is permitted:

To save the life of the woman	Yes
To preserve physical health	Yes
To preserve mental health	Yes
Rape or incest	Yes
Foetal impairment	Yes
Economic or social reasons	Yes
Available on request	Yes

Additional requirements:

An abortion requires the consent of the pregnant woman; it is authorized if performed by a licensed physician in a hospital or other recognized medical institution. Abortion is available on request during the first 12 weeks of gestation. Thereafter, induced abortion is available within 28 weeks from conception on judicial, genetic, vital, broad medical and social grounds, as well as for personal reasons with the special authorization of a commission of local physicians.

REPRODUCTIVE HEALTH CONTEXT

Government view on fertility level:	Satisfactory
Government intervention concerning fertility level:	No intervention
Government policy on contraceptive use:	Direct support provided
Percentage of currently married women using modern contraception (aged 15-44, 1997):	50
Total fertility rate (1995-2000):	1.8
Age-specific fertility rate (per 1,000 women aged 15-19, 1995-2000):	32
Government has expressed particular concern about:	
Morbidity and mortality resulting from induced abortion	Yes
Complications of childbearing and childbirth	Yes
Maternal mortality ratio (per 100,000 live births, 1990):	
National	..
Developed countries	27
Female life expectancy at birth (1995-2000):	72.0

Source: Population Policy Data Bank maintained by the Population Division of the Department of Economic and Social Affairs of the United Nations Secretariat. For additional sources, see list of references.

Republic of Moldova

BACKGROUND

As was the case with all of the former Soviet republics, the Republic of Moldova, known prior to 1992 as the Moldavian Soviet Socialist Republic, observed the abortion legislation and regulations of the former Union of Soviet Socialist Republics. As a result, abortion practices in the Republic of Moldova were similar to those throughout the former USSR.

The description given below pertains to the situation in the Republic of Moldova prior to independence. Since independence there has been no change in the abortion law.

The Soviet Decree of 27 June 1936 prohibited the performance of abortions except in cases of danger to life, serious threat to health, or the existence of a serious disease that could be inherited from the parents. The abortion had to be performed in a hospital or maternity home. Physicians who performed abortions outside a hospital or without the presence of one of these indications were subject to one to two years' imprisonment. If the abortion was performed under unsanitary conditions or by a person with no special medical education, the penalty was no less than three years' imprisonment. A person who induced a woman to have an abortion was subject to two years' imprisonment. A pregnant woman who underwent an abortion was subject to a reprimand and the payment of a fine of up to 300 roubles in the case of a repeat offence.

In its Decree of 23 November 1955, the Government of the former USSR repealed the general prohibition on the performance of abortions contained in the 1936 Decree. Other regulations issued in 1955 specified that abortions could be performed freely during the first twelve weeks of pregnancy if no contraindication existed and after that point when the continuance of the pregnancy and the birth would harm the mother (interpreted to include foetal handicap). The abortion had to be performed in a hospital by a physician and, unless performed in cases of a threat to the mother's health, a fee was charged. Persons who performed an abortion illegally were subject to criminal penalties established by criminal laws such as the Criminal Code. For example, if the abortion was not performed in a hospital, a penalty of up to one year's imprisonment could be imposed, and if it was performed by a person without an advanced medical degree, a penalty of up to two years' imprisonment was possible. In the case of repeat offences or the death or serious injury of the pregnant woman, a higher penalty of up to eight years' imprisonment could be imposed. A woman who underwent an illegal abortion was not penalized.

Despite the approval of the 1955 Decree and regulations, the problem of illegal abortions did not entirely disappear in the former Soviet Union. This situation resulted in part from the Government's conflicted attitude towards contraception. Although, at times, it manifested support for contraception, it did little to make contraception available and in 1974 effectively banned the widespread use of oral contraceptives. The situation was also due in part to a revived pronatalist approach to childbearing adopted at times by the Government, which looked unfavourably on abortion. The result was a reliance on abortion as the primary method of family planning.

Concerned with the high rate of illegal abortions, the Government in 1982 issued a decree allowing abortions for health reasons to be performed through the twenty-eighth week of pregnancy. Continuing this approach of increasing the circumstances under which legal abortions were available, on 31 December 1987 it issued an order setting out a broad range of non-medical indications for abortions performed on request

Source: Population Policy Data Bank maintained by the Population Division of the Department of Economic and Social Affairs of the United Nations Secretariat. For additional sources, see list of references.

through the twenty-eighth week of pregnancy. These included the death of the husband during pregnancy; imprisonment of the pregnant woman or her husband; deprivation of maternity rights; multiparity (the number of children exceeds five); divorce during pregnancy; pregnancy following rape; and child disability in the family. Moreover, the order provided that, with the approval of a commission, an abortion could be performed on any other grounds.

This extension of the grounds for abortion after the first twelve weeks of pregnancy, combined with the ambivalent attitude of the Government towards contraception, led to a dramatic increase in the number of officially reported abortions.

After Moldova's independence, an overall decline in health care services was registered. High rates of maternal and infant mortality as well as complications from abortions resulted. Abortion continued to be favoured as a tool of birth spacing and fertility control because of shortages of high-quality modern contraceptives, a reliance upon traditional methods, a lack of knowledge of family planning among couples and the absence of adequate training for physicians, nurses, teachers and other specialists.

In 1989, the Moldavian Soviet Socialist Republic registered an abortion rate of 93.0 per 1,000 women aged 15-44 years, one of the highest rates in the former Soviet Union. The actual figure was much higher, because this total did not include most abortions performed in departmental health services and commercial clinics, early vacuum aspirations and self-induced abortions. As in other Soviet successor States, the abortion rate fell throughout the 1990s, to 50 abortions per 1,000 women in 1994, and to 38.8 in 1996. The Government reported a further decline to 30.8 abortions per 1,000 in 1998. In the same period, the use of modern contraception increased to 50 per cent of all sexually active women, suggesting that the use of abortion as a tool of fertility control is decreasing. Moldova has a total fertility rate of 1.8 and a population growth rate of 0.02 per cent for the period 1995-2000.

Source: Population Policy Data Bank maintained by the Population Division of the Department of Economic and Social Affairs of the United Nations Secretariat. For additional sources, see list of references.

Romania

ABORTION POLICY

Grounds on which abortion is permitted:

To save the life of the woman	Yes
To preserve physical health	Yes
To preserve mental health	Yes
Rape or incest	Yes
Foetal impairment	Yes
Economic or social reasons	Yes
Available on request	Yes

Additional requirements:

Abortion is permitted on request during the first trimester of pregnancy. Thereafter, a legal abortion can only be performed for therapeutic reasons. A legal abortion must be performed by an obstetrician-gynaecologist in a hospital or dispensary.

REPRODUCTIVE HEALTH CONTEXT

Government view on fertility level:	Too low
Government intervention concerning fertility level:	To raise
Government policy on contraceptive use:	Direct support provided
Percentage of currently married women using modern contraception (aged 15-44, 1993):	14
Total fertility rate (1995-2000):	1.2
Age-specific fertility rate (per 1,000 women aged 15-19, 1995-2000):	36
Government has expressed particular concern about:	
Morbidity and mortality resulting from induced abortion	Yes
Complications of childbearing and childbirth	..
Maternal mortality ratio (per 100,000 live births, 1990):	
National	130
Developed countries	27
Female life expectancy at birth (1995-2000):	73.9

Source: Population Policy Data Bank maintained by the Population Division of the Department of Economic and Social Affairs of the United Nations Secretariat. For additional sources, see list of references

BACKGROUND

Abortion on request was first legalized in Romania in 1957. The abortion had to be performed during the first trimester of pregnancy in a hospital and the pregnant woman was required to pay 30 lei. The Law was enacted by the Government for several reasons in order to protect women's health and to support reproductive self-determination.

In 1966, the Government dramatically altered its policy. Concerned about the low rate of population growth, it introduced a number of measures to increase the fertility rate. These measures made abortion legally available only in certain limited circumstances, restricted access to contraception, and increased allowances for large families. Council of State Decree No. 770 of 29 September 1966 restricted abortion to the following situations: the continuance of the pregnancy posed a serious danger to the life of the pregnant woman that could not otherwise be prevented; one parent suffered from a serious hereditary disease or a disease likely to cause serious congenital malformations; the pregnant woman suffered from a serious physical, mental, or sensory disorder; the pregnancy resulted from rape or incest; the pregnant woman was over age 45 (subsequently lowered to age 40 in 1972 and raised to 42 in 1984); or the pregnant woman had given birth to at least four children that were under her care.

Except for abortions performed to save the life of the pregnant woman, a legal abortion had to be performed within the first trimester of pregnancy by a specialist in obstetrics and gynaecology in a specialized health-care unit, with the approval of a medical board. Women who obtained an illegal abortion, as well as the persons performing it, were subject to fines and imprisonment.

The sudden imposition of severe restrictions on access to legal abortion and modern contraception had an immediate if somewhat short-term impact on fertility levels in Romania. The crude birth rate increased and the number of abortions declined sharply from 973,000 in 1966 to 206,000 in 1967. However, the birth rate began to decrease once again in 1967 and reached the 1966 level (14.3 births per 1,000 population) in 1983. Despite Government restrictions on abortion, the abortion ratio also began to increase in 1967, due in part to the existence of an underground illegal abortion network.

Sensing that its demographic policies had been ineffective, the Government of Romania commenced a new campaign in 1984 to increase the birth rate and restrict abortion. A directive issued by the Central Committee of the Romanian Communist Party in March 1984 included systematic control systems and severe measures. In practice this meant that women of reproductive age were required to undergo regular gynaecological examinations at their place of employment. Pregnant women were monitored until delivery, doctors were required to report all women who became pregnant and gynaecological wards were under continuous surveillance. A special tax was levied on unmarried persons over 25 years of age, as well as on childless couples that did not have a medical reason for being childless. Investigations were carried out to determine the cause of all miscarriages.

In 1985, access to abortion was further restricted. The age required for a legal abortion was increased from 42 to 45 years or older. Similarly, having four children was no longer considered sufficient grounds for obtaining an abortion on request. Decree Number 411 of 26 December 1985 provided that to qualify for an abortion, a woman must have given birth to a minimum of five children that were currently under her care.

Source: Population Policy Data Bank maintained by the Population Division of the Department of Economic and Social Affairs of the United Nations Secretariat. For additional sources, see list of references.

Romania

As a result of the restrictive reproductive health policies enforced in Romania between 1966 and 1989, maternal mortality reached heights unprecedented in Europe. The maternal mortality ratio rose from 85 deaths per 100,000 live births in 1965 to 170 in 1983. Moreover, illegal and unsafe abortion was the major cause of maternal mortality, accounting for more than 80 per cent of maternal deaths between 1980 and 1989. Furthermore, unofficial estimates suggest that nearly 20 per cent of women of reproductive age may have become infertile because, on average, a woman may have undergone at least five illegal abortions by age 40.

On 26 December 1989, one of the first acts of the new transitional Government of Romania was to repeal restrictive abortion legislation. Shortly thereafter, it also repealed restrictions on sterilization and the use of contraception. Romania, however, did not enact new abortion legislation until 1996. Under Law No. 140 of 5 November 1996, an abortion can be freely performed during the first 14 weeks of pregnancy so long as it is carried out with the pregnant woman's consent in a medical institution or surgery approved for that purpose by a physician. An abortion may be performed later in pregnancy if absolutely necessary for therapeutic reasons, according to legal provisions. Abortions performed after 14 weeks with the consent of the pregnant woman are punishable by six months' to three years' imprisonment. If the woman does not consent, the punishment is two to seven years' imprisonment and the suspension of other rights. A physician who performs an illegal abortion is subject to suspension from practising his or her profession.

As a consequence of this legal change in Romania, the abortion rate increased precipitously, while the maternal mortality ratio declined dramatically. The abortion rate rose from 39 abortions per 1,000 women aged 15-44 years in 1989 to 199 in 1990. Although the abortion rate fell to 78 abortions per 1,000 women aged 15-44 by 1996, it remains by far the highest in Europe. The maternal mortality ratio also remains the highest in Europe at a 1990 estimate of 130 deaths per 100,000 live births.

Since the revolution in December 1989, the Romanian Ministry of Health and of the Family has made concerted efforts to improve women's reproductive health and to reduce the incidence of abortion. The implementation of a family planning and sex education programme and the manufacture of locally produced contraceptives are top priorities of the Ministry. However, in its efforts to improve and strengthen reproductive health services, the Government faces major challenges, including the need to educate the population in general and health professionals in particular about contraception. Because the policies pursued by the previous Government prohibited contraception, family planning and sex education, many Romanian women know very little about modern family planning methods and most believe that modern contraceptives have adverse side-effects. The modern contraceptive prevalence rate thus remains low, estimated in 1993 to be 14 per cent. Moreover, because of a lack of experience with modern methods of contraception, many members of the Romanian medical profession have been reluctant to accept the safety of modern contraceptives, and many are unaware of the improvements made in recent years to certain methods, such as oral contraceptives. For the period 1995-2000, Romania's current total fertility rate is estimated at 1.2 children per woman and the country has a negative population growth rate of –0.4 per cent.

Source: Population Policy Data Bank maintained by the Population Division of the Department of Economic and Social Affairs of the United Nations Secretariat. For additional sources, see list of references

ABORTION POLICY

Grounds on which abortion is permitted:

To save the life of the woman	Yes
To preserve physical health	Yes
To preserve mental health	Yes
Rape or incest	Yes
Foetal impairment	Yes
Economic or social reasons	Yes
Available on request	Yes

Additional requirements:

An abortion requires the consent of the pregnant woman; it is authorized if performed by a licensed physician in a hospital or other recognized medical institution. Abortion is available on request during the first 12 weeks of gestation. Thereafter, induced abortion is available within 28 weeks from conception on judicial, genetic, vital, broad medical and social grounds, as well as for personal reasons with the special authorization of a commission of local physicians.

REPRODUCTIVE HEALTH CONTEXT

Government view on fertility level:	Too low
Government intervention concerning fertility level:	To raise
Government policy on contraceptive use:	Direct support provided
Percentage of currently married women using modern contraception (aged 15-44, 1996):	55[a,b]
Total fertility rate (1995-2000):	1.4
Age-specific fertility rate (per 1,000 women aged 15-19, 1995-2000):	45
Government has expressed particular concern about:	
Morbidity and mortality resulting from induced abortion	Yes
Complications of childbearing and childbirth	Yes
Maternal mortality ratio (per 100,000 live births, 1990):	
National	75
Developed countries	27
Female life expectancy at birth (1995-2000):	72.8

[a] Including consensual unions, where possible.
[b] Adjusted from source to exclude breastfeeding.

Source: The Population Policy Data Bank maintained by the Population Division of the Department of Economic and Social Affairs of the United Nations Secretariat. For additional sources, see list of references.

BACKGROUND

As was the case with all of the former Soviet republics, the Russian Federation, known prior to 1992 as the Russian Soviet Socialist Republic, observed the abortion legislation and regulations of the former Union of Soviet Socialist Republics. As a result, abortion practices in the Russian Federation were similar to those throughout the former USSR.

The Soviet Decree of 27 June 1936 prohibited the performance of abortions except in cases of danger to life, serious threat to health, or the existence of a serious disease that could be inherited from the parents. The abortion had to be performed in a hospital or maternity home. Physicians who performed abortions outside a hospital or without the presence of one of these indications were subject to one to two years' imprisonment. If the abortion was performed under unsanitary conditions or by a person with no special medical education, the penalty was no less than three years' imprisonment. A person who induced a woman to have an abortion was subject to two years' imprisonment. A pregnant woman who underwent an abortion was subject to a reprimand and the payment of a fine of up to 300 roubles in the case of a repeat offence.

In its Decree of 23 November 1955, the Government of the former USSR repealed the general prohibition on the performance of abortions contained in the 1936 Decree. Other regulations issued in 1955 specified that abortions could be performed freely during the first twelve weeks of pregnancy if no contraindication existed and after that point when the continuance of the pregnancy and the birth would harm the mother (interpreted to include foetal handicap). The abortion had to be performed in a hospital by a physician and, unless performed in cases of a threat to the mother's health, a fee was charged. Persons who performed an abortion illegally were subject to criminal penalties established by criminal laws under the Criminal Code. For example, if the abortion was not performed in a hospital, a penalty of up to one year's imprisonment could be imposed, and if it was performed by a person without an advanced medical degree, a penalty of up to two years' imprisonment was possible. In the case of repeat offences or the death or serious injury of the pregnant woman, a higher penalty of up to eight years' imprisonment could be imposed. A woman who underwent an illegal abortion was not penalized.

Despite the approval of the 1955 Decree and regulations, the problem of illegal abortions did not entirely disappear in the former Soviet Union. This situation resulted in part from the Government's conflicted attitude towards contraception. Although at times the Government manifested support for contraception, it did little to make contraception available and in 1974 effectively banned the widespread use of oral contraceptives. The situation was also due in part to a revived pronatalist approach to childbearing adopted at times by the Government, which looked unfavourably on abortion. The result was a reliance on abortion as the primary method of family planning.

Concerned with the high rate of illegal abortions, the Government in 1982 issued a Decree allowing abortions for health reasons to be performed through the twenty-eighth week of pregnancy. Continuing this approach of increasing the circumstances under which legal abortions were available, on 31 December 1987 it issued an order setting out a broad range of non-medical indications for abortions performed on request through the twenty-eighth week of pregnancy. These were included the death of the husband during pregnancy; imprisonment of the pregnant woman or her husband; deprivation of maternity rights; multiparity (the number of

---

Source: The Population Policy Data Bank maintained by the Population Division of the Department of Economic and Social Affairs of the United Nations Secretariat. For additional sources, see list of references.

children exceeds five); divorce during pregnancy; pregnancy following rape; and child disability in the family. Moreover, the order provided that, with the approval of a commission, an abortion could performed on any other grounds.

In 1996, the Ministry of Health issued a new order on indications for the performance of abortions on social grounds after the first twelve weeks of pregnancy. The order lists six new indications beyond those mentioned above: they include the husband's disability, the husband or wife's unemployment, the unmarried status of the woman, the woman's precarious financial condition, the woman's lack of housing, and the woman's status as a refugee or a person needing resettlement. On the other hand, the order eliminated the possibility of a woman obtaining an abortion for other reasons if approved by a commission. Further, in July another order was issued reducing from twenty-eight to twenty-two weeks the period in pregnancy in which an abortion could be obtained on social grounds. The changes appear to reflect three factors: (a) the difficult economic and social conditions experienced by women since the break up of the Soviet Union; (b) the ability of women to circumvent the requirements for late-term abortions; and (c) the ability of medical technology to keep a foetus alive outside the mother's body earlier in pregnancy.

Moreover, at about the same time in 1996, the Russian Federation enacted a new Criminal Code with provisions on the performance of illegal abortions. The former Code contained a blanket prohibition on the performance of such abortions. The new Code repeals this provision and now provides that the only time that an abortion will be considered to have been performed illegally is when the person performing it did not have the proper qualifications. The Code, in effect, removes criminal sanctions on the performance of abortions as long as they are carried out by a qualified practitioner.

This extension of the grounds for abortion after the first twelve weeks of pregnancy, combined with the ambivalent attitude of the Government towards contraception, led to a dramatic increase in the number of officially reported abortions. Other factors resulting in a high incidence of abortion have included shortages of high-quality modern contraceptives and reliance upon less reliable traditional methods; a lack of knowledge concerning contraception and the detrimental health consequences of frequent abortions; and the absence of adequate training for physicians, nurses, teachers and other specialists.

In 1990, a total of 3.9 million induced abortions were registered in the Russian Federation, giving an abortion rate of 119.6 per 1,000 women aged 15-44 years, one of the highest in the world. The actual figure is believed to be much higher, because this total does not include most abortions performed in departmental health services and commercial clinics, early vacuum aspirations and self-induced abortions. Owing to the implementation of family planning programmes in the period 1994-1997, abortions declined by 29 per cent according to the International Planned Parenthood Federation. Still, the abortion rate for 1995 was estimated to be 68.4 abortions per 1,000 women aged 15-44. The total number of abortions in the Russian Federation is still estimated to be almost double the number of births.

Maternal mortality ratios in the Russian Federation were 68 per 100,000 births in 1980, 50 in 1988, and 75 in 1990, one of the highest rates in the former Soviet Union and in Europe. More generally, the population growth rate for 1995-2000 was –0.2 per cent with a total fertility rate of 1.4 children per woman. The Government of the Russian Federation finds these rates too low.

As a means of improving the demographic situation, the Committee for the Family and Demographic Policies, under the Council of Ministers of the Russian Federation, formulated the State Programme on Family Planning for the period 1991-1995. The Programme was designed to modify the attitudes of citizens,

Source: The Population Policy Data Bank maintained by the Population Division of the Department of Economic and Social Affairs of the United Nations Secretariat. For additional sources, see list of references.

to make the people aware of their right to family planning, to protect the reproductive health of individuals and couples, and to enable them to have children that are desired and healthy. The Programme provided the basis for regional programmes and accommodated demographic and religious diversity by integrating the activities of various organizations, cooperatives and other institutions. After the International Conference on Population and Development, held in Cairo in 1994, the Government created the Presidential Family Planning Programme and the Presidential Safe Motherhood Programme. By 1999, the Government reported that these programmes had helped reduce the total number of abortions by a third, and abortion-related maternal mortality by 20 per cent.

The modern contraceptive prevalence rate was 55 per cent in 1996 and availability and quality were considered continuing obstacles. The only two condom factories in the Russian Federation reportedly ceased production in 1992 because they could no longer afford to import latex, while the only factory manufacturing IUDs was closed down because of complaints concerning the quality of its products.

Source: The Population Policy Data Bank maintained by the Population Division of the Department of Economic and Social Affairs of the United Nations Secretariat. For additional sources, see list of references.

Rwanda

ABORTION POLICY

Grounds on which abortion is permitted:

To save the life of the woman	Yes
To preserve physical health	Yes
To preserve mental health	Yes
Rape or incest	No
Foetal impairment	No
Economic or social reasons	No
Available on request	No

Additional requirements:

An abortion must be performed by a physician in a public hospital or other authorized health-care facility. Two physicians must confirm in writing that continuation of the pregnancy would seriously endanger the woman's health.

REPRODUCTIVE HEALTH CONTEXT

Government view on fertility level:	Too high
Government intervention concerning fertility level:	To lower
Government policy on contraceptive use:	Direct support provided
Percentage of currently married women using modern contraception (aged 15-49, 1992):	13
Total fertility rate (1995-2000):	6.2
Age-specific fertility rate (per 1,000 women aged 15-19, 1995-2000):	56
Government has expressed particular concern about:	
Morbidity and mortality resulting from induced abortion	..
Complications of childbearing and childbirth	..
Maternal mortality ratio (per 100,000 live births, 1990):	
National	1 300
Eastern Africa	1 060
Female life expectancy at birth (1995-2000):	41.7

Source: Population Policy Data Bank maintained by the Population Division of the Department of Economic and Social Affairs of the United Nations Secretariat. For additional sources, see list of references.

BACKGROUND

Until 1977, abortion was generally illegal in Rwanda. The Criminal Code (Ordinance 43/Just. of 18 May 1970), which was based on the 1940 Penal Code of the Belgian Congo, contained no stated exceptions to the prohibition on the performance of abortions, and an abortion could be carried out only under general criminal law principles of necessity to save the life of the pregnant woman.

In 1977, Rwanda enacted a new Penal Code (Law 21-77 of 18 August 1977) that liberalized to some degree the performance of abortions. The law prohibits abortion except when the continuance of the pregnancy seriously endangers the health of the pregnant woman. In such cases, a second medical opinion is required, and the intervention must be performed by a State physician or physician approved by the State in a public hospital or a private hospital approved by the State.

Any person who induces an abortion is subject to 5-10 years' imprisonment if the woman does not consent and to two to five years' imprisonment if she consents. A person who is employed in a health profession and performs an abortion is subject to suspension from practicing his or her profession for one to five years or, in the case of repeat offenders, for life. A woman inducing her own abortion or consenting to an abortion is subject to two to five years' imprisonment.

Illegal abortions are performed in Rwanda, usually by means of plant extracts or heavy massages. However, abortion is not reported to be widespread. When abortion does occur, it appears to be limited mainly to unmarried women. Rather than relying upon contraception or abortion, women in Rwanda space their births by means of such traditional practices as abstinence due to mourning rites or prolonged breastfeeding.

Family planning efforts in Rwanda date back 30 years. The first family planning programme offering modern contraception was established in 1962, but family planning goals were included for the first time in the Five-Year Plan for the period 1977-1981. In 1974, the Government of Rwanda established the Scientific Council for Socio-demographic Problems, which proposed the creation of an institution that would address population issues on a permanent basis. In 1981, the National Population Office (ONAPO) was established to implement population programmes and to begin a programme to integrate family planning services into all of the health-care facilities in Rwanda.

The Government of Rwanda has long been aware of the major threat that population growth poses for the development of the country. Nevertheless, Government actions were constrained by the strong pronatalist sentiments of the population and by the opposition of religious groups to family planning. However, the pressure of population on agricultural land gradually brought about a change in attitude, and family planning is now considered to be a key element in national development. Religious groups have also acknowledged demographic problems in Rwanda and have begun to soften their opposition. In 1990, the family planning programme was expanded and a national population policy and plan of action were adopted, with the goal of reducing the population growth rate from 3.7 to 2.0 per cent by the year 2000. Related goals were to increase the contraceptive prevalence rate from 2 to 48 per cent and to decrease the total fertility rate from 8.6 to 4.0 births per woman.

Source: Population Policy Data Bank maintained by the Population Division of the Department of Economic and Social Affairs of the United Nations Secretariat. For additional sources, see list of references.

Rwanda

Currently, however, Rwanda is facing overwhelming consequences of its civil war, which led to the death of more than 500,000 people and a massive exodus from the country. The main challenge is to rebuild the health and family planning infrastructure so as to restore the accessibility of services. Victims of sexual abuse during the genocide suffer persistent health problems in the area of reproductive health including the spread of HIV/AIDS. The National Population Office has estimated the "pregnancies of war," "enfants non-desirés" (unwanted children) or "enfants mauvais souvenir" (bad memories children) to be between 2,000 and 5,000. Rape-related pregnancies resulted in a substantial number of induced abortions after the war despite their illegality, and Rwandan doctors have treated women with serious complications resulting from self-induced or clandestine abortions. As a result, there is continuing political pressure to further liberalize abortion law despite a general pronatalist view arising from the genocide's traumatic loss of life.

Rwanda's maternal mortality ratio was estimated at 1,300 deaths per 100,000 live births in 1990. The country has a low level of modern contraceptive use (13 per cent in 1992) and a current total fertility rate of 6.2 children per woman (1995-2000 estimate).

Source: Population Policy Data Bank maintained by the Population Division of the Department of Economic and Social Affairs of the United Nations Secretariat. For additional sources, see list of references.

Saint Kitts and Nevis

ABORTION POLICY

Grounds on which abortion is permitted:

To save the life of the woman	Yes
To preserve physical health	Yes
To preserve mental health	Yes
Rape or incest	No
Foetal impairment	No
Economic or social reasons	No
Available on request	No

Additional requirements:

Legal abortions are usually performed within 28 weeks of gestation.

REPRODUCTIVE HEALTH CONTEXT

Government view on fertility level:	Too high
Government intervention concerning fertility level:	To lower
Government policy on contraceptive use:	Direct support provided
Percentage of currently married women using modern contraception (aged 15-44,* 1984):	37
Total fertility rate (1995-2000):	..
Age-specific fertility rate (per 1,000 women aged 15-19, 1995-2000):	..
Government has expressed particular concern about:	
Morbidity and mortality resulting from induced abortion	..
Complications of childbearing and childbirth	..
Maternal mortality ratio (per 100,000 live births, 1990):	
National	..
Caribbean	400
Female life expectancy at birth (1995-2000):	..

* All sexually active women.

Source: Population Policy Data Bank maintained by the Population Division of the Department of Economic and Social Affairs of the United Nations Secretariat. For additional sources, see list of references.

BACKGROUND

Abortion law in Saint Kitts and Nevis derives from the English Offences against the Person Act of 1861. Under the Act, any person who, intending to procure a miscarriage, regardless of whether the woman is with child, unlawfully administers to her any poison or noxious thing or unlawfully uses any instrument or other means to the same end is subject to life imprisonment, with or without hard labour. A pregnant woman who acts in the same way with respect to her own pregnancy is subject to the same penalty.

Nonetheless, under the Infant Life (Preservation) Act, also based on English legislation, an abortion may be performed to save the life of the pregnant woman. The Act provides that a person who wilfully causes a child capable of being born alive to die before it has an existence independent from its mother shall not be guilty of an offence if the person acted in good faith for the purpose of preserving the life of the mother.

Moreover, Saint Kitts and Nevis, like a number of Commonwealth countries, whose legal systems are based on the English common law, follows the holding of the 1938 English *Rex v. Bourne* decision in determining whether an abortion performed for health reasons is lawful. In the *Bourne* decision, a physician was acquitted of the offence of performing an abortion in the case of a woman who had been raped. The court ruled that the abortion was lawful because it had been performed to prevent the woman from becoming "a physical and mental wreck", thus setting a precedent for future abortion cases performed on the grounds of preserving the pregnant woman's physical and mental health.

The Government of Saint Kitts and Nevis considers the rates of population growth and fertility to be too high and has a policy of intervention directed to reducing those rates. It is extensively involved in family planning and provides contraceptives through the national family planning programme. The Saint Kitts and Nevis Family Planning Association, which was founded in 1966, complements the Government's family planning efforts by distributing contraceptives to government clinics and promoting family planning by means of radio, television and newspapers. The modern contraceptive prevalence rate was estimated in 1984 to be 37 per cent.

The Government of Saint Kitts and Nevis is especially concerned about the problem of teenage pregnancy and its social consequences. In response to those concerns, the Government has introduced specialized family life education and family planning programmes directed at the youth of the country. A relatively low total fertility rate and continuing economic emigration have produced a declining population growth rate of –0.8 per cent per year during 1995-2000. After the 1994 Cairo conference, the Government established a Ministry of Women's Affairs with responsibility for reproductive and sexual rights as well as related health services.

Source: Population Policy Data Bank maintained by the Population Division of the Department of Economic and Affairs of the United Nations Secretariat. For additional sources, see list of references.

ABORTION POLICY

Grounds on which abortion is permitted:

To save the life of the woman	Yes
To preserve physical health	Yes
To preserve mental health	Yes
Rape or incest	No
Foetal impairment	No
Economic or social reasons	No
Available on request	No

Additional requirements:

Information is not readily available.

REPRODUCTIVE HEALTH CONTEXT

Government view on fertility level:	Too high
Government intervention concerning fertility level:	To lower
Government policy on contraceptive use:	Direct support provided
Percentage of currently married women using modern contraception (aged 15-44,* 1988):	46
Total fertility rate (1995-2000):	..
Age-specific fertility rate (per 1,000 women aged 15-19, 1995-2000):	..
Government has expressed particular concern about:	
Morbidity and mortality resulting from induced abortion	No
Complications of childbearing and childbirth	Yes
Maternal mortality ratio (per 100,000 live births, 1990):	
National	..
Caribbean	400
Female life expectancy at birth (1995-2000):	..

* Including visiting unions.

Source: Population Policy Data Bank maintained by the Population Division of the Department of Economic and Social Affairs of the United Nations Secretariat. For additional sources, see list of references.

BACKGROUND

Abortion law in Saint Lucia is governed by the provisions of the Criminal Code, as amended through 1992. Under the Code, abortion is generally illegal and any person who intentionally and unlawfully causes abortion or miscarriage is subject to fourteen years' imprisonment. Nonetheless, the Code allows abortions to be legally performed for medical purposes. It provides that an act performed in good faith and without negligence for the purposes of medical or surgical treatment of a pregnant woman is justifiable although it causes or is intended to cause abortion or miscarriage.

Adolescent fertility is a serious problem in Saint Lucia. Although the birth rate is relatively low, the incidence of adolescent pregnancies and births is very high. It is estimated that teenage fertility accounts for 27 per cent of all births in the country. Therefore, the family planning programme places particular emphasis on adolescents. Saint Lucia had a population growth rate of 1.4 per cent for 1995-2000.

The Government of Saint Lucia directly supports the provision of contraceptives. Activities of the Saint Lucia Planned Parenthood Association complement the Government family planning project. In 1987, the Saint Lucia Family Planning Association observed that the main obstacles to delivering family planning services were traditional and religious practices, the mountainous topography that made some rural villages inaccessible and the high rate of illiteracy in the country.

The Government of Saint Lucia has expressed concern about its rapid population growth, emphasizing that the rate is too high for a small island State that is heavily dependent upon agriculture. The Government response to this concern was the establishment of the Population Planning Unit, which is charged with monitoring population trends and advising the Government on strategies to reduce the population growth rate. Following the International Conference on Population and Development, the Government expanded its sexual and reproductive health services to include counselling on human sexuality, responsible parenthood, effective prevention of sexually transmitted diseases and HIV/AIDS and the promotion, supply and distribution of high quality condoms.

Source: Population Policy Data Bank maintained by the Population Division of the Department of Economic and Social Affairs of the United Nations Secretariat. For additional sources, see list of references.

Saint Vincent and the Grenadines

ABORTION POLICY

Grounds on which abortion is permitted:

To save the life of the woman	Yes
To preserve physical health	Yes
To preserve mental health	Yes
Rape or incest	Yes
Foetal impairment	Yes
Economic or social reasons	Yes
Available on request	No

Additional requirements:

The procedure must be performed by a medical practitioner in an approved hospital or other establishment and two medical practitioners must certify that the legal grounds for abortion have been met. The pregnant woman's actual or reasonably foreseeable environment may be taken into account when deciding the legality of an abortion on health grounds.

REPRODUCTIVE HEALTH CONTEXT

Government view on fertility level:	Too high
Government intervention concerning fertility level:	To lower
Government policy on contraceptive use:	Direct support provided
Percentage of currently married women using modern contraception (aged 15-44,* 1988):	55
Total fertility rate (1995-2000):	..
Age-specific fertility rate (per 1,000 women aged 15-19, 1995-2000):	..
Government has expressed particular concern about:	
Morbidity and mortality resulting from induced abortion	No
Complications of childbearing and childbirth	Yes
Maternal mortality ratio (per 100,000 live births, 1990):	
National	..
Caribbean	400
Female life expectancy at birth (1995-2000):	..

* Including visiting unions.

Source: Population Policy Data Bank maintained by the Population Division of the Department of Economic and Social Affairs of the United Nations Secretariat. For additional sources, see list of references.

BACKGROUND

Until 1988 abortion law in Saint Vincent and the Grenadines, as in most Commonwealth Caribbean countries, was governed by the Indictable Offences Ordinance, which was closely based on the English Offences against the Person Act of 1861. Under this Ordinance, the performance of abortions was generally prohibited, although one could be carried out according to general criminal law principles of necessity to save the life of the pregnant woman.

Moreover, Saint Vincent and the Grenadines, like a number of British Commonwealth countries whose legal systems are based on English common law, followed the holding of the 1938 English *Rex v. Bourne* decision in determining whether an abortion performed for health reasons was lawful. In the *Bourne* decision, a physician was acquitted of the offence of performing an abortion in the case of a woman who had been raped. The court ruled that the abortion was lawful because it had been performed to prevent the woman from becoming "a physical and mental wreck", thus setting a precedent for future abortion cases performed on the grounds of preserving the pregnant woman's physical and mental health.

In 1977, the Minister of Health established a committee to examine the abortion law. The Saint Vincent Medical Association recommended a change in the law to allow for a broad range of indications for the medical termination of pregnancy.

This recommendation was incorporated into the new Criminal Code of 1988 (Act No. 23). Under the Code, abortion is still generally illegal. Any person who, with intent to procure the miscarriage of a woman, whether or not she is pregnant, unlawfully administers or causes her to take any poison or other noxious item, uses force of any kind or uses any other means is guilty of an offence and is subject to imprisonment for 14 years. A pregnant woman who consents to the above or undertakes the same activity with respect to her own miscarriage is subject to seven years' imprisonment. A person who unlawfully supplies poison or other noxious things for any person or uses force or any instrument, knowing that it will be unlawfully used to induce the miscarriage of any woman, whether or not she is pregnant, is guilty of an offence and is subject to imprisonment for five years.

However, a pregnancy may be lawfully terminated by a medical practitioner in a hospital or other establishment approved by the Senior Medical Officer, when two medical practitioners are of the opinion formed in good faith, that (a) continuation of the pregnancy would involve risk to the life of the pregnant woman or injury to her physical or mental health, or to that of any of her existing children, greater than if the pregnancy were terminated; or (b) there is a substantial risk that, if the child were born, it would suffer from a physical or mental abnormality so as to be seriously handicapped. The woman's actual or reasonably foreseeable environment may be taken into consideration in the determination of whether continuation of the pregnancy would involve risk to the life or physical or mental health of the pregnant woman. In an emergency, a registered medical practitioner may perform an abortion without the second opinion of another medical practitioner in a place other than an approved hospital or establishment, if he or she is of the opinion formed in good faith that the abortion is immediately necessary to save the life of the woman or to prevent grave permanent injury to her physical or mental health.

Performance of an abortion is also legal if carried out in an approved hospital or other establishment when the pregnancy results from an act of rape or incest, whether or not any person has been charged with the offence of rape or incest.

Source: Population Policy Data Bank maintained by the Population Division of the Department of Economic and Social Affairs of the United Nations Secretariat. For additional sources, see list of references.

Saint Vincent and the Grenadines

The Government of Saint Vincent and the Grenadines considers the rates of population growth and fertility to be too high and believes that the current population growth rate will severely strain the limited natural resources of the country. The Government's population policy is directed to reducing the rate of population growth to 0.7 per cent by the year 2030. Strongly committed to family planning, the Government seeks to lower fertility levels through a national family planning programme in which the Ministry of Health provides free family planning services in all health-care centres. Adolescent fertility is viewed as a major concern and special emphasis is placed on youth, for whom outreach programmes have been developed. Family planning is a priority in the training of health-care personnel and in health education. The Ministry of Health also conducts an education programme for parents, which includes workshops on sexuality, family planning, family life education and communication skills.

The Government directly supports the provision of modern methods of contraceptives, a wide range of which are available to men and women, including adolescents, regardless of marital status. A 1988 study found the level of modern contraceptive use at 55 per cent. Female sterilization is permitted upon the assurance that the woman will not want more children, with the consent of the spouse and upon consideration of the woman's age and marital status.

Source: Population Policy Data Bank maintained by the Population Division of the Department of Economic and Social Affairs of the United Nations Secretariat. For additional sources, see list of references.

ABORTION POLICY

Grounds on which abortion is permitted:

To save the life of the woman	Yes
To preserve physical health	Yes
To preserve mental health	Yes
Rape or incest	No
Foetal impairment	No
Economic or social reasons	No
Available on request	No

Additional requirements:

Information is not readily available.

REPRODUCTIVE HEALTH CONTEXT

Government view on fertility level:	Too high
Government intervention concerning fertility level:	To lower
Government policy on contraceptive use:	Direct support provided
Percentage of currently married women using modern contraception (aged 15-49):	..
Total fertility rate (1995-2000):	4.2
Age-specific fertility rate (per 1,000 women aged 15-19, 1995-2000):	37
Government has expressed particular concern about:	
Morbidity and mortality resulting from induced abortion	..
Complications of childbearing and childbirth	..
Maternal mortality ratio (per 100,000 live births, 1990):	
National	35
Oceania	680
Female life expectancy at birth (1995-2000):	73.6

Source: Population Policy Data Bank maintained by the Population Division of the Department of Economic and Social Affairs of the United Nations Secretariat. For additional sources, see list of references.

BACKGROUND

The performance of abortions in Samoa is regulated by the Crimes Ordinance of 1961, as amended by the Crimes Amendment Act of 1969. Under the Ordinance, abortion is generally illegal. Anyone who unlawfully uses any means on a woman, whether she is pregnant or not, with intent to procure her miscarriage is subject to up to seven years' imprisonment. A woman who undertakes the same act is subject to the same penalty.

Nonetheless, Article 73 of the Act provides that a person who before or during the birth of any child causes its death by means employed in good faith for the preservation of the life of the mother is not guilty of any crime.

In addition, Samoa, like many Commonwealth countries, whose legal systems are based on the English common law, follows the holding of the 1938 English *Rex v. Bourne* decision in determining whether an abortion performed for health reasons is lawful. In the *Bourne* decision, a physician was acquitted of the offence of performing an abortion in the case of a woman who had been raped. The court ruled that the abortion was lawful because it had been performed to prevent the woman from becoming "a physical and mental wreck", thus setting a precedent for future abortion cases performed on the grounds of preserving the pregnant woman's physical and mental health.

Induced abortion appears socially acceptable in Samoa and has reportedly been performed routinely in cases of rape or incest. Findings from the Western Samoa Family Planning Knowledge, Attitude and Practice Survey (KAP) in 1971 show that induced abortion, although illegal, was considered permissible by 34 per cent of unmarried women, by 28 per cent of married women and by 15 per cent of husbands.

There are no reliable estimates on the frequency of induced abortion in Samoa. Since the early 1970s, the Government of Samoa has made efforts to control the high natural growth rate of its population. In 1971, the Government created the Family Welfare Programme incorporating family planning as an integral part of maternal and child health (MCH) services. High priority has been given to improving maternal and child health, largely through child spacing. Other non-governmental organizations, such as the Samoan Family Health Association, have been active in strengthening and developing MCH care and family planning services, in collaboration with the government programme. Samoa has successfully extended basic health services to all of its population and since the International Conference on Population and Development, held in Cairo in 1994, has focused increasingly on maternal and child health care as well as family planning.

Source: Population Policy Data Bank maintained by the Population Division of the Department of Economic and Social Affairs of the United Nations Secretariat. For additional sources, see list of references.

ABORTION POLICY

Grounds on which abortion is permitted:

To save the life of the woman	Yes*
To preserve physical health	No
To preserve mental health	No
Rape or incest	No
Foetal impairment	No
Economic or social reasons	No
Available on request	No

Additional requirements:

Not applicable.

* Legal interpretation generally permits this ground.

REPRODUCTIVE HEALTH CONTEXT

Government view on fertility level:	Satisfactory
Government intervention concerning fertility level:	No intervention
Government policy on contraceptive use:	Indirect support provided
Percentage of currently married women using modern contraception (aged 15-49):	..
Total fertility rate (1995-2000):	..
Age-specific fertility rate (per 1,000 women aged 15-19, 1995-2000):	..
Government has expressed particular concern about:	
Morbidity and mortality resulting from induced abortion	..
Complications of childbearing and childbirth	No
Maternal mortality ratio (per 100,000 live births, 1990):	
National	..
Developed countries	27
Female life expectancy at birth (1995-2000):	..

Source: Population Policy Data Bank maintained by the Population Division of the Department of Economic and Social Affairs of the United Nations Secretariat. For additional sources, see list of references.

San Marino

BACKGROUND

Under Articles 153 and 154 of the Penal Code of San Marino, abortion is generally prohibited. A woman who procures her own abortion and a person who helps her are subject to imprisonment of the second degree. A person who performs an abortion on a pregnant woman over twenty-one years old with her consent is subject to the same penalty. The penalty of imprisonment of the third degree is imposed if the woman does not consent to the abortion, if the abortion is performed for economic gain, or if the woman dies or is seriously injured. A health professional performing an abortion is subject to imprisonment of the third degree as well as suspension from the practice of his or her profession of the fourth degree. A pregnant woman who because of her honour causes her own abortion or consents to it being caused is subject to imprisonment of the first degree. Nonetheless, under general criminal law principles of necessity, an abortion can be performed to save the life of the pregnant woman.

When the Penal Code of San Marino was modified in 1974, a proposal was submitted for liberalization of the abortion law, which included six grounds on which abortion would have been permitted. Following a lengthy discussion, the Government decided to defer modification of the abortion law in order to permit further debate; the two articles on abortion were maintained unaltered. As of 1999, no new law had been enacted.

San Marino, a small enclave within the territory of Italy, relies upon Italy for some functions. It is therefore likely that women in San Marino desiring an abortion can seek one in neighbouring Italy, which has a more liberal law. The Government reported that it did not wish to modify existing fertility levels. The country is experiencing an ageing population and a decreasing rate of birth. The State provides free health care for all of its 25,000 citizens and residents.

One of the questions raised when the modification of the Penal Code occurred was whether a new abortion law would require new programmes on sex education. A programme of health education, including sex education, was subsequently implemented; it also includes information on contraceptive use.

Source: Population Policy Data Bank maintained by the Population Division of the Department of Economic and Social Affairs of the United Nations Secretariat. For additional sources, see list of references.

ABORTION POLICY

Grounds on which abortion is permitted:

To save the life of the woman	Yes*
To preserve physical health	No
To preserve mental health	No
Rape or incest	No
Foetal impairment	No
Economic or social reasons	No
Available on request	No

Additional requirements:

An abortion may be performed during the first 12 weeks of pregnancy. The decision whether there are grounds to perform an abortion is made by the physician who will perform the abortion. A waiver must be signed by the pregnant woman or by her parents if she is a minor (under 18 years of age).

* Official interpretation generally permits this ground.

REPRODUCTIVE HEALTH CONTEXT

Government view on fertility level:	Too high
Government intervention concerning fertility level:	No intervention
Government policy on contraceptive use:	Direct support provided
Percentage of currently married women using modern contraception (aged 15-49):	..
Total fertility rate (1995-2000):	..
Age-specific fertility rate (per 1,000 women aged 15-19, 1995-2000):	..
Government has expressed particular concern about:	
Morbidity and mortality resulting from induced abortion	..
Complications of childbearing and childbirth	Yes
Maternal mortality ratio (per 100,000 live births, 1990):	
National	..
Middle Africa	950
Female life expectancy at birth (1995-2000):	..

Source: Population Policy Data Bank maintained by the Population Division of the Department of Economic and Social Affairs of the United Nations Secretariat. For additional sources, see list of references.

Sao Tome and Principe

BACKGROUND

Sao Tome and Principe achieved independence from Portugal on 12 July 1975, inheriting the Portuguese legal system. The pre-independence laws of the country were those of Portugal, including the Penal Code of 1886. After independence, this law remained in effect and has not been repealed. Under the Code, there are no stated exceptions to a general prohibition on the performance of abortions, although general criminal law principles of necessity allowed the operation to save the life of a pregnant woman. Any person performing an illegal abortion, including the pregnant woman, is subject to imprisonment.

The de facto policy on abortion is reportedly more liberal and abortion is allowed during the first 12 weeks of pregnancy on medical grounds and in cases of rape, incest or foetal impairment. The decision whether there are grounds to perform an abortion is made by the physician who will perform the abortion.

National development plans have mainly been directed at promoting economic development and improving the health status of the population. The Government of Sao Tome and Principe is concerned about the large number of induced abortions and attributes this situation to the deficiency of the family planning programme. The Government supports family planning activities principally to improve maternal and child health (MCH) and family life conditions. The Government is receiving international assistance for a population programme that has as its immediate goals to expand the provision of integrated MCH and family planning, to increase the contraceptive prevalence rate from 7.6 to 20 per cent, to lower the incidence of abortion, and to expand population education and family life education programmes.

Source: Population Policy Data Bank maintained by the Population Division of the Department for Economic and Social Information and Policy Analysis of the United Nations Secretariat. For additional sources, see list of references.

ABORTION POLICY

Grounds on which abortion is permitted:

To save the life of the woman	Yes
To preserve physical health	Yes
To preserve mental health	Yes
Rape or incest	No
Foetal impairment	No
Economic or social reasons	No
Available on request	No

Additional requirements:

A legal abortion must be performed in a government hospital. A panel of three medical specialists appointed by the hospital director must sign a recommendation before an abortion can be performed. Written consent must be obtained from the patient and her husband or her guardian, using a standard Government-approved form.

REPRODUCTIVE HEALTH CONTEXT

Government view on fertility level:	Satisfactory
Government intervention concerning fertility level:	Maintain
Government policy on contraceptive use:	Indirect support provided
Percentage of currently married women using modern contraception (aged 15-49):	..
Total fertility rate (1995-2000):	5.8
Age-specific fertility rate (per 1,000 women aged 15-19, 1995-2000):	113
Government has expressed particular concern about:	
Morbidity and mortality resulting from induced abortion	No
Complications of childbearing and childbirth	No
Maternal mortality ratio (per 100,000 live births, 1990):	
National	130
Western Asia	320
Female life expectancy at birth (1995-2000):	73.4

Source: Population Policy Data Bank maintained by the Population Division of the Department of Economic and Social Affairs of the United Nations Secretariat. For additional sources, see list of references.

BACKGROUND

Induced abortion is generally illegal in Saudi Arabia under non-codified principles of Islamic law. A person who performs an illegal abortion is subject to the payment of blood money to the relatives of the aborted foetus. However, under article 24 of the Rules of Implementation for Regulations of the Practice of Medicine and Dentistry, Ministerial Resolution No. 218/17/L of 26 June 1989, an abortion may be performed to save the pregnant woman's life, and if the pregnancy is less than four months old and it is proven beyond doubt that continued pregnancy gravely endangers the mother's health. Written consent of the patient and her husband or guardian is required.

Article 24 is based on Resolution No. 140 by the Committee of Senior Ulema, which is reproduced in the above Rules and provides that a pregnancy cannot be aborted at any stage except when legally (according to Islamic Laws) justified and within very narrow limitations.

Resolution No. 140 refers to three stages of pregnancy. Within the first 40 days of pregnancy, an abortion may be allowed if it is deemed necessary to accomplish a legal benefit or to prevent an expected harm. It is not allowed, however, for fear of hardship in child upbringing or inability to secure the cost of living, education, or future, or if the parents decide that they have enough children. At the embryo stage, an abortion is not allowed unless an approved medical committee decides that continuation of the pregnancy endangers the woman's safety and could possibly lead to her death, and if all means to eliminate the danger have been exhausted. After four months of pregnancy, abortion is not allowed unless a panel of approved specialists states that continuation of the pregnancy will cause the woman's death and all means to eliminate the danger have been exhausted. Resolution No. 140 provides that under these conditions, abortion is allowed "to avoid the gravest of two dangers and to accomplish the better of two benefits".

The Government of Saudi Arabia has not formulated a comprehensive policy that specifically considers population issues. However, because the Government views its population problems in the context of ensuring national identity and meeting its labour force requirements, it considers the rate of population growth to be too low and intervenes to increase population growth among its nationals. The Government views its comparatively high level of fertility as satisfactory but pursues a pronatalist policy. The total fertility rate has fallen from 6.8 children per woman (1985-1990) to 5.8 (1995-2000) and the population growth rate has also fallen over the same period from 4.8 per cent to 3.4 per cent.

Source: Population Policy Data Bank maintained by the Population Division of the Department of Economic and Social Affairs of the United Nations Secretariat. For additional sources, see list of references.

ABORTION POLICY

Grounds on which abortion is permitted:

To save the life of the woman	Yes
To preserve physical health	No
To preserve mental health	No
Rape or incest	No
Foetal impairment	No
Economic or social reasons	No
Available on request	No

Additional requirements:

The physician performing the abortion must obtain the written advice of two consulting physicians, one of whom must be taken from a list of experts provided by the Court. The physicians must attest to the fact that the life of the woman cannot be saved by any means other than the intervention contemplated.

REPRODUCTIVE HEALTH CONTEXT

Government view on fertility level:	Too high
Government intervention concerning fertility level:	To lower
Government policy on contraceptive use:	Direct support provided
Percentage of currently married women using modern contraception (aged 15-49, 1997):	8
Total fertility rate (1995-2000):	5.6
Age-specific fertility rate (per 1,000 women aged 15-19, 1995-2000):	119
Government has expressed particular concern about:	
Morbidity and mortality resulting from induced abortion	Yes
Complications of childbearing and childbirth	Yes
Maternal mortality ratio (per 100,000 live births, 1990):	
National	1 200
Western Africa	1 020
Female life expectancy at birth (1995-2000):	54.2

Source: Population Policy Data Bank maintained by the Population Division of the Department of Economic and Social Affairs of the United Nations Secretariat. For additional sources, see list of references.

Senegal

BACKGROUND

The Criminal Code of Senegal is based on article 317 of the French Penal Code of 1810, as amended by the French decree-law of 1939. Under this Code, the performance of an abortion is generally illegal. Anyone performing an abortion on a pregnant woman whether she consents or not is subject to imprisonment for one to five years and to payment of a fine of 20,000-100,000 CFA francs (CFAF). If the person regularly performs abortions, the penalties are increased to imprisonment for 5-10 years and payment of a fine of CFAF 50,000-500,000. A woman who performs her own abortion or consents to its performance is subject to six months' to two years' imprisonment and payment of a fine of CFAF 20,000 to 100,000. In addition to these penalties, health professionals are also subject to five years' to life-long suspension from practising their profession.

Nonetheless, under general criminal law principles of necessity, an abortion can be performed to save the life of a pregnant woman. Moreover, this exception to the general prohibition against the performance of abortions is specifically provided for in the code of medical ethics of Senegal. Under the Code, in such a circumstance, the presiding doctor is required to obtain the approval of two consulting physicians, one of whom must be taken from a list of experts established by the court. They must attest to the fact that the life of the woman can be saved only by the performance of an abortion.

In March 1971, the Parliament declared that it favoured family planning; in April 1974, the Ministry of Health announced the establishment of a new family planning association. In 1980, Law No. 80-49 of 24 December repealed the French anticontraception law of 1920, which prohibited the advertisement and distribution of contraceptives while inserting a new article in the Penal Code prescribing penalties only for incitement to perform abortion and the display or distribution of abortifacients. The National Population Council was also established in 1980 and a family planning programme was initiated and integrated into maternal and child health services. In 1982, the first seminar on Islam and family planning to be held in Senegal was convened; it recognized the compatibility of Islam with family planning and recommended increased accessibility to contraception, according to the Islamic teaching that one must not have more children than one is able to protect and care for.

The Government inaugurated a new approach to population issues through the launching of a comprehensive population policy in 1988, the first francophone Government to do so in the region. An action plan was adopted in 1991, which included a programme for the promotion of women in development, an information programme for adolescents and a more effective strategy on family planning. The National Family Planning Programme involves locally adapted initiatives designed to overcome specific obstacles, as well as attempts to coordinate the activities of the different donors. In 1997, the Government drafted a programme of priority actions and investments in population in response to the International Conference on Population and Development held in Cairo in 1994. Reproductive health was one of three main areas of action. Implementation of these plans is still at an early stage. A national committee on reproductive health worked throughout 1999 on a series of recommendations to the National Assembly on means of removing the legal barriers to reproductive health in Senegal.

Source: Population Policy Data Bank maintained by the Population Division of the Department of Economic and Social Affairs of the United Nations Secretariat. For additional sources, see list of references.

The 1997 contraceptive prevalence rate was estimated at 8 per cent in 1997 and the total fertility rate remains high at 5.6 children per woman for 1995-2000. Adolescent abortion is thought to be quite high in Senegal and surveys have shown that as many as 12 per cent of secondary-school girls have had an abortion. Estimates of the prevalence of clandestine abortions are uncertain, as women suffering from the complications of illegal abortion are usually unwilling to divulge the reasons and the means used. The Government has expressed concern about the number of induced abortions, as they are a major cause of maternal mortality and morbidity. To reduce maternal mortality (1,200 deaths per 100,000 live births in 1990) and morbidity, programmes are under way for training of personnel, renovation of health centres, research and procurement of contraceptives.

Source: Population Policy Data Bank maintained by the Population Division of the Department of Economic and Social Affairs of the United Nations Secretariat. For additional sources, see list of references.

Seychelles

ABORTION POLICY

Grounds on which abortion is permitted:

To save the life of the woman	Yes
To preserve physical health	Yes
To preserve mental health	Yes
Rape or incest	Yes
Foetal impairment	Yes
Economic or social reasons	No
Available on request	No

Additional requirements:

Abortion is legal in Seychelles during the first 16 weeks of gestation on the grounds of saving the life of the mother, preserving her physical and mental health, foetal impairment and rape or incest. The abortion must be performed in Victoria Hospital by a consulting gynaecologist after the proper authorizations based on medical or legal grounds have been obtained.

REPRODUCTIVE HEALTH CONTEXT

Government view on fertility level:	Too high
Government intervention concerning fertility level:	To lower
Government policy on contraceptive use:	Direct support provided
Percentage of currently married women using modern contraception (aged 15-49):	..
Total fertility rate (1995-2000):	..
Age-specific fertility rate (per 1,000 women aged 15-19, 1995-2000):	..
Government has expressed particular concern about:	
Morbidity and mortality resulting from induced abortion	No
Complications of childbearing and childbirth	No
Maternal mortality ratio (per 100,000 live births, 1990):	
National	..
Eastern Africa	1 060
Female life expectancy at birth (1995-2000):	..

Source: Population Policy Data Bank maintained by the Population Division of the Department of Economic and Social Affairs of the United Nations Secretariat. For additional sources, see list of references.

BACKGROUND

Act No. 6 of 3 June 1994, which re-enacts the Termination of Pregnancy Act of 1981, provides that the performance of an abortion is legal in the Seychelles under the following conditions: (1) if three medical practitioners are of the good faith opinion (a) that the continuance of the pregnancy would involve risk to the life or physical or mental health of the pregnant woman greater than if the pregnancy were terminated; or (b) that there is a substantial risk that if the child were born it would suffer from such physical or mental abnormalities as to be seriously handicapped; (2) if the pregnancy is the result of rape, incest or defilement; or (3) if the woman is mentally unfit to have care of the child.

An abortion may only be performed at Victoria Hospital by a consulting gynaecologist. The three medical practitioners referred to above are to consist of the medical practitioner attending the woman, the consultant gynaecologist who is to perform the abortion, and the Director of Health Services. In the case of rape or incest or mental unsuitability to care for a child, a judge must certify the legal grounds. Abortions may be performed during the first 12 weeks of pregnancy; they can be performed later only if there are exceptional grounds.

In 1990, there were 9 therapeutic abortions for every 100 live births in Seychelles. However, the ratio for 1989, when the known number of illegal abortions with complications (treated in the hospital) is included, was almost 21 abortions per 100 live births.

The Government of the Seychelles considers its rates of fertility and population growth to be too high. Concern about the increasing birth rate in the 1960s led to the implementation of family planning services, which came under the direct supervision of the Government in 1978. Services have been provided within the context of the maternal and child health programme in government clinics and social centres and by community health nurses in outlying rural areas. In an effort to lower the high rate of teenage pregnancy, family life and sex education programmes have been integrated into the school curricula. Sterilization is legal in Seychelles.

Source: Population Policy Data Bank maintained by the Population Division of the Department of Economic and Social Affairs of the United Nations Secretariat. For additional sources, see list of references.

Sierra Leone

ABORTION POLICY

Grounds on which abortion is permitted:

To save the life of the woman	Yes
To preserve physical health	Yes
To preserve mental health	Yes
Rape or incest	No
Foetal impairment	No
Economic or social reasons	No
Available on request	No

Additional requirements:

Information is not readily available.

REPRODUCTIVE HEALTH CONTEXT

Government view on fertility level:	Too high
Government intervention concerning fertility level:	To lower
Government policy on contraceptive use:	Indirect support provided
Percentage of currently married women using modern contraception (aged 15-49):	..
Total fertility rate (1995-2000):	6.1
Age-specific fertility rate (per 1,000 women aged 15-19, 1995-2000):	202
Government has expressed particular concern about:	
Morbidity and mortality resulting from induced abortion	..
Complications of childbearing and childbirth	..
Maternal mortality ratio (per 100,000 live births, 1990):	
National	1 800
Western Africa	1 020
Female life expectancy at birth (1995-2000):	38.7

Source: Population Policy Data Bank, maintained by the Population Division, Department of Economic and Social Affairs, United Nations Secretariat. For additional sources, see reference section.

BACKGROUND

Under Sierra Leone law, The English Offences Against the Person Act of 1861 is still in effect. This Act prohibits the performance of all abortions and makes a person performing an abortion and a pregnant woman consenting to the performance of an abortion subject to imprisonment. A law introduced in 1988 to regulate the practice of pharmacy (Pharmacy and Drugs Act of 1988) also prohibits any advertisement of drugs or services that could be used to terminate or influence the course of a human pregnancy.

Nonetheless, under general criminal law principles of necessity an abortion can be performed to save the life of the pregnant woman. In addition, Sierra Leone, like many Commonwealth countries whose legal systems are based on English common law, follows the holding of the 1938 English *Rex v. Bourne* decision in determining whether an abortion performed for health reasons is lawful. In the *Rex v. Bourne* decision, a physician was acquitted of the offence of performing an abortion in the case of a woman who had been raped. The court ruled that the abortion was lawful because it had been performed to prevent the woman from becoming "a physical and mental wreck", thus setting a precedent for future abortion cases performed on the grounds of preserving the pregnant woman's physical and mental health.

The high incidence of induced abortion is a growing concern in Sierra Leone. The problem is more acute among young women, whose high rates of pregnancy force many to seek abortions. It is estimated that 80 per cent of all legal abortions are performed on women aged 15-24. Complications of induced abortion are the most important cause of hospitalization and maternal mortality in Sierra Leone, a situation that has placed strains on an already overburdened health-care system. Sierra Leone suffers the world's highest maternal mortality ratio (1,800 deaths per 100,000 live births) and has an estimated total fertility rate of 6.1 children per woman (1995-2000).

Both knowledge and availability of family planning services are limited, particularly in rural areas, and birth spacing in the form of post-partum abstinence is the main contraceptive method. It is estimated that only 5 per cent of married women use modern contraceptives. In 1992, the Ministry of Health began to play a major role in promoting family planning by including it as a part of maternal and child health services. The Government is committed to integrating population components into development planning. As a result, the National Population Commission was created in 1982 and a national population programme framework (National Population Policy Paper) was formulated in 1989. In 1992, the Government established a national family planning programme in the Department of Health and Social Services. The civil war of the 1990s seriously affected the entire range of governmental population, health and family planning services.

Source: Population Policy Data Bank, maintained by the Population Division, Department of Economic and Social Affairs of the United Nations Secretariat. For additional sources, see reference section.

Singapore

ABORTION POLICY

Grounds on which abortion is permitted:

To save the life of the woman	Yes
To preserve physical health	Yes
To preserve mental health	Yes
Rape or incest	Yes
Foetal impairment	Yes
Economic or social reasons	Yes
Available on request	Yes

Additional requirements:

A legal abortion requires the written consent of the pregnant woman. Abortion is available on request during the first 24 weeks of gestation unless the procedure is immediately necessary to save the life or to prevent grave permanent injury to the physical or mental health of the pregnant woman. A legal abortion is restricted to citizens of Singapore, wives of Singapore citizens and women that have resided in Singapore for a minimum duration of four months. The qualifications required of physicians performing abortion at different stages of pregnancy are defined: if gestation does not exceed 16 weeks, the physician should have a minimum of 24 months' experience in a recognized obstetrics and gynaecological unit; thereafter, additional specialist qualifications are required. A legal abortion must be performed in a government hospital or other approved institution.

REPRODUCTIVE HEALTH CONTEXT

Government view on fertility level:	Too low
Government intervention concerning fertility level:	To raise
Government policy on contraceptive use:	Direct support provided
Percentage of currently married women using modern contraception (aged 15-44, 1982):	73
Total fertility rate (1995-2000):	1.7
Age-specific fertility rate (per 1,000 women aged 15-19, 1995-2000):	7
Government has expressed particular concern about:	
Morbidity and mortality resulting from induced abortion	No
Complications of childbearing and childbirth	No
Maternal mortality ratio (per 100,000 live births):	
National (1990-1994)	4.8
South-eastern Asia (1990)	440
Female life expectancy at birth (1995-2000):	79.3

Source: Population Policy Data Bank, maintained by the Population Division, Department of Economic and Social Affairs of the United Nations Secretariat. For additional sources, see reference section.

BACKGROUND

Until 1969, abortion legislation in Singapore was based on British laws adopted in the nineteenth century. The performance of an abortion was in general a criminal act punishable under sections 312-316 of the Penal Code. However, an abortion was permitted if performed in good faith to preserve the life of the pregnant woman.

The first legislative act designed to liberalize abortion law was enacted on 20 March 1970. The Act permitted an abortion to be performed on broad medical, eugenic, juridical and socio-economic grounds. Abortions carried out on medical or eugenic grounds could be performed during the first 24 weeks of pregnancy, while abortions performed on juridical and socio-economic grounds could be performed only during the first 16 weeks of pregnancy.

In general, before an abortion was performed, it had to receive the approval of a board composed of 11 members (Termination of Pregnancy Authorization Board). Section 5(3) of the Abortion Act, however, permitted a physician to perform an abortion without the Board's authorization if, after consulting another physician, both reached the conclusion that continuance of the pregnancy would involve serious risk to the life of the pregnant woman or serious injury to her physical or mental health. In this case, the Board was to be notified of the performance of the abortion within a two-week period.

The 1970 law required the written consent of all married women regardless of their age and of unmarried women that were at least 18 years of age. The consent of parents/guardians was required for all unmarried women under age 18. The Board was authorized to consent for unmarried women under age 18 if they had no parents/guardians or were so insane or feeble-minded as to be incapable of giving a valid consent.

The Abortion Act of 1974 (Penal Code, chapter 119, sections 312-316), as amended by Act No. 12 of 1980, liberalized Singapore's abortion law further. The Act provides that a person shall not be guilty of an offence under the law relating to abortion when a pregnancy is terminated by a registered physician acting on the request of a pregnant woman and with her written consent during the first 24 weeks of pregnancy. Beyond that time, an abortion may be performed only if immediately necessary to save the life or prevent grave permanent injury to the physical or mental health of the pregnant woman. Except in cases in which an abortion is immediately necessary to save the life of the pregnant woman, she must meet certain residency or citizenship requirements. The new Act abolished the Termination of Pregnancy Authorization Board and the requirement that it consent to the performance of abortions.

The 1974 Act contains a conscience clause permitting medical personnel to be excused from participating in any procedure to terminate a pregnancy, unless the procedure is immediately necessary to save the life of the pregnant woman. Violations of the Act constitute offences punishable by imprisonment and/or payment of a fine.

Under the 1974 Act, a legal abortion must be performed in a government hospital or in an approved institution unless the treatment to terminate the pregnancy consists solely of the use of drugs prescribed by a registered medical practitioner. Regulations issued under the Act define the qualifications required of physicians performing an abortion at different stages of pregnancy. A medical practitioner terminating a pregnancy not exceeding 16 weeks' duration must be registered under the Medical Regulation Act and have at least 24 months' experience in an obstetric and gynaecological unit of a recognized hospital, while a medical

Source: Population Policy Data Bank, maintained by the Population Division, Department of Economic and Social Affairs of the United Nations Secretariat. For additional sources, see reference section.

practitioner terminating a pregnancy of no more than 24 weeks' duration must hold the degree of Master of Medicine (Obstetrics and Gynaecology) of the University of Singapore or the National University of Singapore or be a Member or Fellow of a Royal College of Obstetricians and Gynaecologists. The regulations also require the approval of institutions for the performance of abortions to be renewed every two years and place a duty of confidentiality on such institutions.

In 1987, these regulations were amended to introduce mandatory counselling prior to and following the performance of an abortion. In addition, they require a pregnant woman to wait twenty-four hours after receiving the counselling until the abortion is performed unless performance of the abortion is immediately necessary to save the life or prevent grave permanent injury to the physical or mental health of the pregnant woman. Pre-abortion counselling is reportedly intended to provide women with information that may allow them to continue their pregnancy and post-abortion counselling to discourage them from seeking repeat abortions.

In 1996 the estimated abortion rate was 15.9 abortions per 1,000 women aged 15-44 and the modern contraceptive prevalence rate was estimated most recently in 1982 at 73 per cent.

The Government's concern about below-replacement fertility has led it to implement a number of measures designed to reverse this trend. In 1986 the total fertility rate hit an all-time low of 1.4 children per woman. As a result, the Government set out in 1987 to encourage women to have at least three children: it offered new incentives in the form of tax deductions and rebates, improved maternity leave benefits, childcare subsidies and priority in housing and school registration. The total fertility rate for 1995-2000 rebounded to 1.7 children per woman.

Source: Population Policy Data Bank, maintained by the Population Division, Department of Economic and Social Affairs of the United Nations Secretariat. For additional sources, see reference section.

ABORTION POLICY

Grounds on which abortion is permitted:

To save the life of the woman	Yes
To preserve physical health	Yes
To preserve mental health	Yes
Rape or incest	Yes
Foetal impairment	Yes
Economic or social reasons	Yes
Available on request	Yes

Additional requirements:

Abortion is allowed within 12 weeks of gestation upon written request of the pregnant woman. An abortion may be performed on request only if at least six months have elapsed since a previous abortion, except in the case of a woman that has had two other births or is 35 years of age or older, or in the case of rape. A woman must receive counselling before an abortion is performed. Parental consent is required for minors under 16 years of age; for minors between 16 and 18 years of age, the physician must inform the parents following the intervention. Second-trimester abortion is allowed only for medical and eugenic reasons and in cases of rape or other sexual crimes.

REPRODUCTIVE HEALTH CONTEXT

Government view on fertility level:	Too low
Government intervention concerning fertility level:	To raise
Government policy on contraceptive use:	Indirect support provided
Percentage of currently married women using modern contraception (aged 15-44, 1991):	41
Total fertility rate (1995-2000):	1.4
Age-specific fertility rate (per 1,000 women aged 15-19, 1995-2000):	32
Government has expressed particular concern about:	
Morbidity and mortality resulting from induced abortion	..
Complications of childbearing and childbirth	No
Maternal mortality ratio (per 100,000 live births, 1990):	
National	..
Developed countries	27
Female life expectancy at birth (1995-2000):	76.7

Source: Population Policy Data Bank maintained by the Population Division of the Department of Economic and Social Affairs of the United Nations Secretariat. For additional sources, see list of references.

Slovakia

BACKGROUND

Since the end of the Second World War, Slovakia's abortion law has been amended a number of times, with the general trend being towards liberalization. Law No. 86/1950 (the Penal Code, sections 227-229), effective August 1950, permitted abortion when the pregnant woman's life or health was endangered and in cases of genetic defect. A woman who violated the law was subject to one year's imprisonment, and the person performing the abortion to ten years' imprisonment. In 1957, owing to concern over the negative effects of clandestine abortions on women's health, the Government enacted new legislation broadening the circumstances under which abortions could be legally performed. Law No. 68 of 19 December 1957 specified that abortions could be legally performed on the basis of medical or other important reasons. A commission was required to approve the abortion and the abortion had to be performed in a health establishment. A woman who obtained an illegal abortion was no longer punished, and the sentence for the person performing the abortion was reduced to a maximum of five years.

Following the enactment of Law No. 68 in 1957, a series of ordinances and instructions were issued that specified in greater detail the nature of these "other important reasons" and the procedures that had to be followed to obtain the approval of the commission. By 1983, a woman was allowed to obtain an abortion if she was over 40, if she had at least three living children, if the pregnancy was the result of rape or another crime, if she was in a difficult situation due to an extramarital relationship, if she had lost a husband or her husband was in bad health, if she had difficult housing or material conditions that endangered the standard of living of her family (particularly minor children), or if a documented disintegration of the family had taken place. Authorization would not be granted if the pregnancy was of more than 12 weeks' duration, if it was found that the woman had a condition that would increase the risks of the abortion or if she had undergone an abortion in the past year. Exceptions to these rules were possible. An abortion could be performed despite a risk to her health if continuing the pregnancy would endanger the woman's life. An abortion could be terminated through the sixteenth week of pregnancy if the woman had contracted rubella and through the 26th week of pregnancy if there were genetic problems. Abortion could be performed only up to the twelfth of gestation, except to save the life of the pregnant woman or in the case of known foetal impairment. In the latter case, up to 24 weeks and exceptionally up to 26 weeks of gestation were allowed.

The size of the commission that was to assess whether abortion was warranted was reduced from four to three members in December 1962. The commission included a gynaecologist, a social worker and a deputy from the National Committee. Only abortions performed on medical grounds or in cases of economic duress were performed free of charge.

The most recent amendment to the abortion law was passed on 23 October 1986 and took effect in 1987. It abolished the abortion commissions, leaving the decision to be made between the woman and her doctor. Under current laws, a woman makes a written request to her gynaecologist, whereby the physician will inform her of the possible consequences of the procedure and of the available methods of birth control. If gestation is under 12 weeks and there are no health contraindications for the procedure, the doctor specifies the health centre where the procedure is to be performed. If gestation is over 12 weeks or if other contraindications exist, the request is reviewed by a medical committee. Women who have had an abortion within six months are not permitted to undergo the procedure unless they have had two deliveries, are at least 35 years of age or the pregnancy was the result of a rape. Beyond the first trimester, the pregnancy can be terminated only if the woman's life or health is endangered or in the case of suspected foetal impairment.

Source: Population Policy Data Bank maintained by the Population Division of the Department of Economic and Social Affairs of the United Nations Secretariat. For additional sources, see list of references.

If the woman is under 16 years of age, consent of her legal representative is required. If the woman is between 16 and 18 years of age, her legal representative must be notified. An abortion must be performed in a hospital.

Through the years, abortion has remained the preferred method of birth control in Slovakia. Part of the reason was that abortion was free but contraceptives were not and were also difficult to obtain. The new 1986 law attempted to reduce the use of abortion by providing contraception (excluding condoms) free of charge and discouraging abortion by charging a fee for abortions performed after eight weeks of gestation. The fee was waived only if the abortion was medically indicated.

The abortion rate in Slovakia rose from 30.5 per cent in 1984 to a high of 43.1 in 1988. However, the abortion rate declined substantially in the course of the 1990s. It was estimated at 19.7 abortions per 1,000 women aged 15-44 in 1996. The Government reported a gross abortion rate of 4.9 per cent in 1999.

Slovakia's rate of modern contraceptive usage was 41 per cent in 1991. That rate is thought to have increased after 1991. For example, the International Planned Parenthood Federation reported a five-fold increase in the use of oral contraceptives after 1990. The total fertility rate for 1995-2000 was 1.4 children per woman, and the population growth rate was 0.1 per cent.

Source: Population Policy Data Bank maintained by the Population Division of the Department of Economic and Social Affairs of the United Nations Secretariat. For additional sources, see list of references.

Slovenia

ABORTION POLICY

Grounds on which abortion is permitted:

To save the life of the woman	Yes
To preserve physical health	Yes
To preserve mental health	Yes
Rape or incest	Yes
Foetal impairment	Yes
Economic or social reasons	Yes
Available on request	Yes

Additional requirements:

An abortion must be performed in a hospital or other authorized health-care facility. If the woman is a minor, approval of her parents or guardian is required, unless she has been recognized as fully competent to earn her own living. After the first 10 weeks of pregnancy, special authorization by a commission composed of a gynaecologist/obstetrician, a general physician or a specialist in internal medicine and a social worker or a psychologist is required.

REPRODUCTIVE HEALTH CONTEXT

Government view on fertility level:	Too low
Government intervention concerning fertility level:	To raise
Government policy on contraceptive use:	Direct support provided
Percentage of currently married women using modern contraception (aged 15-49):	..
Total fertility rate (1995-2000):	1.3
Age-specific fertility rate (per 1,000 women aged 15-19, 1995-2000):	17
Government has expressed particular concern about:	
Morbidity and mortality resulting from induced abortion	No
Complications of childbearing and childbirth	No
Maternal mortality ratio (per 100,000 live births, 1990):	
National	..
Developed countries	27
Female life expectancy at birth (1995-2000):	78.2

Source: Population Policy Data Bank maintained by the Population Division of the Department of Economic and Social Affairs of the United Nations Secretariat. For additional sources, see list of references.

BACKGROUND

Although Slovenia achieved independence from the former Socialist Federal Republic of Yugoslavia in 1991, abortion is still regulated by the Law of 7 October 1977. This Law was enacted by Slovenia when it was part of Yugoslavia to implement article 191 of the Federal Constitution of Yugoslavia of 21 February 1974, which proclaims that "it is a human right freely to decide on the birth of children". Under the 1977 law, an abortion may be performed on request during the first 10 weeks of pregnancy. The intervention must be performed in a hospital or other authorized health-care facility. If the woman is a minor, approval of her parents or guardian is required, unless she has been recognized as fully competent to earn her own living. After the first 10 weeks of pregnancy, special authorization by a commission, composed of a gynaecologist/obstetrician, a general physician or specialist in internal medicine, and a social worker or psychologist is required. The commission decides on the basis of whether the procedure entails a risk to the woman's life, health, or future motherhood that is less than the risk to the woman or the child associated with the continuation of the pregnancy or childbirth. The woman can appeal to the Commission of Second Instance if the Commission of First Instance rejects her request.

Medical organizations and persons who violate provisions of the law are subject to criminal punishment. A woman, however, is never held criminally responsible for inducing her own abortion or for cooperating in such a procedure.

In recent years signs of opposition to Slovenia's liberal abortion law have been increasing. In approving the new Slovene Constitution in 1991, the Government modified language on reproductive rights from its previous constitution that had closely resembled language contained in Article 191 of the Federal Constitution of Yugoslavia (see above). Instead of the language "it is a human right freely to decide on the birth of children", the new Constitution simply states that "the decision to bear one's own children is free". This change raised concern that the Government might amend the abortion law to introduce greater restrictions. Furthermore, the new law on Provision of Health Care of 1992 contains a conscience clause, allowing a physician to refuse to perform any medical procedure. Finally, a proposed revision of the Code of Medical Ethics under discussion in 1992 included a conscience clause that a physician could invoke in order to be exempted from performing an abortion or sterilization if no medical emergency existed.

Beginning in 1952, abortion legislation in the former Yugoslavia was liberalized in response to the significant increase in illegal abortions associated with high levels of morbidity and mortality. The subsequent changes in the abortion laws—general principles were adopted at the federal level and laws were implemented at the local level—were expressly directed to facilitating access to legal abortion in order to discourage illegal practices. For instance, a significant decline in the number of illegal abortions is attributed to the decision in 1969 to eliminate the requirement of a commission's approval for termination of pregnancies of less than 10 weeks, a requirement that had been a practical and psychological obstacle to abortion. The policy of liberalizing legal regulations with regard to abortion was facilitated by increased numbers of medical facilities, better access to information on abortion services and higher levels of education. Although abortion rates continued to be high, the former Government essentially achieved its objective: illegal abortions were practically eliminated, and the country experienced a significant decline in maternal morbidity and mortality related to abortion. For example, in Slovenia, mortality associated with abortion declined from 52 maternal deaths per 100,000 abortions in 1960 to 5 per 100,000 in 1976.

Source: Population Policy Data Bank maintained by the Population Division of the Department of Economic and Social Affairs of the United Nations Secretariat. For additional sources, see list of references.

Slovenia

High rates of abortion, as well as a high rate of repeat abortions, an increase in second-trimester abortions and an increase in abortions among adolescents were problems experienced throughout the former Yugoslavia. These trends demonstrated that women relied upon abortion as a contraceptive method, with consequent health risks. Slovenia, however, has a very low incidence of second-trimester abortions; during the period 1965-1980, they accounted for only 1.7-3.4 per cent of all legal abortions. As concerns its overall abortion rate, Slovenia is in the middle range among the former Yugoslav republics. The abortion rate has declined over the last fifteen years, from 40.3 abortions per 1,000 women aged 15-44 in the early 1980's, to 31 in 1991, and to 23.2 in 1996.

Family planning services were a part of the regular medical services in the former Yugoslavia from the mid-1950s onward. A family planning institution was established in 1963 at the national and local levels, and the Family Planning Association, affiliated with the International Planned Parenthood Federation, has existed since 1966. However, sex education in the schools and family planning counselling have not been systematically developed, and family planning has encountered continuing resistance throughout the country. As a result, insufficient knowledge and fear of modern methods of contraception remain widespread.

In the late 1980s, the former Government indicated deep concern about the high abortion rates and low rates of usage of modern contraceptive methods. In the Resolution on Population, Development and Family Planning of 1989, which set out general principles and directions with regard to population matters, special emphasis was given to fertility and family planning. The resolution, while reconfirming the right of each person to decide freely on the number and spacing of children, as established in the Constitution of 1974, was directed to attaining replacement-level fertility in all areas of the country. In part to reduce the incidence of abortion and in part to reduce fertility in some republics, specific measures to disseminate contraceptive information and supplies more widely were taken at the federal level. Social welfare measures, such as prolonged maternity leave, child allowances and childcare facilities, were also strengthened in areas of the country where fertility was below replacement level. In the former Yugoslavia, the republics and autonomous provinces were responsible for implementing within their borders the general principles of population policy adopted by the Federal Assembly. However, the republics and autonomous provinces often abstained from executing federally adopted policies.

Concerned by the declining rate of fertility, which fell to 1.6 children per woman in 1989, Slovenia had, prior to independence, implemented measures to halt the decline. However, the total fertility rate continued to decline, to 1.3 children per woman for the period 1995-2000, while the population growth rate fell to –0.05 per cent.

Source: Population Policy Data Bank maintained by the Population Division of the Department of Economic and Social Affairs of the United Nations Secretariat. For additional sources, see list of references.

ABORTION POLICY

Grounds on which abortion is permitted:

To save the life of the woman	Yes
To preserve physical health	No
To preserve mental health	No
Rape or incest	No
Foetal impairment	No
Economic or social reasons	No
Available on request	No

Additional requirements:

Two physicians must approve an abortion in order for it to be performed. In addition, written consent of the patient's spouse or next of kin is required before any operation can be performed. Parental consent is required if the girl is a minor. There is no time limit for an abortion to be performed except the one imposed by medical practice, which is usually the first trimester of pregnancy, in order to avoid serious medical risk to the mother. Abortion is free of charge when performed at a government hospital.

REPRODUCTIVE HEALTH CONTEXT

Government view on fertility level:	Too high
Government intervention concerning fertility level:	To lower
Government policy on contraceptive use:	Direct support provided
Percentage of currently married women using modern contraception (aged 15-49):	..
Total fertility rate (1995-2000):	4.9
Age-specific fertility rate (per 1,000 women aged 15-19, 1995-2000):	94
Government has expressed particular concern about:	
Morbidity and mortality resulting from induced abortion	..
Complications of childbearing and childbirth	..
Maternal mortality ratio (per 100,000 live births, 1990):	
National	..
Oceania	680
Female life expectancy at birth (1995-2000):	73.9

Source: Population Policy Data Bank maintained by the Population Division of the Department of Economic and Social Affairs of the United Nations Secretariat. For additional sources, see list of references.

Solomon Islands

BACKGROUND

Abortion in the Solomon Islands is governed by the Penal Code of 1963 (Chapter 26 of the 1996 Revised Laws of the Solomon Islands), which makes the performance of abortions generally illegal. Under the Code, any person who unlawfully uses any means with the intent to procure the miscarriage of a woman, whether pregnant or not, is subject to life imprisonment. A pregnant woman who undertakes the same act or consents to it is subject to the same penalty.

Nonetheless, the Code allows an abortion to be performed to save the life of a pregnant woman. It provides that a person is not criminally responsible for performing in good faith and with reasonable care and skill a surgical operation upon an unborn child for the preservation of the mother's life, if the performance of the operation is reasonable, having regard to the patient's state at the time and to all the circumstances of the case.

Two physicians must reportedly approve an abortion in order for it to be performed. In addition, written consent of the patient's spouse or next of kin is required before any operation can be performed. Parental consent is required if the girl is a minor. There is no time limit for an abortion to be performed except that imposed by medical practice, which is usually the first trimester of pregnancy, in order to avoid serious medical risk to the mother. Abortion is free of charge when performed at a government hospital.

Two legal systems, customary and general law, exist side by side in the Solomon Islands. According to custom, a birth is a gift from God and is generally accepted, as such even if not desired. In addition, among the native population, the stigma attached to out-of-wedlock pregnancies is less than in many other cultures, and adoption is a common solution for unplanned births. Demand for abortion is therefore relatively low. On the other hand, it has been recognized that frequent pregnancies with short birth intervals and subsequent complications are a major cause of maternal morbidity and mortality. Fertility levels in the Solomon Islands remain high, with the total fertility rate estimated at 4.9 births per woman for the period 1995-2000.

Since the 1970s, the Government has sought to reduce the rate of population growth (which was estimated at 3.1 per cent for the period 1995-2000), mainly through family planning. The family planning programme, which is directed both to improving the health of mothers and children and to reducing population growth, has achieved significant progress. A national population policy was approved by the Government in 1987 and reformulated after the International Conference on Population and Development. In recent years, the Solomon Islands Planned Parenthood Association has successfully introduced community-based contraceptive distribution programmes in a few areas on a pilot basis. Although there is growing acceptance of family planning among community and traditional leaders, some religious leaders and groups still remain opposed to it. As a result, the Government is developing information programmes to increase awareness of the negative effects of rapid population growth and closely spaced pregnancies.

Source: Population Policy Data Bank maintained by the Population Division of the Department of Economic and Social Affairs of the United Nations Secretariat. For additional sources, see list of references.

ABORTION POLICY

Grounds on which abortion is permitted:

To save the life of the woman	Yes
To preserve physical health	No
To preserve mental health	No
Rape or incest	No
Foetal impairment	No
Economic or social reasons	No
Available on request	No

Additional requirements:

Information is not readily available.

REPRODUCTIVE HEALTH CONTEXT

Government view on fertility level:	Satisfactory
Government intervention concerning fertility level:	No intervention
Government policy on contraceptive use:	Indirect support provided
Percentage of currently married women using modern contraception (aged 15-49):	..
Total fertility rate (1995-2000):	7.3
Age-specific fertility rate (per 1,000 women aged 15-19, 1995-2000):	213
Government has expressed particular concern about:	
Morbidity and mortality resulting from induced abortion	Yes
Complications of childbearing and childbirth	Yes
Maternal mortality ratio (per 100,000 live births, 1990):	
National	1 600
Eastern Africa	1 060
Female life expectancy at birth (1995-2000):	48.6

Source: Population Policy Data Bank maintained by the Population Division of the Department of Economic and Social Affairs of the United Nations Secretariat. For additional sources, see list of references.

Somalia

BACKGROUND

Owing to the breakdown of central Government in Somalia, current abortion law and policy of the country are unclear.

Before this breakdown, abortion was governed by the provisions of the Somalia Penal Code of 16 December 1962 (articles 418-422 and 424), which in general, prohibits the performance of abortions. The penalty for performing an abortion without the woman's consent is three to seven years' imprisonment; if the abortion results in injury to the woman, the person performing it is subject to three to eight years' imprisonment and, if the woman dies, 10-15 years' imprisonment. Anyone performing an abortion on a woman who is incapable of giving consent, or whose consent is extorted by violence, threat, undue influence or fraud, is subject to the same penalties.

If the woman consents to the abortion, the person performing it is subject to one to five years' imprisonment; if the abortion results in injury to the woman, the person performing it is subject to two to six years' imprisonment; and if the abortion results in her death, four to eight years' imprisonment. A woman consenting to or causing her own abortion is subject to one to five years' imprisonment. Any person instigating a pregnant woman to perform an abortion by administering to her appropriate means thereto is subject to six months' to two years' imprisonment.

Nonetheless, under general criminal law principles of necessity, an abortion may be performed to save the life of a pregnant woman. Moreover, the Penal Code provides that if an abortion is performed to safeguard one's own honour or that of a near relative, the penalties shall be reduced by one half to two thirds. On the other hand, if the person performing the abortion exercises a medical profession, the penalty shall be increased. Repeat offenders who are medical professionals shall be permanently barred from medical practice.

Somalia's estimated total fertility rate for 1995-2000 is 7.3 children per woman with a population growth rate of 4.2 per cent. Maternal mortality remains high at an estimated 1,600 deaths per 100,000 live births.

Source: Population Policy Data Bank maintained by the Population Division of the Department of Economic and Social Affairs of the United Nations Secretariat. For additional sources, see list of references.

South Africa

ABORTION POLICY

Grounds on which abortion is permitted:

To save the life of the woman	Yes
To preserve physical health	Yes
To preserve mental health	Yes
Rape or incest	Yes
Foetal impairment	Yes
Economic or social reasons	Yes
Available on request	Yes

Additional requirements:

A legal abortion must be performed by a physician in a government hospital or other approved medical institution with the permission of the hospital superintendent. Abortion requires the approval of two independent physicians (besides the physician performing the abortion), one of whom must be a psychiatrist if abortion is sought on mental health grounds or a district surgeon if the pregnancy resulted from unlawful intercourse. One of the consenting physicians must have practised medicine for at least four years. The law prohibits consenting physicians from participating or assisting in the abortion. Authority for an abortion on the grounds of rape, incest or intercourse with a mentally retarded woman may not be granted without a certificate from the local magistrate.

REPRODUCTIVE HEALTH CONTEXT

Government view on fertility level:	Too high
Government intervention concerning fertility level:	To lower
Government policy on contraceptive use:	Direct support provided
Percentage of currently married women using modern contraception (under age 50, 1988):	48
Total fertility rate (1995-2000):	3.3
Age-specific fertility rate (per 1,000 women aged 15-19, 1995-2000):	68
Government has expressed particular concern about:	
Morbidity and mortality resulting from induced abortion	No
Complications of childbearing and childbirth	Yes
Maternal mortality ratio (per 100,000 live births, 1990):	
National	230
Southern Africa	260
Female life expectancy at birth (1995-2000):	58.1

Source: Population Policy Data Bank maintained by the Population Division of the Department of Economic and Social Affairs of the United Nations Secretariat. For additional sources, see list of references.

BACKGROUND

Up to 1975, abortion law in South Africa was governed by Roman-Dutch common law, which permitted abortion only when the life of the mother would be endangered by continuation of the pregnancy. In practice, however, physicians often performed abortions on other grounds without prosecution by law enforcement agencies. In 1968, for example, it was estimated that at least 28 per cent of therapeutic abortions were performed for reasons other than saving the life of the mother.

In 1975, The Abortion and Sterilization Act of 1975 (Act No. 2 of 1975) was enacted, which extended the grounds under which an abortion could be legally obtained in South Africa. Under the Act, as amended in 1982, abortions could be performed in the following cases: (a) when the continued pregnancy endangered the woman's life; (b) when the continued pregnancy constituted a serious threat to the woman's physical or mental health; (c) when there was a serious risk that the child to be born would suffer from a physical or mental defect of such a nature as to be irreparably seriously handicapped; and (d) when the pregnancy was the result of unlawful intercourse such as rape or incest, or with an "idiot or imbecile". The abortion had to be approved by three physicians and performed in a State-designated institution and was subject to other procedural requirements depending on the indication. For example, when the abortion was requested because the pregnancy resulted from unlawful intercourse, the magistrate in whose district the offence was alleged to have occurred was required to provide the hospital superintendent with a certificate attesting to the fact that the alleged offence was reported to the police, or if no complaint was lodged, that there was a good and acceptable reason for it.

Although the Act in theory legalized abortion under a broad series of indications, in effect, very few legal abortions were performed after its enactment. Estimates are that under 1,000 legal abortions were carried out each year. Most abortions, estimated to be at least 200,000 a year, continued to be performed illegally. Some 45,000 of these resulted in hospitalization due to incomplete abortion and led to 1,500 to 3,000 deaths per year. In addition, the vast majority of these were performed on white women, who made up only a small percentage of the population seeking abortions. The preponderance of white women among the women who obtained legal abortions was evidently due to the strict procedural requirements imposed by the 1975 Act. These worked to the advantage of those with money, skill in dealing with government bureaucracy, and access to urban medical facilities.

This legal situation was dramatically altered in 1994 after the transition from the apartheid regime to full democracy and the victory of the African National Congress (ANC) in the first fully democratic elections in South Africa. The ANC had campaigned on a platform of liberalized abortion and, once it came to power, it proceeded to fulfill its campaign pledge on this issue. After receiving the report of the Ad Hoc Select Committee on Abortion and Sterilisation, appointed to review this matter, the Government introduced draft legislation in Parliament to allow abortions to be performed on request during the first fourteen weeks of pregnancy. The proposed legislation provoked a heated debate between pro-choice and pro-life groups, and the latter held numerous rallies to protest suggested changes. Despite polls indicating that the great majority of the population did not support the legislation and considerable opposition among legislators both within and without the ruling ANC party, the legislation (the Choice on Termination of Pregnancy Act) was enacted in 1996, with almost one quarter of the legislators absent.

In its enacted form, the new abortion law is slightly different from the legislation initially proposed. Like much abortion legislation, it is based on a time-frame model. During the first twelve weeks of pregnancy, a woman may obtain an abortion upon request. From the thirteenth to the twentieth week of pregnancy, an

Source: Population Policy Data Bank maintained by the Population Division of the Department of Economic and Social Affairs of the United Nations Secretariat. For additional sources, see list of references.

abortion may be performed in the following circumstances: if a medical practitioner is of the opinion that the continued pregnancy would pose a risk of injury to the woman's physical or mental health; if there is a substantial risk that the foetus would suffer from a severe physical or mental abnormality; if the pregnancy resulted from rape or incest; or if the continued pregnancy would significantly affect the social or economic circumstances of the woman. After the twentieth week of pregnancy, an abortion may be performed if two medical practitioners or one medical practitioner and a midwife are of the opinion that the continued pregnancy would endanger the woman's life, would result in severe malformation of the foetus or would pose a risk of injury to the foetus.

Although all abortions must be performed in government-designated facilities, during the first twelve weeks an abortion may be performed by a medical practitioner or a midwife; after this period only a medical practitioner is qualified to carry out an abortion. While non-directive and non-mandatory counselling is encouraged, it is in no case mandated, and all women requesting an abortion are to be informed of their rights under the Act. As long as the woman is mentally competent, no parental or spousal consent is required, even in the case of a minor. If the woman is mentally incompetent or in a state of continuous unconsciousness, an abortion may be carried out with the consent of her guardian or spouse and the fulfilment of various other procedural requirements. The Act contains detailed notification and recordkeeping requirements and imposes penalties of a fine or up to ten years' imprisonment on those who perform abortions in contravention of its provisions or who prevent the lawful termination of a pregnancy or obstruct access to a facility for the termination of pregnancy.

The 1996 abortion law is now the most liberal in Africa and, indeed, the world, authorizing the performance of abortions not only during the first trimester of pregnancy on request, but also through the twentieth week of pregnancy on very broad grounds, including socio-economic grounds. Although the preamble to the law stresses that abortion is not considered a form of contraception or population control, it also makes clear that the law is firmly based on a notion of individual human rights. The preamble provides that South Africa's Constitution protects the right of persons to make decisions concerning reproduction and to achieve security in and control over their bodies; that both men and women have the right to have access to safe, effective, and acceptable methods of fertility control of their choice; and that women have a right of access to appropriate health care services to ensure safe pregnancy and childbirth. It also makes the State responsible for providing reproductive health to all, contraception and termination of pregnancy services, as well as safe conditions under which the right of choice can be exercised without fear or harm.

Nevertheless, opposition to the law has persisted. Shortly after its approval, the Christian Lawyers Association and other right-to-life groups brought an action against the Government claiming that, in authorizing the taking of life, the law violated the right to life of human beings, which, they asserted, starts at conception. They based their claim on Section 11 of South Africa's new Constitution, which provides that "everyone has the right to life," arguing that the phrase "everyone" applies to an unborn child. In 1998 in a procedural ruling before trial, the Transvaal Provisional Division of the High Court dismissed the suit (*Christian Lawyers Association v. Minister of Health*, 1998). It held that there was no express provision in the Constitution, including Section 11, affording the foetus or embryo legal personality or protection and that to interpret "everyone" as encompassing a foetus would ascribe to the word a meaning different from that which it bears everywhere else in the Constitution. Moreover, the Court concluded that to afford the foetus the status of a legal person might impinge on the rights of women that are expressly guaranteed in the Constitution. Although the ruling constitutes a forceful endorsement of the abortion law, the issue has not been fully settled since the plaintiffs have appealed the decision.

After the reform of the law, the number of legally performed abortions rose quickly. Within the first six months (January to June 1997), the number of abortions reported was twice that of the total number legally

---

Source: Population Policy Data Bank maintained by the Population Division of the Department of Economic and Social Affairs of the United Nations Secretariat. For additional sources, see list of references.

conducted during the eight-year period 1984-1991. The abortion rate was estimated in 1997 at 2.7 abortions per 1,000 women aged 15-44. In October 1999, the National Medicines Control Council announced that abortifacients would be made available in the country in mid-2000.

The South African Government views the fertility rate as too high. It has expressed particular concern about the high level of adolescent fertility and illegal abortion. The Government target is to reduce the total fertility rate from 3.3 births per woman in 1995-2000 to 2.1 by 2010 and to increase contraceptive use from 48 per cent (as estimated in 1988) to 80 per cent of fertile women. The Government supports family planning services, and contraceptives are provided free of charge at all government medical establishments.

Source: Population Policy Data Bank maintained by the Population Division of the Department of Economic and Social Affairs of the United Nations Secretariat. For additional sources, see list of references.

Spain

ABORTION POLICY

Grounds on which abortion is permitted:

To save the life of the woman	Yes
To preserve physical health	Yes
To preserve mental health	Yes
Rape or incest	Yes
Foetal impairment	Yes
Economic or social reasons	No
Available on request	No

Additional requirements:

An abortion must be performed by or under the supervision of a physician in an approved public or private health centre or establishment, provided the pregnant woman gives her express consent and one of the legal indications for abortion is met. A qualified specialist, other than the physician performing or supervising the abortion, must certify that the abortion is necessary to avoid a serious risk to the physical or mental health of the pregnant woman. If the pregnancy is a result of rape, the rape must first be reported to the police and the abortion must be performed within the first 12 weeks of pregnancy. In case of foetal impairment, two specialists from an approved health centre, other than the physician performing or supervising the abortion, must certify that the foetus, if carried to term, would suffer from severe physical or mental defects. Such an abortion must be performed within the first 22 weeks of pregnancy. In case of an emergency involving a risk to the life of the mother, an abortion may be performed without the expressed opinion of the physician and without the consent of the woman. All abortions must be reported to the national health authorities.

REPRODUCTIVE HEALTH CONTEXT

Government view on fertility level:	Too low
Government intervention concerning fertility level:	No intervention
Government policy on contraceptive use:	Direct support provided
Percentage of currently married women using modern contraception (aged 18-49*,995):	67
Total fertility rate (1995-2000):	1.2
Age-specific fertility rate (per 1,000 women aged 15-19, 1995-2000):	8
Government has expressed particular concern about:	
Morbidity and mortality resulting from induced abortion	..
Complications of childbearing and childbirth	No
Maternal mortality ratio (per 100,000 live births, 1990):	
National	7
Developed countries	27
Female life expectancy at birth (1995-2000):	81.5

* Respondents whose contraceptive status is unknown are considered non-users of contraception. The percentage of respondents in this category is 0.1 in Spain.

Source: Population Policy Data Bank maintained by the Population Division of the Department of Economic and Social Affairs of the United Nations Secretariat. For additional sources, see list of references.

BACKGROUND

Under Spanish criminal law provisions first enacted in the 1800s and in effect until 1985, there were no stated exceptions to the prohibition against the performance of abortions, although one could be carried out on the grounds of necessity under general principles of criminal law to save the life of the pregnant woman. A person who performed an illegal abortion was subject to imprisonment, as was a woman who performed her own abortion or consented to its performance. Various medical personnel who performed illegal abortions were subject to harsher penalties.

In 1983, the Government of Spain enacted legislation that allowed the performance of abortions in cases of a serious threat to life or health, pregnancy resulting from rape and serious foetal impairment. Before the legislation could take effect, however, its validity was challenged by legislators opposed to its enactment. In 1985, the Constitutional Court held that the legislation was unconstitutional because it did not adequately protect prenatal life. It objected, in particular, to the lack of procedural safeguards to protect such life and suggested provisions that could be included in future legislation to establish such safeguards.

On 5 July 1985, new abortion legislation was adopted (Organic Law No. 9 of 1985), containing more extensive procedural safeguards than the old legislation. Under the legislation, an abortion can be legally performed by or under the direction of a physician in an approved public or private health centre or establishment, provided that the woman gives her express consent to the procedure and one of the following conditions is met: (a) the abortion is necessary to avert a serious risk to the physical or mental health of the pregnant woman, in accordance with an opinion expressed prior to the abortion by a physician, other than the one performing the abortion or under whose direction the abortion is to be performed, and who holds an appropriate specialist qualification; (b) the pregnancy is the result of rape, provided that the rape has been reported to the police and the abortion is performed within the first 12 weeks of pregnancy; or (c) the foetus, if carried to term, will suffer from severe physical or mental defects, provided that the abortion is performed within the first 22 weeks of pregnancy and the medical opinion, communicated prior to the abortion, is expressed by two specialists of an approved public or private health centre or establishment, neither of whom is the physician by whom or under whom the abortion is to be performed.

Under the above circumstances, a pregnant woman is penalized if the abortion is not performed in an approved public or private health centre or establishment, or if the prescribed medical opinions have not been expressed. In the case of an emergency that involves a risk to the life of the pregnant woman, an abortion can be performed without the expressed opinion of a second physician and without the consent of the woman.

Further procedural requirements were established in an Order of 31 July 1985 on the practice of abortion in health centres or establishments. The Order prescribed the minimum staff and resource requirements for accreditation and the guidelines for specialists and methods employed in the diagnosis of serious physical or psychological handicaps in the foetus. The Order required the creation of a commission of evaluation in each health centre or establishment to facilitate the performance of all legal provisions, provide advice whenever problems surfaced and gather statistical information. It also required health centres and establishments to keep clinical histories and documents that record the consent of the woman to an abortion.

By Order of the Ministry of Health of 16 June 1986, all voluntary interruptions of pregnancy carried out in conformity with Organic Law No. 9 of 1985 must be reported to the national health authorities by the Ministry of Health of each Autonomous Community upon receipt of a form filled out by the physician performing the abortion. In order to preserve the confidentiality of the pregnant woman, the form does not require the woman to provide her name; moreover, no individualized data obtained in the forms can be made

Source: Population Policy Data Bank maintained by the Population Division of the Department of Economic and Social Affairs of the United Nations Secretariat. For additional sources, see list of references.

public. The national health authorities are required to provide local authorities with information concerning abortions, specifying the characteristics of the women on whom abortions are performed.

Crown Decree No. 2409/1986 of 21 November 1986 repealed the Order of 31 July 1985 and set forth new provisions on the practice of abortions in accredited health centres. Sections 1 and 2 are similar to Sections 1 and 2 of the 1985 Order and deal with accreditation of health centres and establishments. Section 4 requires accredited public and private health centres and establishments to retain the case history and the assessments, reports and other documents required for the legal practice of abortion, and the form indicating the express consent of the pregnant woman. This information must be kept confidential. Section 5 provides that the health authority in each Autonomous Community is responsible for assuring the availability of the necessary services, including access to the emergency diagnostic techniques needed for abortion to be performed within the established time-limits. Section 6 provides that in cases where the abortion is performed to avert a serious danger to the life or physical or mental health of the pregnant woman, physicians in the corresponding speciality are considered accredited in respect of the opinion. When the abortion is performed on the grounds of foetal impairment, the opinion is to be issued by two medical specialists on the staff of a public or private health centre or of an establishment accredited for that purpose. This accreditation is to be granted by the competent agency of the Autonomous Community and is distinct from and independent of the accreditation for performing abortion. Section 9 requires health professionals to inform applicants for abortion of the medical, psychological and social consequences of continuation of pregnancy and of its termination, as well as of the existence of social assistance and family counselling available to applicants. Applicants must also be informed of the various requirements that must be fulfilled, the date of the abortion and the name of the health centre or establishment where it can be performed. A woman must immediately be notified if abortions are not carried out in the department that she attends, so that she may have sufficient time to consult another physician. The confidentiality of consultations must be guaranteed in all cases.

In January 1991, the Supreme Court of Spain sanctioned abortion for the first time on social grounds. The Court dismissed a criminal case brought against a married couple and the friend who helped them, concluding that if the woman had been forced to give birth, her right to the free development of her person would have been violated. The Court pointed to the fact that the couple could not support another child and that the woman was suffering both physically and mentally. This decision, however, does not mean that the abortion law in Spain has changed, especially since the Court upheld the conviction of the physician. It indicates that, in some cases, if a court so chooses, it may exonerate a pregnant woman from guilt on the basis of social grounds.

Since 1991 several attempts have been made to enact legislation liberalizing Spain's abortion law further, including the publication of a draft Penal Code permitting abortions to be performed on socio-economic grounds and the submission to Parliament of a bill allowing abortion to be performed on request after a compulsory three-day waiting period. None has received final approval by Parliament.

There are no public clinics that offer family planning and abortion services; as a result, most abortions in Spain are performed in private clinics. In 1988, an estimated 94 per cent of all abortions were carried out in private clinics. Approximately 85 per cent of the abortions performed in private clinics are performed on the grounds of averting severe danger to the woman's physical or mental health (especially mental health), which may conceal reasons prohibited by law. The relatively large proportion of hospitals where only a few abortion procedures are performed reflects a general tendency in those institutions to perform abortions only on medical indications. The abortion rate in 1996 was estimated to be 5.7 abortions per 1,000 women aged 15-44.

Source: Population Policy Data Bank maintained by the Population Division of the Department of Economic and Social Affairs of the United Nations Secretariat. For additional sources, see list of references.

The Government of Spain considers fertility to be an individual matter and has no explicit policy of intervention with regard to population growth and fertility, although it is aware that various social and economic policies designed to improve the situation of families with children and working mothers can have an impact on demographic trends. The total fertility rate for the period 1995-2000 was 1.2 children per woman. The Government desires to achieve lower levels of infant and maternal mortality through an improved health-care system, including maternal health care during pregnancy. Health promotion activities include programmes connected with family planning and sex education. In fact, Government priorities are directed towards improving the health situation in the country through a network of family planning centres. The Government believes that instruction, information and assistance should be made accessible to the entire population so that couples may decide the number and spacing of their children. Contraception was legalized in Spain in 1978, and sterilization has been permitted since 1983. The contraceptive prevalence rate for modern methods was estimated at 67 per cent in 1995.

Source: Population Policy Data Bank maintained by the Population Division of the Department of Economic and Social Affairs of the United Nations Secretariat. For additional sources, see list of references.

Sri Lanka

ABORTION POLICY

Grounds on which abortion is permitted:

To save the life of the woman	Yes
To preserve physical health	No
To preserve mental health	No
Rape or incest	No
Foetal impairment	No
Economic or social reasons	No
Available on request	No

Additional requirements:

The Penal Code contains no procedural requirements for the legal termination of pregnancy, except that the pregnant woman's consent is necessary. There are no provisions specifying the qualifications of those authorized to perform abortions nor the type of facilities in which the procedures are to be performed.

REPRODUCTIVE HEALTH CONTEXT

Government view on fertility level:	Satisfactory
Government intervention concerning fertility level:	To lower
Government policy on contraceptive use:	Direct support provided
Percentage of currently married women using modern contraception (aged 15-49,* 1993):	44
Total fertility rate (1995-2000):	2.1
Age-specific fertility rate (per 1,000 women aged 15-19, 1990-1995):	20
Government has expressed particular concern about:	
Morbidity and mortality resulting from induced abortion	No
Complications of childbearing and childbirth	Yes
Maternal mortality ratio (per 100,000 live births, 1990):	
National	140
South-central Asia	560
Female life expectancy at birth (1995-2000):	75.4

* Excluding areas containing roughly 15 per cent of the population.

Source: Population Policy Data Bank maintained by the Population Division of the Department of Economic and Affairs of the United Nations Secretariat. For additional sources, see list of references.

BACKGROUND

Abortion is generally illegal in Sri Lanka under the Penal Code of 1883, which is based on the Indian Penal Code. Section 303 of the Penal Code provides that anyone voluntarily causing a woman with child to miscarry is subject to up to three years' imprisonment and/or payment of a fine, unless the miscarriage was caused in good faith in order to save the life of the mother. The penalty is imprisonment for up to seven years and payment of a fine if the woman is "quick with child", a term which, while not defined in the Code, refers to an advanced stage of pregnancy when there is perception of foetal movement, as opposed to "woman with child", which simply refers to "being pregnant". A woman who induces her own miscarriage is subject to the same penalties. If the miscarriage is caused without the consent of the woman, whether or not she is quick with child, the person causing it is subject to up to 20 years' imprisonment and payment of a fine (Section 304). The same penalty is imposed if the woman's death results from any act carried out with intent to bring about a miscarriage, whether or not the offender knew that the act was likely to cause death (Section 305).

In 1973, the abortion legislation of the country was studied by a committee of the Medical Legal Society of Sri Lanka, which recommended that the law should be liberalized to allow abortions to be performed to prevent grave injury to the physical and mental health of the mother, in cases where pregnancy resulted from rape or incest, and in cases where there was substantial risk that the child, if born, would suffer from severe physical or mental abnormalities that would cause it to be seriously handicapped for life. No legislative action, however, resulted from these recommendations. The Ministry of Health has begun, however, to publicize the linkage between illegal abortion and maternal mortality as a means of giving support to a liberalization of the abortion law.

Despite rigid statutory provisions, Sri Lankan women from higher income households who desire to terminate their pregnancies find little or no difficulty in doing so. They often consult a psychiatrist for severe mental depression combined with suicidal tendencies. The psychiatrist may advise an abortion in order to save the life of the mother, and the pregnancy may then be terminated in a private or government hospital by a qualified medical practitioner. Women from middle-income and lower income households, however, must often resort to abortions performed by "back-door abortionists" under primitive and unhygienic conditions, resulting in high maternal mortality and chronic ill health.

Although any abortion wilfully induced without the specific intent to save the life of the mother constitutes illegal abortion in Sri Lanka, in practice, indictments for criminal abortion rarely occur and convictions are even rarer. The incidence of abortion is believed to be considerably higher than is commonly acknowledged. A rural survey suggests that 54 abortions per 1,000 population are performed each year.

The Government of Sri Lanka considers the rates of fertility and population growth to be too high and hoped to achieve a target of replacement-level fertility by the year 2000. Sri Lanka has a current total fertility rate of 2.1 children per woman and a population growth rate of 1 per cent, a rate satisfactory to the Government. Recognizing that a reduction in fertility will enhance socio-economic development, the Government has sought to strengthen and expand the delivery of family planning services, to provide incentives for controlling population growth and to promote population education. Family planning services are part of a comprehensive family health programme that provides a variety of subsidized clinical and contraceptive services. Existing maternal and child health and family planning services are being enhanced, especially in rural and poor urban areas. The modern contraceptive prevalence rate was estimated at 44 per cent in 1993. Local health officials estimated the 1999 maternal mortality rate to be 250 deaths per 100,000 live births, 25 per cent of them related to unsafe abortions.

Source: Population Policy Data Bank maintained by the Population Division of the Department of Economic and Social Affairs of the United Nations Secretariat. For additional sources, see list of references.

Sudan

ABORTION POLICY

Grounds on which abortion is permitted:

To save the life of the woman	Yes
To preserve physical health	No
To preserve mental health	No
Rape or incest	Yes
Foetal impairment	No
Economic or social reasons	No
Available on request	No

Additional requirements:

Information is not readily available.

REPRODUCTIVE HEALTH CONTEXT

Government view on fertility level:	Too high
Government intervention concerning fertility level:	To lower
Government policy on contraceptive use:	Direct support provided
Percentage of currently married women using modern contraception (aged 15-49, 1992/93):	7*
Total fertility rate (1995-2000):	4.6
Age-specific fertility rate (per 1,000 women aged 15-19, 1995-2000):	52
Government has expressed particular concern about:	
Morbidity and mortality resulting from induced abortion	..
Complications of childbearing and childbirth	..
Maternal mortality ratio (per 100,000 live births, 1990):	
National	660
Northern Africa	340
Female life expectancy at birth (1995-2000):	56.4

* Data refer to Northern Sudan.

Source: Population Policy Data Bank maintained by the Population Division of the Department of Economic and Social Affairs of the United Nations Secretariat. For additional sources, see list of references.

BACKGROUND

Until 1983, abortion was governed in Sudan by the provisions of the Penal Code of 1 August 1925 (sections 262-267). Under the Code, abortion was prohibited except when performed to save the life of the pregnant woman. A person performing an abortion with the woman's consent was subject to imprisonment for a term not exceeding three years and/or payment of a fine if the pregnancy had not reached the stage of "quickening". A woman performing her own abortion was subject to the same penalties. Harsher penalties were applied if the abortion was performed without the consent of the pregnant woman, if the pregnancy had reached the stage of "quickening", or if the abortion resulted in the death of the pregnant woman. On the other hand, if the unmarried woman performed an abortion on herself in order to conceal her dishonour, the punishment was reduced.

In 1983, this Code was replaced by new criminal legislation designed to conform more closely to the principles of Islamic law than had the 1925 Penal Code. The performance of abortions was still prohibited except to save the life of the pregnant woman; but the punishment had been changed to reflect the Islamic penalty of payment of blood money. Persons who violated the law were subject to the payment of compensation, as well as to imprisonment and payment of fines. The payment was to be made to the relatives of the foetus and/or mother depending on the circumstances of the abortion.

In 1991, the Penal Code of Sudan was amended once again, resulting in changes in the abortion law. The major change was the expansion of the circumstances under which the performance of an abortion was legal. A person who intentionally causes a woman to miscarry is not guilty of an offence where (a) the miscarriage is necessary to save the mother's life; (b) the pregnancy is the result of rape which has occurred not more than 90 days before the pregnant woman has desired to have the abortion; or (c) it is proved that the quick unborn child has died in the mother's womb. If the pregnancy is of less than 90 days' duration, the person who performs the illegal abortion is subject to up to three years' imprisonment and/or payment of a fine. If the pregnancy is of more than 90 days' duration, the penalty is increased to up to five years' imprisonment and payment of a fine. In both cases, the person may be subject to the payment of compensation. As of 1991, the new legislation did not apply to largely Christian Southern Sudan.

Information on the incidence of induced abortion in the Sudan is scarce. However, a survey conducted in Khartoum between 1974 and 1976 found that the largest proportions of gynaecological admissions were due to complications of induced abortion. A similar observation has been made in Southern Sudan, and studies have found abortion to be one of the major causes of maternal death in the Sudan, estimated at 660 deaths per 100,000 live births in 1990.

The Government of the Sudan provides direct access to modern methods of family planning. Family planning services were introduced in the country in 1965 when the Sudan Family Planning Association was founded. The maternal and child health and family planning project within the Ministry of Health was established in 1975 and the Sudan Fertility Control Association in 1976. The Sudan Family Planning Association and the Sudan Fertility Control Association provide family planning services throughout the country. The main rationale for family planning is to improve MCH. Family planning services are provided free of charge, and there are no legal restrictions on the importation of contraceptives. Recent studies show that the level of contraceptive use is low but has increased slightly. The percentage of women using modern methods of contraception in Northern Sudan rose, for example, from 4 per cent in 1977-1978 to 6 per cent in 1989 and 7 per cent in 1992-1993. The total fertility rate for the Sudan has fallen in the last decade from 5.4 children per woman to 4.6 in the period 1995-2000.

Source: Population Policy Data Bank maintained by the Population Division of the Department of Economic and Social Affairs United Nations Secretariat. For additional sources, see list of references.

Suriname

ABORTION POLICY

Grounds on which abortion is permitted:

To save the life of the woman	Yes
To preserve physical health	No
To preserve mental health	No
Rape or incest	No
Foetal impairment	No
Economic or social reasons	No
Available on request	No

Additional requirements:

Information is not readily available.

REPRODUCTIVE HEALTH CONTEXT

Government view on fertility level:	Satisfactory
Government intervention concerning fertility level:	No intervention
Government policy on contraceptive use:	Direct support provided
Percentage of currently married women using modern contraception (aged 15-49):	..
Total fertility rate (1995-2000):	2.2
Age-specific fertility rate (per 1,000 women aged 15-19, 1995-2000):	22
Government has expressed particular concern about:	
Morbidity and mortality resulting from induced abortion	No
Complications of childbearing and childbirth	No
Maternal mortality ratio (per 100,000 live births, 1990):	
National	..
South America	260
Female life expectancy at birth (1995-2000):	72.7

Source: Population Policy Data Bank maintained by the Population Division of the Department of Economic and Affairs of the United Nations Secretariat. For additional sources, see list of references.

BACKGROUND

Under Suriname's criminal code, abortion is generally illegal. A woman who intentionally causes the abortion or death of her unborn child or allows another person to cause it is subject to up to three years' imprisonment. The other person is subject to up to four years and six months' imprisonment if the woman consents to the abortion and up to twelve years' imprisonment if she does not consent. In the first of these cases, if the woman dies, the penalty is increased to up to six years' imprisonment and in the second to up to fifteen years' imprisonment. If the person performing the abortion is a medical practitioner, midwife or pharmacist, the above-mentioned penalties may be increased by one third and the person can be barred from practising his or her profession.

In addition, the code prohibits a person from intentionally treating a woman or providing treatment to her knowing that thereby her pregnancy may be destroyed. The law subjects such a person to up to three years' imprisonment or payment of a fine of up to three thousand guilders. If the person has acted out of profit, or has acted professionally or regularly, or is a medical practitioner, midwife or pharmacist, the penalty may be increased by one third.

Nonetheless, an abortion may be performed under general criminal law principles of necessity to save the life of the pregnant woman.

Although the provision of contraceptives and contraceptive information is illegal under the country's criminal law, the laws are not enforced, and there has been no legal interference with the activities of the country's family planning organization, the Stichting Lobi (LOBI). The Stichting Lobi works to integrate family planning into the Government's primary health-care system and to include sex education in the school curriculum. Founded in 1969, it operates clinics, provides family planning services through private physicians, offers medical/clinical services, conducts sex education classes in schools, offers counselling services, trains health workers, educates patients at prenatal clinics and conducts a wide range of community education activities. It is also involved in various research projects to assess attitudes and constraints on contraceptive use, and it sponsors media campaigns on family planning.

The total fertility rate has fallen substantially in the last two decades and was estimated at 2.2 children per woman for 1995-2000. The Government of Suriname considers the current rate of fertility and population growth to be satisfactory. Although it has no official population policy, the Government supports the availability of accessible and affordable health services, focusing on the development of primary health care and supporting the provision of contraceptives. Although 70 per cent of the population is concentrated in or around the capital Paramaribo, beyond it physical geography has been a barrier to the access to health services by the poor and indigenous populations.

Source: Population Policy Data Bank maintained by the Population Division of the Department of Economic and Social Affairs of the United Nations Secretariat. For additional sources, see list of references.

ABORTION POLICY

Grounds on which abortion is permitted:

To save the life of the woman	Yes
To preserve physical health	No
To preserve mental health	No
Rape or incest	No
Foetal impairment	No
Economic or social reasons	No
Available on request	No

Additional requirements:

Although there are no legal provisions specifying by whom or where a legal abortion must be performed or the gestational limits to be observed, practice suggests that legal abortions are performed by registered physicians in government hospitals, private clinics or other approved institutions and may be performed up to 20 weeks of gestation.

REPRODUCTIVE HEALTH CONTEXT

Government view on fertility level:	Too high
Government intervention concerning fertility level:	To lower
Government policy on contraceptive use:	Direct support provided
Percentage of currently married women using modern contraception (aged 15-49,* 1988):	17
Total fertility rate (1995-2000):	4.7
Age-specific fertility rate (per 1,000 women aged 15-19, 1995-2000):	90
Government has expressed particular concern about:	
Morbidity and mortality resulting from induced abortion	No
Complications of childbearing and childbirth	Yes
Maternal mortality ratio (per 100,000 live births, 1990):	
National	560
Southern Africa	260
Female life expectancy at birth (1995-2000):	62.5

* Including never-married women who have a child.

Source: Population Policy Data Bank maintained by the Population Division of the Department of Economic and Social Affairs of the United Nations Secretariat. For additional sources, see list of references.

BACKGROUND

There is no statutory law in Swaziland governing the performance of abortions. Instead, abortion is a matter of common law, which is patterned after Roman-Dutch common law. Under this law, which was also in effect in South Africa prior to the enactment of its Abortion and Sterilization Act (1975), abortion is prohibited except in cases of necessity. There is some disagreement, however, as to what constitutes a case of necessity. The majority position of commentators is that a case of necessity exists only when an abortion is performed to save the life of the pregnant woman. However, it is possible that a case of necessity need not be so serious and that an abortion could be performed in cases of serious threat to both physical and mental health, foetal defect and rape. There is no case law on this issue in Swaziland.

Because there is no statutory law on abortion in Swaziland, there are no legal provisions dealing with the professional qualifications required to perform an abortion, the place where the procedure must be performed or the period during pregnancy when an abortion can be performed. Abortions are reportedly usually performed by a registered physician in a government hospital or other approved institution and may be performed within 20 weeks of pregnancy. Swazi physicians generally seek permission from the Ministry of Health prior to performing an abortion. Although this permission is not a legal requirement, it is a precaution that physicians have chosen to take in order to protect themselves and to prove their good faith. In practice, the person performing the abortion must usually be satisfied that the woman's physical or mental health is endangered by the birth and must act in good faith for therapeutic purposes only. There are no data concerning the number of legally induced abortions, but it is believed that the numbers are small.

The high incidence of illegal abortion is a growing concern in Swaziland. Induced abortion is a particularly significant problem among teenage girls. Faced with the prospect of an unwanted pregnancy, many teenage girls resort to abortion to avoid expulsion from school. Unmarried teenage women are more likely to have unwanted pregnancies because of the barriers they face in obtaining contraceptives. For example, it is reported that health workers often require proof of the husband's authorization before dispersing contraceptives, even though this is not a legal requirement.

Swaziland had a total fertility rate of 4.7 children per woman and a population growth rate of 2.9 per cent for 1995-2000. The Government recognizes that the current levels of population growth and fertility are too high and its goal is to reduce the level of fertility in order to improve family well-being and maternal and child health. Contraceptives are provided at all government health-care centres. The national family planning programme, which was launched in 1973, provides family planning services at all its service delivery centres and mobile units. The family planning programme has achieved a certain measure of success. By 1988 more than 80 per cent of women knew at least one effective contraceptive method, and 17 per cent of all women reported use of a modern contraceptive method, up from about 5 per cent in 1985.

Following the International Conference on Population and Development, held in Cairo in 1994, Swaziland launched the National Population Council in 1998. Both a national population policy and a comprehensive reproductive health programme were reported under formulation in 2000.

Source: Population Policy Data Bank maintained by the Population Division of the Department of Economic and Social Affairs of the United Nations Secretariat. For additional sources, see list of references.

ABORTION POLICY

Grounds on which abortion is permitted:

To save the life of the woman	Yes
To preserve physical health	Yes
To preserve mental health	Yes
Rape or incest	Yes
Foetal impairment	Yes
Economic or social reasons	Yes
Available on request	Yes

Additional requirements:

Abortion is legal in Sweden on a wide variety of grounds, including on request, up to 18 weeks of gestation, provided that the procedure will not seriously endanger the woman's life or health. For pregnancies between 12 and 18 weeks of gestation, the pregnant women is required to discuss the abortion with a social worker; after 18 weeks, permission must be obtained from the National Board of Health and Welfare. The abortion must be performed by a licensed medical practitioner and, except in cases of emergency, in a general hospital or other approved health-care establishment. Abortion is subsidized by the Government.

REPRODUCTIVE HEALTH CONTEXT

Government view on fertility level:	Satisfactory
Government intervention concerning fertility level:	No intervention
Government policy on contraceptive use:	Direct support provided
Percentage of currently married women using modern contraception (aged 20-44* 1981):	71
Total fertility rate (1995-2000):	1.6
Age-specific fertility rate (per 1,000 women aged 15-19, 1995-2000):	7
Government has expressed particular concern about:	
Morbidity and mortality resulting from induced abortion	No
Complications of childbearing and childbirth	No
Maternal mortality ratio (per 100,000 live births, 1990):	
National	7
Developed countries	27
Female life expectancy at birth (1995-2000):	80.8

* All sexually active women.

Source: Population Policy Data Bank maintained by the Population Division of the Department of Economic and Social Affairs of the United Nations Secretariat. For additional sources, see list of references.

Sweden

BACKGROUND

Performance of an abortion was considered a crime in Sweden at the beginning of the twentieth century except to save the life of a pregnant woman or protect her from serious health consequences. Both the sale of contraceptives and the dispensing of information on contraceptives were prohibited by law in 1910. In 1938, Sweden enacted legislation permitting the termination of pregnancy under broader circumstances. The 1938 Abortion Act, which remained in force until 1975, provided that abortion, although prohibited in principle, could be legally performed on a wide range of grounds. In addition to health indications, an abortion was permitted for eugenic reasons, in cases where the pregnancy was the result of a crime, and in cases of medical-social hardship, designated as "frailty of the mother". An abortion performed for medical reasons could be performed at any time during pregnancy, after the approval of two physicians. Abortions performed on other grounds required the approval of a health authorities board and had to be performed during the first 20 weeks of pregnancy. Women who did not meet the requirements and wished to terminate their pregnancies resorted to illegal abortions.

The 1938 Act was amended in 1946 to enlarge the definition of medical-social hardship so as to allow abortions to be performed when, taking into consideration the living conditions and other circumstances, the physical or mental strength of the mother would be seriously weakened by the birth or rearing of the child. The amendment stipulated that a woman seeking an abortion had to consult a social worker, who would investigate the woman's situation and help her prepare the application. Social workers were expected to offer social and economic assistance so that a woman could reconsider her decision or provide her with support if the application for abortion was refused. In addition, the period during which abortions could be legally performed on other than health indications was extended to 24 weeks of pregnancy. In 1963, the Abortion Act was amended again to include the existence of "prenatal injury in the foetus" as a ground for the termination of pregnancy.

In 1965, a government committee was assigned to study the application of the 1938 Abortion Act and to consider alternatives for future legislation. The committee's report proposed that a woman should have an unconditional right, without any time limit, to decide whether to terminate her pregnancy. The report also contained many suggestions about family planning services in the public-health system.

The final version of the committee's recommendations was approved by the Swedish Parliament and became known as the Swedish Abortion Law of 14 June 1974. The law, which came into effect in 1975, permits the interruption of pregnancy on request, provided there are no medical contraindications (that is, that the procedure will not seriously endanger the woman's life or health), during the first 18 weeks of pregnancy. For pregnancies between 12 and 18 weeks of pregnancy, the pregnant woman is required to discuss the abortion with a social worker. An abortion may be performed only on Swedish citizens or residents, or in cases where the National Board of Health and Welfare grants the authorization on special grounds. Only persons licensed to practise medicine may perform an abortion. Except in cases of emergency, the procedure must be carried out in a general hospital or in another health-care establishment approved by the National Board of Health and Welfare. Abortion is provided free of charge up to 18 weeks of pregnancy.

An abortion performed after 18 weeks of pregnancy is legal only if the National Board of Health and Welfare authorizes the procedure based on special reasons. In general, such an abortion may not be performed if there is reason to suppose that the embryo is viable. However, if there is a serious threat to the life or health of the pregnant woman, an abortion may be authorized at any time during pregnancy. In

---

Source: Population Policy Data Bank maintained by the Population Division of the Department of Economic and Social Affairs of the United Nations Secretariat. For additional sources, see list of references.

cases of emergency, a person authorized to practise medicine may perform an abortion without authorization. The abortion law makes no specific provision for consent.

Non-physicians who perform an abortion are subject to a fine or imprisonment for a maximum of one year. This penalty does not apply to a woman who terminates her own pregnancy or cooperates in a illegal termination. In 1995, the Abortion Law was amended to remove the requirement that a woman desiring to obtain an abortion between 12 and 18 weeks of pregnancy should discuss the abortion with a social worker.

After the new Abortion Act went into effect in 1975, the procedure for having an abortion in Sweden was simplified, making it possible for more women to obtain an abortion early in their pregnancy. Ninety-five per cent of abortions are performed during the first 12 weeks of gestation. Since 1975, between 30,000 and 37,000 abortions have been performed annually in Sweden, constituting 18-21 abortions per 1,000 women aged 15-44 years, or 24-26 per cent of known pregnancies. In 1996, for example, there were 32,100 reported abortions, producing a rate of 18.7 abortions per 1,000 women aged 15-44. Illegal abortion is very rare in Sweden.

For the period 1995-2000, Sweden registered a total fertility rate of 1.6 children per woman and a population growth rate of 0.3 per cent. In its response to the *Eighth United Nations Inquiry among Governments on Population and Development*, the Government of Sweden said it had no official position on the fertility rate and no policy to influence the rate. Population is integrated within development planning, and various government agencies are responsible for taking population variables into account. The Swedish social welfare system lessens the financial burdens of childbearing and child-rearing. Maternity and paternity leave is available for up to 290 days, during which time 90 per cent of wages are paid. Sixty days of paid leave are also provided annually if a family is caring for a sick child. Until the child reaches the age of 16, a system of family allowances pays 750 Swedish kronor (SKr) a month for one child, SKr 1,500 for two children, SKr 2,625 for three children, SKr 4,125 for four children and SKr 6,000 for five children.

Family planning services, integrated within maternal and child health care, have been established throughout the country. The emphasis is on preventive measures and a reduction in the number of abortions. Sweden has a high rate of modern contraceptive use, estimated in 1981 at 71 per cent of all sexually active women aged 20-44. Sterilization is available upon request in Sweden to those 25 years of age or over and with medical approval to those under age 25. The combination of health education on sexuality and family planning, easy access to contraceptive services, and free abortion on request is thought to have helped reduce both teenage birth rates and abortion rates in Sweden.

Source: Population Policy Data Bank maintained by the Population Division of the Department of Economic and Social Affairs of the United Nations Secretariat. For additional sources, see list of references.

Switzerland

ABORTION POLICY

Grounds on which abortion is permitted:

To save the life of the woman	Yes
To preserve physical health	Yes
To preserve mental health	Yes
Rape or incest	No
Foetal impairment	No
Economic or social reasons	No
Available on request	No

Additional requirements:

An abortion must be performed by a physician, with the woman's written consent, and except in an emergency, with the written approval of a second physician. Swiss law does not set a time-limit for therapeutic abortion, nor does it require compulsory counselling or a waiting period before an abortion can be performed.

REPRODUCTIVE HEALTH CONTEXT

Government view on fertility level:	Too low
Government intervention concerning fertility level:	No intervention
Government policy on contraceptive use:	No support provided
Percentage of currently married women using modern contraception (age 20-49*, 1994/95)	78
Total fertility rate (1995-2000):	1.5
Age-specific fertility rate (per 1,000 women aged 15-19, 1995-2000):	4
Government has expressed particular concern about:	
Morbidity and mortality resulting from induced abortion	No
Complications of childbearing and childbirth	No
Maternal mortality ratio (per 100,000 live births, 1990):	
National	6
Developed countries	27
Female life expectancy at birth (1995-2000):	81.8

* Including women in partnerships

Source: Population Policy Data Bank, maintained by the Population Division of the Department of Economic and Social Affairs of the United Nations Secretariat. For additional sources, see reference section.

BACKGROUND

Switzerland's abortion law, which is contained in the Penal Code of 21 December 1937, is one of the oldest abortion laws still in effect in Europe. The Code, in general, prohibits the performance of abortions. Under Article 118 of the Code, a woman who performs her own abortion or lets it be performed is subject to imprisonment. Article 119 provides that any person who performs an abortion on a consenting woman is subject to up to five years' imprisonment. If the woman does not consent the penalty is increased to up to ten years' imprisonment. If the abortion is performed for economic gain or the woman dies as a result of the abortion and this was foreseeable by the person performing the abortion, he or she is subject to a minimum of three years' imprisonment.

Nonetheless, an abortion may be legally performed for therapeutic reasons. Under article 120 of the Code, a pregnancy may be terminated by a licensed physician, with the woman's written consent, in order to avoid a danger to her life or serious danger of severe and lasting injury to her health that cannot otherwise be avoided. Before the abortion is performed, the physician must obtain a written opinion from a second physician who is familiar with the woman's condition and who is designated by the authorities in the canton where the woman resides or where the abortion will be performed. If the woman is incapable of giving consent, the written consent of her legal representative is required. In case of an emergency, an abortion may be performed without a consenting second opinion, with the stipulation that the physician notify the cantonal authorities within 24 hours following the operation. A physician who fails to notify the authorities after performing an emergency abortion is subject to detention or a fine.

Swiss law does not set a time limit during pregnancy within which an abortion may be performed. Nor does it require parental consent for minors. In practice, however, physicians are reluctant to perform an abortion during the second trimester. The abortion rate was estimated at 8.4 abortions per 1,000 women aged 15-44 in 1996.

Although the abortion provisions of the Swiss Penal Code are highly restrictive and have not changed since it came into force in 1942, they are subject to major differences in interpretations among the cantons of the country due to the fact that implementation of the law has been left to the cantons. Some cantons view serious danger to health very broadly as encompassing a threat to mental health and socio-economic welfare, while other cantons view serious danger to health quite narrowly. Indeed, abortion practices began to evolve differently in the various cantons soon after the enactment of the Penal Code and within a few years, six cantons already had very liberal abortion practices. This trend towards liberalization has continued over the years. Currently, psychosocial grounds for the termination of pregnancy are broadly accepted, accounting for more than 95 per cent of abortions. In fact, in the more liberal cantons, it is rare for a woman requesting an abortion to be refused; virtually any woman wishing to terminate her pregnancy is able to have a legal abortion. Nonetheless, in a few cantons, it is still almost impossible to obtain a legal abortion.

In some cantons, abortions are performed by physicians (both gynaecologists and general practitioners) in their private offices or in private clinics under local anaesthesia and on an out-patient basis. In other cantons, abortions are performed mainly in public hospitals or private clinics, usually under general anaesthesia, with a hospital stay of from one to three (or more) days.

Source: Population Policy Data Bank, maintained by the Population Division of the Department of Economic and Social Affairs of the United Nations Secretariat. For additional sources, see reference section.

Switzerland

Prior to the 1970s, Swiss abortion practices were among the most liberal in Western Europe. As a result, pregnant women from other countries sought safe, legal abortions in the Swiss cantons where "health" was interpreted more broadly. Attempts in the 1970s to reformulate Swiss abortion law along the lines of the more liberal abortion legislation then being adopted in other Western European countries were not successful. The debate on whether to relax or restrict the abortion law, which lasted more than 15 years, had very little impact at the legislative level. Two laws were passed in 1981, however: one obliged cantons to create counselling services for pregnant women, and the other ordered health insurance to reimburse (without exception) the cost of legal abortion. In 1998 the Conseil National (the house of representatives) adopted a bill providing for abortion on request in the first 14 weeks of pregnancy. In 2000, similar bill was sent to the floor by the Judiciary Committee of the Conseil des Etats (the senate).

Prior to the enactment of the Swiss Penal Code, illegally performed abortions were seldom prosecuted, despite the fact that they were widely practised. In 1929, there were 72 convictions in Switzerland; after the passage of the abortion law in 1937, the number rose sharply and peaked in 1950 with 667 convictions. Subsequently, the increasingly liberal interpretation of the law resulted in a decline in the number of prosecutions. In the late 1960s, there were, on average, 150 prosecutions per annum, and after the initiation of public discussions to decriminalize abortion in 1971, prosecutions declined further to only a few each year. Very few illegal abortions were being performed in Switzerland in the early 1990s, with most of them consisting of abortions performed by physicians who failed to obtain the mandatory second opinion. There are no reported cases of women entering hospitals in Switzerland as a result of complications following clandestine abortions. Since 1973, there have been no reported deaths resulting from abortion.

There is a high rate of modern contraceptive usage, estimated by the Office Federal de la Statistique in 1999 at 88 per cent of sexually active persons aged 20-49 years. In terms of method, 38 per cent use the pill, 21 per cent the condom and 6 per cent the IUD, and 17 per cent have undergone sterilization.

The Government of Switzerland considers the rate of population growth to be satisfactory but the fertility level to be too low. The total fertility rate for 1995-2000 was estimated at 1.5 children per woman. The Government intends indirectly to increase the fertility rate by establishing an atmosphere of economic security and well-being for children and families in all socio-economic sectors. Family assistance services, family counselling, marriage guidance centres and pregnancy advisory services were expanded in the 1980s. Maternity allowances introduced in 1987 include an entitlement of 16 weeks beginning at the time of confinement. A system of family allowances exists at both the federal and the cantonal level, with the amount varying according to region, occupation, canton and number of children.

Source: Population Policy Data Bank, maintained by the Population Division of the Department of Economic and Social Affairs of the United Nations Secretariat. For additional sources, see reference section.

ABORTION POLICY

Grounds on which abortion is permitted:

To save the life of the woman	Yes
To preserve physical health	No
To preserve mental health	No
Rape or incest	No
Foetal impairment	No
Economic or social reasons	No
Available on request	No

Additional requirements:

Authorization for an abortion must be issued by two physicians. Written consent is required from the woman and her spouse or guardian.

REPRODUCTIVE HEALTH CONTEXT

Government view on fertility level:	Satisfactory
Government intervention concerning fertility level:	No intervention
Government policy on contraceptive use:	Direct support provided
Percentage of currently married women using modern contraception (aged 15-49, 1993):	28*
Total fertility rate (1995-2000):	4.0
Age-specific fertility rate (per 1,000 women aged 15-19, 1995-2000):	44
Government has expressed particular concern about:	
Morbidity and mortality resulting from induced abortion	..
Complications of childbearing and childbirth	..
Maternal mortality ratio (per 100,000 live births):	
National	180
Western Asia	320
Female life expectancy at birth (1995-2000):	71.2

* Preliminary or provisional.

Source: Population Policy Data Bank, maintained by the Population Division of the Department of Economic and Social Affairs of the United Nations Secretariat. For additional sources, see reference section.

Syrian Arab Republic

BACKGROUND

Induced abortion is generally illegal in the Syrian Arab Republic. Under the Penal Code of 22 June 1949, there are no stated exceptions to a general prohibition of abortion. A person who performs an abortion on a woman with her consent is subject to one to three years' imprisonment. If she does not consent, the penalty is increased to at least five years' forced labour. A woman who performs her own abortion or consents to its performance is subject to six months' to three years' imprisonment. Harsher penalties are applied if the abortion results in the death of the woman or if the person performing the abortion is a health professional. Penalties are reduced if the abortion is performed by the woman to save her honour or another person performs the abortion to save the honour of a descendant or a relative to the second degree.

Nonetheless, under general criminal law principles of necessity, an abortion can be legally performed to save the life of the pregnant woman. Moreover, the law on the exercise of health professions specifically allows an abortion to be performed by a physician or midwife when continuation of the pregnancy poses a danger to the life of the woman. In this case, the performance of the abortion must be approved by another physician. Before the operation, a record must be drawn up certifying the necessity of the abortion; and the record must be signed by the two physicians and the patient or her spouse or guardian.

Data on the incidence of induced abortion in the Syrian Arab Republic are scarce. However, one study of family formation and pregnancy outcome conducted in 1981 found that out of 31,567 pregnancies reported by 5,621 women, 9.6 per cent terminated in abortion.

The Government's involvement in family planning began in 1974, when it announced plans to integrate family planning into its health-care programme by establishing the Family Planning Unit as a component of its maternal and child health programme. The Family Planning Unit works in collaboration with the Syrian Family Planning Association, which began providing family planning services in the Syrian Arab Republic in 1974. The Government supports family planning activities through a network of MCH centres. It sets no major limits on contraceptives and directly supports their use. National statistics report 94,513 new acceptors and 460,258 clinic visits to the family planning programme in 1988, numbers that have risen steadily over the years. In 1988, 71 per cent of new acceptors chose oral contraceptives, 17 per cent used an intrauterine device and 11 per cent chose other methods. Efforts are under way to provide a wider mix of contraceptives and to reduce the dependence upon oral contraceptives. The modern contraceptive prevalence rate rose to 28 per cent by 1993. To improve the success of the family planning programme, local leaders have been consulted, and greater use has been made of traditional birth attendants. Cooperation has been encouraged among a wide variety of organizations, such as women and youth groups, and literacy and agricultural extension programmes have been used to disseminate information.

Source: Population Policy Data Bank, maintained by the Population Division of the Department of Economic and Social Affairs of the United Nations Secretariat. For additional sources, see reference section.

ABORTION POLICY

Grounds on which abortion is permitted:

To save the life of the woman	Yes
To preserve physical health	Yes
To preserve mental health	Yes
Rape or incest	Yes
Foetal impairment	Yes
Economic or social reasons	Yes
Available on request	Yes

Additional requirements:

An abortion requires the consent of the pregnant woman; it is authorized if performed by a licensed physician in a hospital or other recognized medical institution. Abortion is available on request during the first 12 weeks of gestation. Thereafter, induced abortion is available within 28 weeks from conception on judicial, genetic, vital, broad medical and social grounds, as well as for personal reasons with the special authorization of a commission of local physicians.

REPRODUCTIVE HEALTH CONTEXT

Government view on fertility level:	Too high
Government intervention concerning fertility level:	No intervention
Government policy on contraceptive use:	Direct support provided
Percentage of currently married women using modern contraception (aged 15-49):	..
Total fertility rate (1995-2000):	4.2
Age-specific fertility rate (per 1,000 women aged 15-19, 1995-2000):	35
Government has expressed particular concern about:	
Morbidity and mortality resulting from induced abortion	Yes
Complications of childbearing and childbirth	Yes
Maternal mortality ratio (per 100,000 live births, 1990):	
National	..
South-central Asia	560
Female life expectancy at birth (1995-2000):	70.2

Source: Population Policy Data Bank maintained by the Population Division of the Department of Economic and Social Affairs of the United Nations Secretariat. For additional sources, see list of references.

Tajikistan

BACKGROUND

As was the case with all of the former Soviet republics, Tajikistan, known prior to 1992 as the Tajik Soviet Socialist Republic, observed the abortion legislation and regulations of the former Union of Soviet Socialist Republics. As a result, abortion practices in Tajikistan were similar to those throughout the former USSR.

The description given below pertains to the situation in Tajikistan prior to independence. Since independence there has been no change in the abortion law.

The Soviet Decree of 27 June 1936 prohibited the performance of abortions except in cases of danger to life, serious threat to health, or the existence of a serious disease that could be inherited from the parents. The abortion had to be performed in a hospital or maternity home. Physicians who performed abortions outside a hospital or without the presence of one of these indications were subject to one to two years' imprisonment. If the abortion was performed under unsanitary conditions or by a person with no special medical education, the penalty was no less than three years' imprisonment. A person who induced a woman to have an abortion was subject to two years' imprisonment. A pregnant woman who underwent an abortion was subject to a reprimand and the payment of a fine of up to 300 roubles in the case of a repeat offence.

In its Decree of 23 November 1955, the Government of the former USSR repealed the general prohibition on the performance of abortions contained in the 1936 Decree. Other regulations issued in 1955 specified that abortions could be performed freely during the first twelve weeks of pregnancy if no contraindication existed and after that point when the continuance of the pregnancy and the birth would harm the mother (interpreted to include foetal handicap). The abortion had to be performed in a hospital by a physician and, unless performed in cases of a threat to the mother's health, a fee was charged. Persons who performed an abortion illegally were subject to criminal penalties established by criminal laws under the Criminal Code. For example, if the abortion was not performed in a hospital, a penalty of up to one year's imprisonment could be imposed and if it was performed by a person without an advanced medical degree, a penalty of up to two years' imprisonment was possible. In the case of repeat offences or the death or serious injury of the pregnant woman, a higher penalty of up to eight years' imprisonment could be imposed. A woman who underwent an illegal abortion was not penalized.

Despite the approval of the 1955 Decree and regulations, the problem of illegal abortions did not entirely disappear in the former Soviet Union. This situation resulted in part from the Government's conflicted attitude towards contraception. Although at time the Government manifested support for contraception, it did little to make contraception available and in 1974 effectively banned the widespread use of oral contraceptives. The situation was also due in part to a revived pronatalist approach to childbearing adopted at times by the Government, which looked unfavourably on abortion. The result was a reliance on abortion as the primary method of family planning.

Concerned with the high rate of illegal abortions, the Government in 1982 issued a decree allowing abortions for health reasons to be performed through the twenty-eighth week of pregnancy. Continuing this approach of increasing the circumstances under which legal abortions were available, on 31 December 1987 it

Source: Population Policy Data Bank maintained by the Population Division of the Department of Economic and Social Affairs of the United Nations Secretariat. For additional sources, see list of references.

issued an order setting out a broad range of non-medical indications for abortions performed on request through the twenty-eighth week of pregnancy. These included the death of the husband during pregnancy; imprisonment of the pregnant woman or her husband; deprivation of maternity rights; multiparity (the number of children exceeds five); divorce during pregnancy; pregnancy following rape; and child disability in the family. Moreover, the order provided that, with the approval of a commission, an abortion could be performed on any other grounds.

This extension of the grounds for abortion after the first 12 weeks of pregnancy, combined with the ambivalent attitude of the Government towards contraception, led to a dramatic increase in the number of officially reported abortions. Other factors resulting in a high incidence of abortion have included shortages of high-quality modern contraceptives and reliance upon less reliable traditional methods; a lack of knowledge among couples of contraception and of the detrimental health consequences of frequent abortions; and the absence of adequate training for physicians, nurses, teachers and other specialists. Data from the All-Union sample survey of contraceptive use conducted in 1990 indicate that in Tajikistan, 15 per cent of all women aged 15-49 years regularly used contraception, 6 per cent sometimes used contraception, 59 per cent did not use any contraceptive method and 18 per cent knew nothing about contraception.

In 1990, the abortion rate was estimated to be 49.1 per 1,000 women aged 15-44 (including spontaneous abortions). The actual figure is much higher, because this total does not include most abortions performed in departmental health services and commercial clinics, early vacuum aspirations or self-induced abortions. In 1989, illegal abortions, calculated on the basis of their registered complications, accounted for 40 per cent of all abortions and 61 per cent of all abortions among primigravidae. Among women under age 17, they accounted for 24 per cent of all induced abortions.

Maternal mortality ratios in Tajikistan were 43.6 per 100,000 live births in 1988, 65 per cent of which were due to unknown or "other" causes. The civil war that broke out in 1992 had disastrous consequences for the country's development and for its maternal and child health services in particular. Tajikistan is recovering from the civil war, and the socio-economic situation continues to stabilize. The total fertility rate was 4.2 children per woman in 1995-2000.

Source: Population Policy Data Bank maintained by the Population Division of the Department of Economic and Social Affairs of the United Nations Secretariat. For additional sources, see list of references.

ABORTION POLICY

Grounds on which abortion is permitted:

To save the life of the woman	Yes
To preserve physical health	Yes
To preserve mental health	Yes
Rape or incest	Yes
Foetal impairment	No
Economic or social reasons	No
Available on request	No

Additional requirements:

A legal abortion must be performed by a physician.

REPRODUCTIVE HEALTH CONTEXT

Government view on fertility level:	Satisfactory
Government intervention concerning fertility level:	To maintain
Government policy on contraceptive use:	Direct support provided
Percentage of currently married women using modern contraception (aged 15-44, 1993):	72
Total fertility rate (1995-2000):	1.7
Age-specific fertility rate (per 1,000 women aged 15-19, 1995-2000):	70
Government has expressed particular concern about:	
Morbidity and mortality resulting from induced abortion	Yes
Complications of childbearing and childbirth	Yes
Maternal mortality ratio (per 100,000 live births, 1990):	
National	200
South-eastern Asia	440
Female life expectancy at birth (1995-2000):	72.0

Source: Population Policy Data Bank maintained by the Population Division of the Department of Economic and Social Affairs of the United Nations Secretariat. For additional sources, see list of references.

Thailand

BACKGROUND

Abortion law in Thailand is governed by the provisions of Sections 301-305 of the Thai Penal Code of 13 November 1956. Under the Code, the performance of abortions is generally prohibited. A woman who causes her own abortion or allows any other person to procure her abortion is subject to up to three years' imprisonment and/or payment of a fine not exceeding 6,000 baht. A person who procures an abortion for a woman with her consent is subject to up to five years' imprisonment and/or payment of a fine not exceeding 10,000 baht. If this act causes grievous bodily harm to the woman, the penalty is increased to up to seven years' imprisonment and/or payment of a fine not exceeding 14,000 baht; and if the act causes the woman's death, the penalty is increased to up to ten years' imprisonment and payment of a fine not exceeding 20,000 baht. A person who procures an abortion for a woman without her consent is subject to up to seven years' imprisonment and/or payment of a fine not exceeding 14,000 baht. If the act causes grievous bodily harm, the penalty is increased to one to ten years' imprisonment and payment of a fine of 2,000 to 20,000 baht. If the act causes the death of the woman, the penalty is increased to five to twenty years' imprisonment and payment of a fine of 10,000 to 40,000 baht.

Nonetheless, the performance of an abortion is legal under the Code if carried out by a medical practitioner and (a) the abortion is necessary for the sake of the woman's health or (b) the woman is pregnant as a result of a criminal offence.

In practice, the law is not rigorously enforced. The prevalence of illegal abortion has been widely documented, particularly in the rural areas of the country. One estimate suggests that, in the late 1970s, at least 300,000 illegal abortions were performed in rural Thailand. Most illegal abortions are performed by non-medical personnel, such as self-trained practitioners, within the first trimester of pregnancy. Whereas abortions can be obtained in urban hospitals using vacuum curretage, the most frequently used procedure in rural areas is traditional massage abortion, followed by uterine injections. Some studies have shown that for a majority of women in rural areas, the stated reason for obtaining an abortion was to limit family size. A significant proportion of women also expressed the need for child spacing.

Although maternal mortality in Thailand has been considerably reduced over the past two decades, wide disparities remain between urban and rural areas with regard to maternal and child health care. Because the increasing number of illegal abortions are performed under unsanitary conditions by unqualified practitioners, hospitalization for complications from illegal abortion has been rising in many hospitals in Thailand. One study conducted in 1981 found that in Ramathibodi Hospital at Bangkok, one fourth of maternal deaths were due to complications from induced abortions improperly performed outside the hospital. In another study conducted in 1979 on the health consequences of induced abortion in north-eastern Thailand, the abortion rate in the rural province of Chayapoom was estimated to be as high as 107 per 1,000 women of reproductive age (15-49); the same study estimated a complication rate of about 25 per cent. An increasing trend has also been observed for adolescent pregnancies and abortions in Thailand. A 1982 study indicated that more than 25 per cent of the women that received abortions were aged 15-20 years.

Since the 1960s, the Government of Thailand has sponsored an active and effective integrated national family planning programme. The service network of the Thai Family Planning Programme has tried to provide complete, accessible family planning services free of charge. The modern contracteptive pravelence rate is high, estimated in 1993 at 72 per cent. Consequently, fertility has fallen dramatically in Thailand, in

---

Source: Population Policy Data Bank maintained by the Population Division of the Department of Economic and Social Affairs of the United Nations Secretariat. For additional sources, see list of references.

both urban and rural areas from 6.4 children per woman in 1965 to 2.6 by 1990 and 1.7 by 2000. The population growth rate is currently 0.9 per cent (2000). Despite the ready availability of contraceptives, however, several studies have shown that a significant proportion of abortion patients were not practising any method of contraception prior to the most recent abortion. In addition, changes in social and sexual lifestyles and the challenges of migration have translated into an increase in unwanted pregnancies, unsafe abortions, HIV/AIDS and sexually-transmitted diseases. The Government has attempted to direct family planning programmes increasingly towards the poor and uneducated in order to ensure access to contraceptive services by these high-risk groups.

Source: Population Policy Data Bank maintained by the Population Division of the Department of Economic and Social Affairs of the United Nations Secretariat. For additional sources, see list of references.

ABORTION POLICY

Grounds on which abortion is permitted:

To save the life of the woman	Yes
To preserve physical health	Yes
To preserve mental health	Yes
Rape or incest	Yes
Foetal impairment	Yes
Economic or social reasons	Yes
Available on request	Yes

Additional requirements:

An abortion must be performed in a hospital or other authorized health-care facility. If the woman is a minor, approval of her parents or guardian is required, unless she has been recognized as fully competent to earn her own living. After the first 10 weeks of pregnancy, special authorization by a commission composed of a gynaecologist/obstetrician, a general physician or a specialist in internal medicine and a social worker or a psychologist is required.

REPRODUCTIVE HEALTH CONTEXT

Government view on fertility level:	Too high
Government intervention concerning fertility level:	To lower
Government policy on contraceptive use:	Direct support provided
Percentage of currently married women using modern contraception (aged 15-49):	..
Total fertility rate (1995-2000):	2.1
Age-specific fertility rate (per 1,000 women aged 15-19, 1995-2000):	42
Government has expressed particular concern about:	
Morbidity and mortality resulting from induced abortion	No
Complications of childbearing and childbirth	No
Maternal mortality ratio (per 100,000 live births, 1990):	
National	..
Developed countries	27
Female life expectancy at birth (1995-2000):	75.3

Source: Population Policy Data Bank maintained by the Population Division of the Department of Economic and Social Affairs of the United Nations Secretariat. For additional sources, see list of references.

The former Yugoslav Republic of Macedonia

BACKGROUND

The former Yugoslav Republic of Macedonia achieved independence from the former Socialist Federal Republic of Yugoslavia in 1993 and ratified a new constitution. However, abortion is still regulated by the Law of 1977 enacted by the Republic when it was still part of Yugoslavia to implement article 191 of the Federal Constitution of Yugoslavia of 21 February 1974, which proclaims that "it is a human right to decide freely and responsibly on the number and timing of offspring". Under the law of the former Yugoslav Republic of Macedonia, abortion is allowed on request during the first 10 weeks of pregnancy. The intervention must be performed in a hospital or other authorized health-care facility. If the woman is a minor, approval of her parents or guardian is required. After the first 10 weeks of pregnancy, special authorization by a commission, composed of a gynaecologist/obstetrician, a second physician and a social worker or nurse, is required. The commission decides on the basis of the existence of medical, eugenic, juridical or socioeconomic grounds. The woman can appeal to the Commission of Second Instance if the Commission of First Instance rejects her request.

Penal provisions are imposed on medical organizations and persons that violate provisions of the law. However, a woman is never held criminally responsible for inducing her own abortion or for cooperating in such a procedure.

Beginning in 1952, abortion legislation in the former Yugoslavia was liberalized in response to the high levels of morbidity and mortality associated with a significant increase in illegal abortions. The subsequent changes in the abortion laws (general principles were adopted at the federal level and laws were implemented at the local level) were expressly directed to facilitating access to legal abortion in order to discourage illegal practices. For instance, a significant decline in the number of illegal abortions is attributed to the decision in 1969 to eliminate the requirement of a commission's approval for termination of pregnancies of less than 10 weeks, a requirement that had been a practical and psychological obstacle to abortion. The policy of liberalizing legal regulations with regard to abortion was facilitated by increased numbers of medical facilities, better access to information on abortion services and higher levels of education.

The former Yugoslavia registered high rates of abortion, a high rate of repeat abortions, increased second-trimester abortions and increased abortions among adolescents. These trends suggest that abortion continued to be used as a contraceptive method, with all the attendant health risks. In the late 1980s, the former Government indicated deep concern about these trends and the low rates of usage of modern contraceptive methods.

In the former Government's Resolution on Population, Development and Family Planning of 1989, which set out general principles and directions with regard to population matters, special emphasis was given to fertility and family planning. The resolution, while reconfirming the right of each person to decide freely on the number and spacing of children, as established in the Constitution of 1974, was directed to attaining replacement-level fertility in all areas of the country. In part to reduce the incidence of abortion and in part to reduce fertility in some republics, specific measures to disseminate contraceptive information and supplies more widely were taken at the federal level. Social welfare measures, such as prolonged maternity leave, child allowances and childcare facilities, were also strengthened in areas of the country where fertility was below replacement level.

Source: Population Policy Data Bank maintained by the Population Division of the Department of Economic and Social Affairs of the United Nations Secretariat. For additional sources, see list of references.

Although abortion rates continued to be very high, the former Government of Yugoslavia essentially achieved its objective through the legal liberalization of abortion: illegal abortions were practically eliminated and the country experienced a significant decline in maternal morbidity and mortality related to abortion. In the former Yugoslav Republic of Macedonia itself, maternal mortality associated with abortion declined from 35 per 100,000 abortions in 1969 to 3 per 100,000 in 1986. Although the abortion rates did not begin declining until the late 1980s, when they did fall, they did so dramatically, from a 1986 peak of 70.6 abortions per 1,000 women aged 15-44 to 28.5 only a decade later in 1996.

Family planning services had been a part of the regular medical services in the former Yugoslavia since the mid-1950s. A family planning institution was established in 1963 at the national and local levels, and the Family Planning Association, affiliated with the International Planned Parenthood Federation, has existed since 1966. However, sex education in the schools and family planning counselling were not systematically developed, and family planning has encountered continuing resistance throughout the country. As a result, insufficient knowledge and fear of modern supply methods of contraception remain widespread.

Source: Population Policy Data Bank maintained by the Population Division of the Department of Economic and Social Affairs of the United Nations Secretariat. For additional sources, see list of references.

Togo

ABORTION POLICY

Grounds on which abortion is permitted:

To save the life of the woman	Yes
To preserve physical health	No*
To preserve mental health	No*
Rape or incest	No*
Foetal impairment	No*
Economic or social reasons	No
Available on request	No

Additional requirements:

The decision to interrupt a pregnancy is made under the authority of the physician, who requires the permission of the family of the pregnant woman in order to proceed. The intervention may take place up to the third month of pregnancy.

* Official interpretation generally permits these grounds.

REPRODUCTIVE HEALTH CONTEXT

Government view on fertility level:	Satisfactory
Government intervention concerning fertility level:	To maintain
Government policy on contraceptive use:	Direct support provided
Percentage of currently married women using modern contraception (aged 15-49, 1998):	7
Total fertility rate (1995-2000):	6.1
Age-specific fertility rate (per 1,000 women aged 15-19, 1995-2000):	120
Government has expressed particular concern about:	
Morbidity and mortality resulting from induced abortion	..
Complications of childbearing and childbirth	Yes
Maternal mortality ratio (per 100,000 live births, 1990):	
National	640
Western Africa	1 020
Female life expectancy at birth (1995-2000):	50.1

Source: Population Policy Data Bank maintained by the Population Division of the Department of Economic and Social Affairs of the United Nations Secretariat. For additional sources, see list of references.

BACKGROUND

The exact status of abortion law in Togo is unclear. In 1981, the Government of Togo enacted a new criminal code explicitly repealing the French Penal Code of 1810, which was in force at the time of independence and which generally prohibited the performance of abortions. The new code omits reference to abortion altogether. Under the usual rules of legislative interpretation which provide that where there is no law there is no punishment, such an omission would imply that the performance of abortions has been depenalized completely.

There are reports, however, that this is not the case. While the removal of the abortion provisions from the Penal Code may have liberalized abortion law in Togo, it appears not to have eliminated it. Reportedly the performance of abortion is possible through the third month of pregnancy when the woman's life or health would be endangered by continuation of the pregnancy, as well as when there is evidence of foetal impairment or when the pregnancy results from rape or incest. The decision to interrupt a pregnancy is made under the authority of the physician, who is said usually to require the permission of the family of the pregnant woman in order to proceed.

Illegal abortion appears to occur in Togo, and backstreet interventions are reported to be performed outside authorized facilities. The practice is not widespread, however, owing to the existence of customary, traditional, moral and religious practices that strongly condemn abortion. In a 1975 survey, only 6 per cent of women reported that they would resort to induced abortion for unwanted pregnancy, although the strong social disapproval of abortion suggests that the incidence may be widely under-reported.

The French anticontraception law of 1920 forbidding the advertisement, manufacture, transport, sale and importation of contraceptives has apparently not been repealed in Togo. However, it does not appear to be enforced. The Togolese Association for Family Welfare, an affiliate of the International Planned Parenthood Federation, was given legal status in 1976 and participated in the Government's national family planning programme. In 1989, the *Programme national du bien-être familial* received the United Nations Population Award in recognition of its achievements in the family planning field. Nevertheless, surveys show a continuing lack of knowledge of family planning methods. Abstinence is still the most frequently used method of spacing births, frequently by the woman moving away from her husband. In addition, the delivery of family planning services is uneven: a 1994 survey found that of 375 health centres, only 190 offered family planning services and 59 provided all contraceptive methods.

The use of modern contraceptives improved from 3 per cent of married women in 1988 to 7 per cent in 1998. The total fertility rate has only recently begun to decline, from 6.6 children per woman in 1990-1995 to a projected 6.0 children per woman for the period 1995-2000. Given the low contraceptive prevalence rate, this decline has been cited as potential evidence of an increase in either traditional contraceptive methods or induced abortion. There is, however, to date no data supporting either conclusion. The maternal mortality ratio (640 maternal deaths per 100,000 live births in 1990) remains significantly below the regional average of 1,020.

The Government of Togo has expressed deep concern about the growing number of teenage pregnancies. In a 1984 decree, the President of Togo established that "Whosoever makes a girl pregnant if she is a regular member of a school or training college . . ." is subject to imprisonment for from six months to three years and

Source: Population Policy Data Bank maintained by the Population Division of the Department of Economic and Social Affairs of the United Nations Secretariat. For additional sources, see list of references.

to a fine of 500,000 CFA francs. Adolescents are also a target group for the family planning programme, although only married couples appear to have relatively easy access to family planning services in Togo. After the International Conference on Population and Development, the Government recommitted itself to population issues through the formulation of a national population policy and the establishment of regional programmatic implementation committees on reproductive health and family planning.

Source: Population Policy Data Bank maintained by the Population Division of the Department of Economic and Social Affairs of the United Nations Secretariat. For additional sources, see list of references.

ABORTION POLICY

Grounds on which abortion is permitted:

To save the life of the woman	Yes
To preserve physical health	No
To preserve mental health	No
Rape or incest	No
Foetal impairment	No
Economic or social reasons	No
Available on request	No

Additional requirements:

Information is not readily available.

REPRODUCTIVE HEALTH CONTEXT

Government view on fertility level:	Satisfactory
Government intervention concerning fertility level:	To maintain
Government policy on contraceptive use:	Direct support provided
Percentage of currently married women using modern contraception (aged 15-49):	..
Total fertility rate (1995-2000):	..
Age-specific fertility rate (per 1,000 women aged 15-19, 1995-2000):	..
Government has expressed particular concern about:	
Morbidity and mortality resulting from induced abortion	..
Complications of childbearing and childbirth	..
Maternal mortality ratio (per 100,000 live births, 1990):	
National	..
Oceania	680
Female life expectancy at birth (1995-2000):	..

Source: Population Policy Data Bank maintained by the Population Division of the Department of Economic and Social Affairs of the United Nations Secretariat. For additional sources, see list of references.

Tonga

BACKGROUND

Sections 103-105 of the Criminal Offences Act regulate abortion in Tonga. Under these sections, there are no exceptions to a prohibition against the performance of all abortions. A person who with intent to procure a miscarriage administers any drug or noxious thing or unlawfully uses any means is subject to up to seven years' imprisonment. A woman who undertakes the same act or allows it to be undertaken with respect to her with intent to cause her own miscarriage is subject to up to three years' imprisonment. Nonetheless, under general criminal law principles of necessity, an abortion can be legally performed to save the life of a pregnant woman.

Since the 1960s, the Government has strongly supported maternal and child health care and family planning. Two voluntary organizations, the Tonga Family Planning Association and the Catholic Family Planning Centre, have been offering family planning services throughout most of the country. By the mid-1980s, about 28 per cent of women of reproductive age practised family planning. By the late 1990s, the International Planned Parenthood Federation reported that an estimated 70 per cent of the population had some knowledge of family planning.

Tonga comprises 36 inhabited islands; remoteness thus presents a continuing barrier to the delivery of reproductive health care services, including family planning. The low rate of contraceptive usage is also attributed to enduring traditional, cultural and religious beliefs. In 1999, the Government expressed its concern that the sustainability of population policies and programmes was threatened by the lack of adequate human and financial resources, particularly in the face of emerging challenges in the areas of adolescent pregnancy, sexually transmitted diseases and HIV/AIDS.

Tonga has a relatively high total fertility rate, but it has been offset by heavy emigration under the impact of inflation and unemployment, increasingly producing what is thought to be a negative population growth rate. The World Health Organization estimated the annual population growth rate average for the entire 1990-1999 period to be 0.3 per cent.

Source: Population Policy Data Bank maintained by the Population Division of the Department of Economic and Social Affairs of the United Nations Secretariat. For additional sources, see list of references.

ABORTION POLICY

Grounds on which abortion is permitted:

To save the life of the woman	Yes
To preserve physical health	Yes
To preserve mental health	Yes
Rape or incest	No
Foetal impairment	No
Economic or social reasons	No
Available on request	No

Additional requirements:

Information is not readily available.

REPRODUCTIVE HEALTH CONTEXT

Government view on fertility level:	Too high
Government intervention concerning fertility level:	To lower
Government policy on contraceptive use:	Direct support provided
Percentage of currently married women using modern contraception (aged 15-49,* 1987):	44
Total fertility rate (1995-2000):	1.7
Age-specific fertility rate (per 1,000 women aged 15-19, 1995-2000):	40
Government has expressed particular concern about:	
Morbidity and mortality resulting from induced abortion	..
Complications of childbearing and childbirth	Yes
Maternal mortality ratio (per 100,000 live births, 1990):	
National	90
Caribbean	400
Female life expectancy at birth (1995-2000):	76.2

* Including visiting unions.

Source: Population Policy Data Bank maintained by the Population Division of the Department of Economic and Social Affairs of the United Nations Secretariat. For additional sources, see list of references.

BACKGROUND

The performance of abortions is generally illegal in Trinidad and Tobago under the Offences Against the Person Act of 3 April 1925, as amended. Any person who, with intent to procure the miscarriage of a woman, unlawfully administers to her any noxious thing or unlawfully uses any means is subject to four years' imprisonment. A woman who undertakes the same act with respect to herself is subject to the same penalty. Any person who unlawfully supplies means to procure an abortion knowing that it is intended for that purpose is subject to two years' imprisonment.

Nonetheless, under general criminal law principles of necessity, an abortion can be legally performed to save the life of a pregnant woman. Moreover, Trinidad and Tobago, like a number of Commonwealth countries, whose legal systems are based on the English common law, follows the holding of the 1938 English *Rex v. Bourne* decision in determining whether an abortion performed for health reasons is lawful. In the *Bourne* decision, a physician was acquitted of the offence of performing an abortion in the case of a woman who had been raped. The court ruled that the abortion was lawful because it had been performed to prevent the woman from becoming " physical and mental wreck" thus setting a precedent for future abortion cases performed on the grounds of preserving the pregnant woman' physical and mental health.

Although statistics on abortion in Trinidad and Tobago are not accurate, the practice is believed to be widespread and abortion is a major cause of maternal mortality and hospital admissions.

The Government of Trinidad and Tobago considers the rates of fertility and population growth to be too high, and its population policy since the late 1960s has consisted primarily of a national family planning programme designed to lower fertility, reduce excessive pressure on natural resources and ease the resulting problems of housing, unemployment and unequal income distribution. The national family planning programme has focused on integrating maternal and child health and information and education programmes at the community level. Through the Health Sector Reform Programme, the national health system in Trinidad and Tobago has been further decentralized. As a result, well over 100 government health centres offer family planning as a part of their maternal and child health care programme.

According to the Demographic and Health Survey conducted in 1987 by the Family Planning Association of Trinidad and Tobago, knowledge of modern methods of contraception is nearly universal, with 83 per cent of women in a union having used a method at some time and 44 per cent practising modern contraception. Oral contraceptives, the condom and female sterilization are the most widely used methods of contraception among couples in Trinidad and Tobago. However, a decline in modern contraception utilization was recorded in clinics during the 1990s. This decline is presumably related to the limited range of available methods, to supply problems, or to the increasing availability of over-the-counter contraception. The total fertility rate for the period 1995-2000 was 1.7 children per woman.

In 1989 the Government reconstituted its national population council, and after the 1994 ICPD in Cairo, Trinidad and Tobago adopted a national population policy in 1996. More recently, the Population Programme Unit of the Ministry of Health completed a nation-wide training programme for nurses to improve the quality of reproductive health care. Adolescent pregnancy and adolescent HIV/AIDS have evolved into major concerns of the Government.

Source: Population Policy Data Bank maintained by the Population Division of the Department of Economic and Social Affairs of the United Nations Secretariat. For additional sources, see list of references.

ABORTION POLICY

Grounds on which abortion is permitted:

To save the life of the woman	Yes
To preserve physical health	Yes
To preserve mental health	Yes
Rape or incest	Yes
Foetal impairment	Yes
Economic or social reasons	Yes
Available on request	Yes

Additional requirements:

The intervention must be performed during the first trimester of pregnancy by a physician legally practising his profession in a hospital, health-care establishment or authorized clinic.

REPRODUCTIVE HEALTH CONTEXT

Government view on fertility level:	Too high
Government intervention concerning fertility level:	To lower
Government policy on contraceptive use:	Direct support provided
Percentage of currently married women using modern contraception (aged 15-49, 1994/95):	51*
Total fertility rate (1995-2000):	2.6
Age-specific fertility rate (per 1,000 women aged 15-19, 1995-2000):	13
Government has expressed particular concern about:	
Morbidity and mortality resulting from induced abortion	No
Complications of childbearing and childbirth	Yes
Maternal mortality ratio (per 100,000 live births, 1990):	
National	170
Northern Africa	340
Female life expectancy at birth (1995-2000):	70.7

* Preliminary or provisional.

Source: Population Policy Data Bank maintained by the Population Division of the Department of Economic and Social Affairs of the United Nations Secretariat. For additional sources, see list of references.

Tunisia

BACKGROUND

In 1965, Tunisia was the first Muslim country to liberalize its abortion law. The Tunisian Penal Code of 1913 and the legislative decrees of 1920 and 1940, which amended the abortion provisions of the Code, had all prohibited the performance of abortions, except to save the life of the pregnant woman. Law No. 65-24 of 1 July 1965 amended the Code to allow abortions to be performed during the first three months of pregnancy, if a couple had at least five living children and the woman had been pregnant for less than three months, and at any time during pregnancy if the continuance of pregnancy posed a danger to the health of the pregnant woman.

Tunisia's current abortion law dates from 1973 when the new Penal Code was enacted. Article 214 of the Code authorizes the performance of abortions on request during the first three months of pregnancy. After this period, an abortion may be performed when there is a risk that the health or mental balance of the mother will be compromised by the continuation of the pregnancy or a risk that the unborn child will suffer from a serious disease or infirmity. During the first three months of pregnancy, an abortion must be performed by a physician in a hospital or health establishment or authorized clinic. After this period, an abortion must be performed in an establishment approved for this purpose and the treating physician must present a report to the physician who will perform the abortion. The performance of abortions is subsidized by the Government in the same way as all other medical services, and those entitled to receive free health care can obtain an abortion free of charge in public hospitals.

Persons who perform an abortion in violation of the provisions of the Code are subject to five years' imprisonment and/or payment of a fine of 10,000 dinars. A woman who performs an abortion on herself in violation of the law or consents to its performance is subject to two years' imprisonment and/or payment of a fine of 2,000 dinars.

The liberalization of abortion in the penal law is only one element of the global policy of the Tunisian Government with regard to fertility and population growth. Tunisia was the first country in Africa (or the Middle East) to adopt an official national policy directed to reducing fertility as a means of improving socio-economic development. After Tunisia attained independence from France in 1956, the Government enacted a number of legislative changes in order to change public opinion concerning the status of women. Legislation enacted in 1956 provided equal rights for women, while the Personal Status Code abolished polygamy and repudiation, introduced women's right to divorce and set a minimum age for marriage. In 1961, the Government added to its goals the reduction of fertility and passed a law that repealed the French anticontraception law of 1920, stating that the importation, sale and advertising of contraceptives would be henceforth regulated by the legislation governing other pharmaceutical products. In 1964, the minimum age at marriage was raised, the number of children entitled to receive family allowances was limited to four and the National Family Planning Programme was implemented in a few regions, before being implemented throughout the country in 1966. In 1965, the first liberalization of abortion took place; however, the law was soon considered to be too restrictive and not in conformity with the family planning and fertility objectives of the country.

In 1973, when the new abortion law was approved, the Office National de la Famille et de la Population was created to direct the family planning programme. It was also charged with conducting demographic research and with informing and educating the public about family planning and family health. Subsequently,

Source: Population Policy Data Bank maintained by the Population Division of the Department of Economic and Social Affairs of the United Nations Secretariat. For additional sources, see list of references.

in 1988, the number of children entitled to receive family allowances was further limited to three. All along, legislative action was complemented by other measures intended to raise the status of the woman and decrease fertility, such as providing schooling for both sexes, affirming the right of women to practise contraception and using the media to encourage family planning. Family planning was fully integrated into the basic health care system and maternal care centers were created to provide abortions and other services. In the Eighth Plan, for the period 1992-1996, the Government identified the demographic targets of increasing contraceptive prevalence from 53 per cent in 1991 to 64 by 2001 and of reducing the total fertility rate to 2.6, with the view of achieving a rate of 2.1 by 2026.

Through its comprehensive approach, the Tunisian Government has achieved significant results, with the total fertility rate decreasing from 7.2 children per woman in 1965 to 3.4 in 1991 and 2.6 by 2000. The population growth rate also decreased from 2.6 per cent in 1985 to 1.4 per cent for 1995-2000. The fertility drop is ascribed to a high rate of contraceptive use. In 1994-1995, 51 per cent of women used a modern method of contraception. Despite the success of the national family planning programme, however, acceptors enter the programme at a relatively advanced age, indicating that contraception and abortion are used mainly to prevent subsequent births once the desired number of children has been reached. The average Tunisian acceptor of family planning is aged 30 years; has 3.7 living children and has been married nine years. Although high parity is no longer a requirement to obtain an abortion, the majority of women have four or more children when they seek an abortion.

Since its liberalization in 1973, abortion has been practised by an increasing number of women and is currently the third most commonly used method of birth control, after intrauterine devices and oral contraceptives. The 1996 rate of 8.6 abortions per 1,000 women aged 15-44 is relatively modest. Official statistics, however, omit legal abortions performed in the private sector. In 1980, official abortions were estimated to account for 15-20 per cent of the total number of reported abortions. Tunisia also has a maternal mortality ratio of 170 deaths per 100,000 live births, about half the regional average.

Although there was little religious opposition to the liberalization of abortion in 1973, it is often difficult for a woman openly to seek a legal abortion. Surveys have shown that people continue to be misinformed about the availability of abortion. Moreover, abortion for unmarried women continues to be a taboo subject in traditional communities. Therefore, illegal abortion continues to be practised, especially in the case of extramarital pregnancy and in rural areas. Illegal abortions are often self-induced, either by vegetable products, by drugs obtained from pharmacists or by vinegar or salt injections.

Source: Population Policy Data Bank maintained by the Population Division of the Department of Economic and Social Affairs of the United Nations Secretariat. For additional sources, see list of references.

Turkey

ABORTION POLICY

Grounds on which abortion is permitted:

To save the life of the woman	Yes
To preserve physical health	Yes
To preserve mental health	Yes
Rape or incest	Yes
Foetal impairment	Yes
Economic or social reasons	Yes
Available on request	Yes

Additional requirements:

Abortion is available on request during the first 10 weeks of pregnancy. Thereafter, a legal abortion is permitted only to save the life or health of the pregnant woman and in cases of foetal impairment. The procedure must be performed by a gynaecologist with additional training in abortion procedures. The pregnant woman must consent to the abortion. Parental consent is required if the pregnant woman is a minor. If a woman has a legal guardian because she is either a minor or is mentally incompetent, the consent of the guardian, of a justice of the peace and of the woman must be obtained. The law requires a married woman to obtain spousal authorization prior to obtaining an abortion. The consent requirements are waived if the woman's life is in immediate danger.

REPRODUCTIVE HEALTH CONTEXT

Government view on fertility level:	Too high
Government intervention concerning fertility level:	To lower
Government policy on contraceptive use:	Direct support provided
Percentage of currently married women using modern contraception (aged 15-49, 1998):	38*
Total fertility rate (1995-2000):	2.5
Age-specific fertility rate (per 1,000 women aged 15-19, 1995-2000):	44
Government has expressed particular concern about:	
Morbidity and mortality resulting from induced abortion	No
Complications of childbearing and childbirth	Yes
Maternal mortality ratio (per 100,000 live births, 1990):	
National	180
Western Asia	320
Female life expectancy at birth (1995-2000):	71.7

* Preliminary or provisional.

Source: Population Policy Data Bank maintained by the Population Division of the Department of Economic and Social Affairs of the United Nations Secretariat. For additional sources, see list of references.

BACKGROUND

Until 1983, abortion in Turkey was permitted only to save the life or preserve the health of the pregnant woman and in cases of foetal impairment. (Penal Code of 1 March 1936; Law No. 557 of 1 January 1965, and Ordinance of 12 June 1967).

Anyone performing an illegal abortion with the woman's consent was subject to two to five years' imprisonment. A woman inducing her own abortion was subject to one to four years' imprisonment, while a woman consenting to an abortion performed by another person was subject to one to five years' imprisonment. Any person performing an abortion without the woman's consent was subject to 7-12 years' imprisonment; a similar penalty was applied if the consenting woman was under 14 years of age or if her consent was obtained by violence, threat or deception.

In the early 1980s, the growing incidence of unsafe abortion in Turkey and the resulting morbidity and mortality led the Government to liberalize the law further and make abortion widely available. Under the Population Planning Law of 24 May 1983 (Law Number 2827, sections 5 and 6, and Ordinance No. 83/7395 of 14 November 1983, issued under the Law) an abortion may be performed on the request of the pregnant woman within 10 weeks of pregnancy. Thereafter, the performance of an abortion is permitted to save the life or preserve the health of the woman and in cases of foetal impairment. The existence of these indications must, however, be confirmed by a specialist in obstetrics and gynaecology and by a specialist in another related field. This requirement is waived if the pregnancy poses an immediate risk to the woman's life, provided that the performing physician informs the Directorate of Health and Welfare in provincial centres of the name and address of the patient, the intervention performed and the justification for the intervention, either prior to the procedure or within 24 hours following the abortion.

A legal abortion must be performed by a gynaecologist/obstetrician or, in the case of menstrual regulation, by a general practitioner with special training under the supervision and control of a gynaecologist/obstetrician. The pregnant woman must consent to the abortion, and the consent of her legal representative is also required if she is a minor. If the pregnant woman has a legal guardian because she is a minor or is mentally incompetent, the consent of her legal guardian and of a justice of the peace, as well as her consent, must be obtained. The current law requires married women to obtain spousal authorization prior to obtaining an abortion. The consent requirements are waived, however, if the pregnancy poses an immediate danger to the life of the woman.

Despite the liberal nature of abortion laws in Turkey, the number of legal abortions performed in the country has been sharply restricted by the requirement that the procedure be carried out only by or under the supervision of gynaecologists. This factor is especially critical in rural Turkey, where medical specialists of any type are scarce or non-existent. Many rural health facilities that are without a trained specialist are excluded from providing services. Consequently, a rural Turkish woman seeking an abortion within the first ten weeks of pregnancy may not be able to obtain one.

Although abortion has been legal in Turkey only since 1983, several studies indicate that abortion has been widely practised in the country for a considerable period. The Turkish Fertility Survey, which was conducted in 1978 before abortion became widely available, found that 34 per cent of Turkish women had

Source: Population Policy Data Bank maintained by the Population Division of the Department of Economic and Social Affairs of the United Nations Secretariat. For additional sources, see list of references.

had at least one induced abortion by the time of the survey. The Turkish Population and Health Survey in 1983 found that 37 per cent of ever-married women had had at least one abortion and estimated that 12 per cent of all pregnancies were artificially terminated. Similarly, the Population and Health Survey conducted in 1988 found that 24 per cent of the respondents had had at least one induced abortion. Most recently, in 1993 the abortion rate was estimated at 25 abortions per 1,000 women (based on ever-married women aged 15-49). Several studies have shown that urban women with higher educational levels are more likely to have had an abortion than less educated rural women.

The total fertility rate declined from 3.8 children per woman in 1990-1995 to 2.5 in 1995-2000, as has the population growth rate, from 2.2 per cent to 1.7. Despite these declines, the Turkish Government still considers the rates of fertility and population growth to be too high. Efforts at fertility reduction continue. For example, in 1996-1997, the Social Marketing for Change project in Turkey targeted for contraception education those women who were seeking or had had an abortion. Although Turkey has a socialized public-health system that provides free medical care to all of its citizens that require it, traditional and religious attitudes have prevented modern family planning methods from becoming widely accepted. The use of modern contraceptives was estimated in 1998 at 38 per cent of currently married women. Finally, Turkey's maternal mortality ratio (180 deaths per 100,000 live births in 1990) remained significantly under the regional average of 320.

In 1982, the Government adopted a population policy providing family planning as a means of improving family health and welfare. In addition to legalizing abortion, the Population Planning Law of 24 May 1983 legalized all family planning services, including permitting sterilization, which is permitted with spousal consent. In 1995, following the International Conference on Population and Development, the Government revised its National Action Plan for Women's Health and Family Planning.

Source: Population Policy Data Bank maintained by the Population Division of the Department of Economic and Social Affairs of the United Nations Secretariat. For additional sources, see list of references.

Turkmenistan

ABORTION POLICY

Grounds on which abortion is permitted:

To save the life of the woman	Yes
To preserve physical health	Yes
To preserve mental health	Yes
Rape or incest	Yes
Foetal impairment	Yes
Economic or social reasons	Yes
Available on request	Yes

Additional requirements:

An abortion requires the consent of the pregnant woman; it is authorized if performed by a licensed physician in a hospital or other recognized medical institution. Abortion is available on request during the first 12 weeks of gestation. Thereafter, induced abortion is available within 28 weeks from conception on judicial, genetic, vital, broad medical and social grounds, as well as for personal reasons with the special authorization of a commission of local physicians.

REPRODUCTIVE HEALTH CONTEXT

Government view on fertility level:	Satisfactory
Government intervention concerning fertility level:	No intervention
Government policy on contraceptive use:	No support provided
Percentage of currently married women using modern contraception (aged 15-49):	..
Total fertility rate (1995-2000):	3.6
Age-specific fertility rate (per 1,000 women aged 15-19, 1995-2000):	20
Government has expressed particular concern about:	
Morbidity and mortality resulting from induced abortion	Yes
Complications of childbearing and childbirth	Yes
Maternal mortality ratio (per 100,000 live births, 1990):	
National	..
South-central Asia	560
Female life expectancy at birth (1995-2000):	68.9

Source: Population Policy Data Bank maintained by the Population Division of the Department of Economic and Social Affairs of the United Nations Secretariat. For additional sources, see list of references.

BACKGROUND

As is the case with all the former Soviet republics, Turkmenistan, known prior to 1992 as the Turkmen Soviet Socialist Republic, observed the abortion legislation and regulations of the former Union of Soviet Socialist Republics. As a result, abortion practices in Turkmenistan were similar to those throughout the former USSR. The description given below pertains to the situation in Turkmenistan prior to independence. Since independence there has been no change in the abortion law.

The Soviet Decree of 27 June 1936 prohibited the performance of abortions except in cases of danger to life, serious threat to health, or the existence of a serious disease that could be inherited from the parents. The abortion had to be performed in a hospital or maternity home. Physicians who performed abortions outside a hospital or without the presence of one of these indications were subject to one to two years' imprisonment. If the abortion was performed under unsanitary conditions or by a person with no special medical education, the penalty was no less than three years' imprisonment. A person who induced a woman to have an abortion was subject to two years' imprisonment. A pregnant woman who underwent an abortion was subject to a reprimand and the payment of a fine of up to 300 roubles in the case of a repeat offence.

In its Decree of 23 November 1955, the Government of the former USSR repealed the general prohibition on the performance of abortions contained in the 1936 Decree. Other regulations also issued in 1955 specified that abortions could be performed freely during the first 12 weeks of pregnancy if no contraindication existed and after that point when the continuance of the pregnancy and the birth would harm the mother (interpreted to include foetal handicap). The abortion had to be performed in a hospital by a physician and, unless performed in cases of a threat to the mother's health, a fee was charged. Persons who performed an abortion illegally were subject to criminal penalties established by criminal laws under the Criminal Code. For example, if the abortion was not performed in a hospital, a penalty of up to one year's imprisonment could be imposed and if it was performed by a person without an advanced medical degree, a penalty of up to two years' imprisonment was possible. In the case of repeat offences or the death or serious injury of the pregnant woman, a higher penalty of up to eight years' imprisonment could be imposed. A woman who underwent an illegal abortion was not penalized.

Despite the approval of the 1955 Decree and regulations, the problem of illegal abortions did not entirely disappear in the former Soviet Union. This situation was due partly to the Government's conflicted attitude towards contraception. Although at times it manifested support for contraception, it did little to make contraception available and in 1974 effectively banned the widespread use of oral contraceptives. The situation was also due in part to a revived pronatalist approach to childbearing adopted at times by the Government, which looked unfavourably on abortion. The result was a reliance on abortion as the primary method of family planning.

Concerned with the high rate of illegal abortions, the Government in 1982 issued a decree allowing abortions for health reasons to be performed through the twenty-eighth week of pregnancy. Continuing this approach of increasing the circumstances under which legal abortions were available, on 31 December 1987 it issued an order setting out a broad range of non-medical indications for abortions performed on request through the twenty-eighth week of pregnancy. These included the death of the husband during pregnancy;

Source: Population Policy Data Bank maintained by the Population Division of the Department of Economic and Social Affairs of the United Nations Secretariat. For additional sources, see list of references.

imprisonment of the pregnant woman or her husband; deprivation of maternity rights; multiparity (the number of children exceeds five); divorce during pregnancy; pregnancy following rape; and child disability in the family. Moreover, the order provided that, with the approval of a commission, an abortion could be performed on any other grounds.

This extension of the grounds for abortion after the first 12 weeks of pregnancy, combined with the ambivalent attitude of the Government towards contraception, led to a dramatic increase in the number of officially reported abortions. Other factors resulting in a high incidence of abortion have included shortages of high-quality modern contraceptives and reliance upon less reliable traditional methods.

The abortion rate was estimated at 44.9 abortions per 1,000 women aged 15-44 (including spontaneous abortions) in 1990. However, that abortion rate reportedly fell 27 per cent between 1990 and 1995. In 1989 the President adopted a comprehensive health plan and a family planning service was established. In terms of reproductive health, 12 centers and 49 units were opened around the country. The Government was considering the creation of a national coordination body on population issues in 1999. The total fertility rate declined from 4.0 children per woman in 1990-1995 to 3.6 in 1995-2000, with a current population growth rate of 1.8 per cent.

Source: Population Policy Data Bank maintained by the Population Division of the Department of Economic and Social Affairs of the United Nations Secretariat. For additional sources, see list of references.

Tuvalu

ABORTION POLICY

Grounds on which abortion is permitted:

To save the life of the woman	Yes
To preserve physical health	No
To preserve mental health	No
Rape or incest	No
Foetal impairment	No
Economic or social reasons	No
Available on request	No

Additional requirements:

Information is not readily available.

REPRODUCTIVE HEALTH CONTEXT

Government view on fertility level:	Too high
Government intervention concerning fertility level:	To lower
Government policy on contraceptive use:	Direct support provided
Percentage of currently married women using modern contraception (aged 15-49):	..
Total fertility rate (1995-2000):	..
Age-specific fertility rate (per 1,000 women aged 15-19, 1995-2000):	..
Government has expressed particular concern about:	
Morbidity and mortality resulting from induced abortion	..
Complications of childbearing and childbirth	..
Maternal mortality ratio (per 100,000 live births, 1990):	
National	..
Oceania	680
Female life expectancy at birth (1995-2000):	..

Source: Population Policy Data Bank maintained by the Population Division of the Department of Economic and Social Affairs of the United Nations Secretariat. For additional sources, see list of references.

BACKGROUND

Abortion in Tuvalu is governed by the provisions of the Penal Code of 18 October 1865, as amended. Under the abortion provisions of the Code (sections 150-152), which are based on the English Offences against the Person Act of 1861, any person who, with intent to procure the miscarriage of a woman, unlawfully administers any noxious thing or uses any means is subject to imprisonment for ten years. A pregnant woman who undertakes the same act or consents to its performance is subject to life imprisonment. Any person who unlawfully supplies means to procure an abortion knowing that it is unlawfully intended for that purpose is subject to five years' imprisonment.

Nonetheless, an abortion may be performed to save the life of a pregnant woman. Section 227 of the Code provides that a person is not criminally responsible for performing in good faith and with reasonable care and skill a surgical operation upon an unborn child for the preservation of the mother's life if the performance of the operation is reasonable having regard to the patient's state at the time, and to all the circumstances of the case. In addition, Section 214 of the Code provides that no person shall be guilty of the offence of causing by wilful act a child to die before it has an independent existence from its mother if the act was carried out in good faith for the purpose of preserving the mother's life.

Little information exists on the legal status and incidence of abortion in Tuvalu. Although the 1982 Penal Code does not contain a section on abortion, two sections (214 and 215) concern the destruction of the life of a child capable of being born alive, which could be applicable to abortion. Based on these sections, it appears that no one will be guilty of an offence unless it is proved that the act that caused the child's death was not done in good faith for the purpose of preserving the mother's life.

There is a long-standing tradition of family planning in Tuvalu. The Family Planning Association was established in the late 1960s and the Government has made efforts to integrate family planning into its maternal and child health services. Family planning programmes are being carried out throughout the country, with a clinic on the central island of Funafuti and a nurse in each dispensary in the outer islands who is responsible for teaching and encouraging couples to use family planning methods. The Government acknowledges that existing family planning programmes need to be broadened to include single men and women, because the number of births to single mothers has been increasing. Moreover, family planning education is necessary in order to overcome the continuing lack of awareness with regard to the availability of family planning services. Additional obstacles include the lack of reliable transportation to outer islands and the fact that sterilization can only be done currently at the hospital on Funafuti. A contraceptive prevalence rate of 30 per cent was reported in 1983. The Government's 1995-1998 National Development Strategy placed considerable emphasis on family planning, and since 1998 the Ministry of Health has increased its collaboration with women and youth NGOs in the areas of family planning awareness, education, and training.

Source: Population Policy Data Bank maintained by the Population Division of the Department of Economic and Social Affairs of the United Nations Secretariat. For additional sources, see list of references.

Uganda

ABORTION POLICY

Grounds on which abortion is permitted:

To save the life of the woman	Yes
To preserve physical health	Yes
To preserve mental health	Yes
Rape or incest	No
Foetal impairment	No
Economic or social reasons	No
Available on request	No

Additional requirements:

A legal abortion must be performed by a registered physician. Although the law does not require the approval of a committee, the consent of two physicians is usually sought before a legal abortion can be performed.

REPRODUCTIVE HEALTH CONTEXT

Government view on fertility level:	Too high
Government intervention concerning fertility level:	To lower
Government policy on contraceptive use:	Direct support provided
Percentage of currently married women using modern contraception (aged 15-49, 1995):	8
Total fertility rate (1995-2000):	7.1
Age-specific fertility rate (per 1,000 women aged 15-19, 1995-2000):	180
Government has expressed particular concern about:	
Morbidity and mortality resulting from induced abortion	Yes
Complications of childbearing and childbirth	Yes
Maternal mortality ratio (per 100,000 live births, 1990):	
National	1 200
Eastern Africa	1 060
Female life expectancy at birth (1995-2000):	40.4

Source: Population Policy Data Bank maintained by the Population Division of the Department of Economic and Social Affairs of the United Nations Secretariat. For additional sources, see list of references.

BACKGROUND

Under the Ugandan Penal Code of 15 June 1950 (sections 136-138, 205 and 217) the performance of abortions is generally prohibited. Any person who, with intent to procure the miscarriage of a woman, unlawfully administers any noxious thing or uses any means is subject to imprisonment for fourteen years. A pregnant woman who undertakes the same act or consents to its performance is subject to seven years' imprisonment. Any person who unlawfully supplies means to procure an abortion knowing that it is unlawfully intended for that purpose is subject to three years' imprisonment.

Nonetheless, under other provisions of the Penal Code an abortion may be performed to save the life of a pregnant woman. Section 217 of the Code provides that a person is not criminally responsible for performing in good faith and with reasonable care and skill a surgical operation upon an unborn child for the preservation of the mother's life if the performance of the operation is reasonable, having regard to the patient's state at the time and to all the circumstances of the case. In addition, Section 205 of the Code provides that no person shall be guilty of the offence of causing by willful act a child to die before it has an independent existence from its mother if the act was carried out in good faith for the purpose of preserving the mother's life.

Moreover, Uganda, like a number of Commonwealth countries, whose legal systems are based the English common law, follows the holding of the 1938 English *Rex v. Bourne* decision in determining whether an abortion performed for health reasons is lawful. In the *Bourne* decision, a physician was acquitted of the offence of performing an abortion in the case of a woman who had been raped. The court ruled that the abortion was lawful because it had been performed to prevent the woman from becoming "a physical and mental wreck", thus setting a precedent for future abortion cases performed on the grounds of preserving the pregnant woman's physical and mental health. The liberalization and legality of abortion in Uganda has been complicated by the use of rape as a weapon of war and terror by rebel groups in the region.

Illegal abortions are common in Uganda. As a result, there is a high level of maternal mortality, estimated in 1990 at 1,200 deaths per 100,000 live births. A 1986 study found that 35 per cent of maternal deaths were linked to complications from unsafe abortion. Induced abortion has been ranked as the second leading cause of maternal mortality in the main referral hospital in Uganda. Illegal abortion is more prevalent among young women. A survey carried out in 1988 among women aged 15-24 years found that 23 per cent of all the women that had ever been pregnant had had one or more abortions. The Government has expressed serious concern over these trends. The high level of induced abortion among young women in Uganda has led the Government to establish family life education programmes in primary and secondary schools.

Uganda has a very high total fertility rate, 7.1 children per woman for the period 1995-2000. For the same period, the population growth rate was 2.8 per cent. In recognition of the negative consequences of rapid population growth on per capita incomes and social services, the Government launched a comprehensive population program in 1988 and adopted the National Population Policy for Sustainable Development in 1995. The main focus of these policies is to strengthen maternal and child health and family planning services and to expand population and family life education campaigns. One objective was to increase the contraceptive prevalence rate from 5 to 20 per cent by the year 2000. The modern contraceptive rate was estimated in 1995 to be 8 per cent.

Contraceptive services in Uganda are available at government clinics and at clinics operated by the Family Planning Association of Uganda. Increased condom use in the late 1990s was successful in reducing the rate of HIV/AIDS infection but has not significantly reduced the number of unwanted pregnancies and therefore abortions.

Source: Population Policy Data Bank maintained by the Population Division of the Department of Economic and Social Affairs of the United Nations Secretariat. For additional sources, see list of references.

Ukraine

ABORTION POLICY

Grounds on which abortion is permitted:

To save the life of the woman	Yes
To preserve physical health	Yes
To preserve mental health	Yes
Rape or incest	Yes
Foetal impairment	Yes
Economic or social reasons	Yes
Available on request	Yes

Additional requirements:

An abortion requires the consent of the pregnant woman; it is authorized if performed by a licensed physician in a hospital or other recognized medical institution. Abortion is available on request during the first 12 weeks of gestation. Thereafter, induced abortion is available within 28 weeks from conception on judicial, genetic, vital, broad medical and social grounds, as well as for personal reasons with the special authorization of a commission of local physicians.

REPRODUCTIVE HEALTH CONTEXT

Government view on fertility level:	Too low
Government intervention concerning fertility level:	To raise
Government policy on contraceptive use:	Direct support provided
Percentage of currently married women using modern contraception (aged 15-49):	..
Total fertility rate (1995-2000):	1.4
Age-specific fertility rate (per 1,000 women aged 15-19, 1995-2000):	36
Government has expressed particular concern about:	
Morbidity and mortality resulting from induced abortion	Yes
Complications of childbearing and childbirth	Yes
Maternal mortality ratio (per 100,000 live births, 1990):	
National	50
Developed countries	27
Female life expectancy at birth (1995-2000):	73.7

Source: Population Policy Data Bank maintained by the Population Division of the Department of Economic and Social Affairs of the United Nations Secretariat. For additional sources, see list of references.

BACKGROUND

As was the case with all of the former Soviet republics, Ukraine, known prior to 1992 as the Ukrainian Soviet Socialist Republic, observed the abortion legislation and regulations of the Union of Soviet Socialist Republics. As a result, abortion practices in Ukraine were similar to those throughout the former USSR. The description given below pertains to the situation in Ukraine prior to independence. Since independence there has been no change in the abortion law.

The Soviet Decree of 27 June 1936 prohibited the performance of abortions except in cases of a danger to life, a serious threat to health, or the existence of a serious disease that could be inherited from the parents. The abortion has to be performed in a hospital or maternity home. Physicians who performed abortions outside a hospital or without the presence of one of these indications were subject to one to two years' imprisonment. If the abortion was performed under unsanitary conditions or by a person with no special medical education, the penalty was no less than three years' imprisonment. A person who induced a woman to have an abortion was subject to two years' imprisonment. A pregnant woman who underwent an abortion was subject to a reprimand and the payment of a fine of up to 300 roubles in the case of a repeat offence.

In its Decree of 23 November 1955, the Government of the former USSR repealed the general prohibition on the performance of abortions contained in the 1936 Decree. Other regulations issued in 1955 specified that abortions could be performed freely during the first 12 weeks of pregnancy if no contraindication existed and after that point when the continuance of the pregnancy and the birth would harm the mother (interpreted to include foetal handicap). The abortion had to be performed in a hospital by a physician and, unless performed in cases of threat to the mother's health, a fee was charged. Persons who performed an abortion illegally were subject to criminal penalties established by criminal laws under the Criminal Code. For example, if the abortion was not performed in a hospital, a penalty of up to one year's imprisonment could be imposed, and if it was performed by a person without an advanced medical degree, a penalty of up to two years' imprisonment was possible. In the case of repeat offences or the death or serious injury of the pregnant woman, a higher penalty of up to eight years' imprisonment could be imposed. A woman who underwent an illegal abortion was not penalized.

Despite the approval of the 1955 Decree and regulations, the problem of illegal abortions did not entirely disappear in the former Soviet Union. This situation resulted in partly from the Government's conflicted attitude towards contraception. Although at times the Government manifested support for contraception, it did little to make contraception available and in 1974 effectively banned the widespread use of oral contraceptives. The situation was also due in part to a revived pronatalist approach to childbearing adopted at times by the Government, which looked unfavourably on abortion. The result was a reliance on abortion as the primary method of family planning.

Concerned with the high rate of illegal abortions, the Government in 1982 issued a decree allowing abortions for health reasons to be performed through the twenty-eighth week of pregnancy. Continuing this approach of increasing the circumstances under which legal abortions were available, on 31 December 1987 it issued an order setting out a broad range of non-medical indications for abortions performed on request through the twenty-eighth week of pregnancy. These included the death of the husband during pregnancy;

Source: Population Policy Data Bank maintained by the Population Division of the Department of Economic and Social Affairs of the United Nations Secretariat. For additional sources, see list of references.

imprisonment of the pregnant woman or her husband; deprivation of maternity rights; multiparity (the number of children exceeds five); divorce during pregnancy; pregnancy following rape; and child disability in the family. Moreover, the order provided that, with the approval of a commission, an abortion could be performed on any other grounds.

This extension of the grounds for abortion after the first 12 weeks of pregnancy, combined with the ambivalent attitude of the Government towards contraception, led to a dramatic increase in the number of officially reported abortions. The rising incidence of abortion has been attributed to a number of factors, including a shortage of high-quality modern contraceptives, the recourse to less reliable methods, a lack of knowledge among couples of contraception, and the absence of adequate training for physicians, nurses, teachers and other specialists.

The abortion rate declined dramatically in the 1990s, from 109 abortions per 1,000 women aged 15-44 in 1986 to 80.9 in 1991 and 57.2 in 1996. This decline reportedly results from the expansion of contraceptive services. However, the uneven quality, inconsistent supply and cost of contraception have ensured that abortion remains a central method of fertility control in Ukraine.

In terms of population growth, Ukraine has fallen below replacement fertility levels. With a total fertility rate that declined between 1990 and 2000 from 2 children per woman to 1.4, the country's current population growth rate is –0.4 per cent. After the International Conference on Population and Development, held in Cairo in 1994, the Government implemented a special plan of action on population issues and a series of national programmes, including one on family planning.

Source: Population Policy Data Bank maintained by the Population Division of the Department of Economic and Social Affairs of the United Nations Secretariat. For additional sources, see list of references.

ABORTION POLICY

Grounds on which abortion is permitted:

To save the life of the woman	Yes
To preserve physical health	No
To preserve mental health	No
Rape or incest	No
Foetal impairment	No
Economic or social reasons	No
Available on request	No

Additional requirements:

A gynaecologist may perform the abortion with the approval of a physician familiar with the condition that makes the abortion necessary and with the written consent of the woman's husband or guardian.

REPRODUCTIVE HEALTH CONTEXT

Government view on fertility level:	Satisfactory
Government intervention concerning fertility level:	No intervention
Government policy on contraceptive use:	No support provided
Percentage of currently married women using modern contraception (aged 15-49, 1995):	24*
Total fertility rate (1995-2000):	3.4
Age-specific fertility rate (per 1,000 women aged 15-19, 1995-2000):	73
Government has expressed particular concern about:	
Morbidity and mortality resulting from induced abortion	..
Complications of childbearing and childbirth	..
Maternal mortality ratio (per 100,000 live births, 1990):	
National	26
Western Asia	320
Female life expectancy at birth (1995-2000):	76.5

* Preliminary or provisional.

Source: Population Policy Data Bank maintained by the Population Division of the Department of Economic and Social Affairs of the United Nations Secretariat. For additional sources, see list of references.

United Arab Emirates

BACKGROUND

Under the Penal Code of 20 December 1987, there are no stated exceptions to a general prohibition on the performance of abortion in the United Arab Emirates. A person who intentionally induces an abortion by providing medicines or other means is subject to up to five years' imprisonment. The maximum penalty is increased to seven years if the abortion is performed without the woman's consent.

However, under general criminal law principles of necessity, as expressed in article 64 of the Penal Code, an abortion may be performed to save the life of the pregnant woman. Moreover, Law No. 7 of 1975 on the practice of human medicine permits an abortion to be performed when continuation of the pregnancy endangers the life of the pregnant woman. The abortion must be carried out by a gynaecologist with the approval of a physician who is a specialist in the condition rendering the abortion necessary and with the written consent of the woman's husband or guardian.

Very little reliable information is available on the incidence of abortion, both legal and illegal, in the United Arab Emirates.

Although the Government has not adopted an official population policy, population issues are important and included in planning activities such as achieving high levels of health care. Because citizens account for only 15 to 20 per cent of the total number of residents, the size and growth rate of the national population in relation to the expatriate population remains a sensitive issue.

The United Arab Emirates does not have an official family planning programme. Access to contraceptive methods is officially restricted only for unmarried adolescents. Among citizens, the modern contraceptive prevalence rate was estimated at 24 per cent of married women 15-49 in 1995. The United Arab Emirates made substantial improvements in the availability of contraception from private as well as public sources in the 1990s, mainly in response to the growing demand for contraception among its relatively wealthy and educated population.

For the period 1995-2000, the total fertility rate was 3.4 children per woman while the population growth rate was estimated at 2 per cent.

Source: Population Policy Data Bank maintained by the Population Division of the Department of Economic and Social Affairs of the United Nations Secretariat. For additional sources, see list of references.

United Kingdom of Great Britain and Northern Ireland

ABORTION POLICY

Grounds on which abortion is permitted:

To save the life of the woman	Yes
To preserve physical health	Yes
To preserve mental health	Yes
Rape or incest	No
Foetal impairment	Yes
Economic or social reasons	Yes
Available on request	No

Additional requirements:

Abortion is legal in England, Wales and Scotland when two registered medical practitioners (only one in an emergency) certify that the required medical grounds as set forth in the Abortion Act of 1967 have been met. The termination of pregnancy must be carried out (except in an emergency) in a National Health Service hospital or in a nursing home, private hospital or other approved place. Abortion is legal during the first 24 weeks of gestation. The consent of the spouse is not a prerequisite of the medical termination of pregnancy. The Abortion Act of 1967 does not apply in Northern Ireland.

REPRODUCTIVE HEALTH CONTEXT

Government view on fertility level:	Satisfactory
Government intervention concerning fertility level:	No intervention
Government policy on contraceptive use:	Direct support provided
Percentage of currently married women using modern contraception (aged 16-49, 1993):	82*
Total fertility rate (1995-2000):	1.7
Age-specific fertility rate (per 1,000 women aged 15-19, 1995-2000):	29
Government has expressed particular concern about:	
Morbidity and mortality resulting from induced abortion	No
Complications of childbearing and childbirth	No
Maternal mortality ratio (per 100,000 live births, 1990):	
National	9
Developed countries	27
Female life expectancy at birth (1995-2000):	79.8

* Data refer to Great Britain.

Source: Population Policy Data Bank maintained by the Population Division of the Department of Economic and Social Affairs of the United Nations Secretariat. For additional sources, see list of references.

BACKGROUND

Until 1967, abortion in the United Kingdom was governed by a combination of statute and court decision, as interpreted by jurists (common law). Before the nineteenth century, there were no statutes relating to abortion and it was not considered a crime to kill a child in the womb so long as it had not reached the stage of "quickening", the point in pregnancy when the movement of the foetus was felt. After that point during pregnancy, the performance of an abortion was considered an offence, although there were very few prosecutions.

The first abortion statute was enacted in 1803. It provided for the death penalty for a person performing an abortion after quickening and a sentence of up to fourteen years' deportation or lashing with a whip for a person performing an abortion before quickening. Although the law was amended in 1837, it was not until 1861, with the enactment of the Offences against the Person Act, that statutory abortion law achieved the form that it was to keep for over 100 years. Under the Offences against the Person Act, any person who, with intent to procure the miscarriage of a woman, unlawfully administered any noxious thing or used any means was subject to imprisonment for fourteen years. A pregnant woman who undertook the same act or consented to its performance was subject to the same penalty.

Although there were no stated exceptions in the Act to the prohibition against the performance of abortions, the use of the word "unlawfully" by the Act implied that some abortions were not unlawful, and, indeed, it was the general opinion that the performance of abortion would not be unlawful to save the life of a pregnant woman.

In the twentieth century, this situation was clarified somewhat by two developments. The first was the enactment of the Infant Life (Preservation) Act of 1929 which introduced the offence of "child destruction", the killing of a child capable of being born alive (gestation age of 28 weeks or more) unless the act that caused the death of the child was done in good faith for the sole purpose of preserving the life of the mother. Although the Act dealt only with abortions performed after the 28th week of pregnancy, it strongly implied that abortions performed earlier in pregnancy to save the life of the pregnant woman were also lawful.

The second development was the 1938 judicial decision of *Rex v. Bourne*, which dealt with the issue of whether an abortion performed for health reasons was lawful. In the *Bourne* decision, a physician was acquitted of the offence of performing an abortion in the case of a woman who had been raped. The court ruled that the abortion was lawful because it had been performed to prevent the woman from becoming "a physical and mental wreck", thus setting a precedent for future abortion cases performed on the grounds of preserving the pregnant woman's physical and mental health.

Neither the Offences Against the Persons Act of 1861 nor the Infant Life (Preservation) Act of 1929 applied in Scotland. Abortion was defined as a criminal offence by Scottish common law, but prosecutions typically were not brought in cases where the operation had been performed for "reputable medical reasons", a term that was never officially or judicially defined. In Northern Ireland, the law was the same as in England and Wales until 1968.

Source: Population Policy Data Bank maintained by the Population Division of the Department of Economic and Social Affairs of the United Nations Secretariat. For additional sources, see list of references.

United Kingdom of Great Britain and Northern Ireland

Abortion in England, Scotland and Wales is currently regulated by the Abortion Act of 1967, as amended by the Human Fertilization and Embryology Act of 1990, which permits abortion to be performed on broad grounds, as certified by two physicians. The two physicians must be of the opinion formed in good faith: (a) that the pregnancy has not exceeded 24 weeks and continuance of the pregnancy would involve a risk, greater than if the pregnancy were terminated, of injury to the physical or mental health of the pregnant woman or any existing children of her family; (b) or that the termination is necessary to prevent grave permanent injury to the physical or mental health of the woman; (c) or that the continuance of the pregnancy would involve risk to the life of the woman, greater than if the pregnancy were terminated; (d) or that there is a substantial risk that if the child were born, it would suffer from such physical or mental abnormalities as to be seriously handicapped. In assessing the risk to the health of the woman and her existing children, physicians may take into account the woman's "actual or reasonably foreseeable environment". Owing to this provision and a broad interpretation about what constitutes a threat to health, abortions are available virtually on request in the United Kingdom.

Within the National Health Service, the provision of abortion services, as with other medical services, is controlled by the individual health-care authorities. Approval to perform abortions in private medical facilities is vested in the Secretary of State for Health. Currently, there is no statutory duty on the part of the Health Authorities to provide a particular level of abortion service. Traditionally, the provision of abortion services, as part of the gynaecological services, has been a matter for local determination by the Health Authorities according to local circumstances.

Except in cases of emergency, a legal abortion must be obtained in National Health Service hospitals or in approved institutions operating as private abortion clinics. The abortion is available free of charge through the National Health Service, or it may be paid for privately. The abortion must be performed by a registered medical practitioner; however, a nurse may also induce the abortion if delegated by a physician as part of a team. The consent of the spouse is not a prerequisite of the termination of pregnancy; a husband has no right to prevent his wife from having a legal abortion.

According to figures from the Office for National Statistics, a total of 187,402 legal abortions were performed in England and Wales in 1998, an increase of 4.3 per cent from 1997. The overall abortion rate for women resident in England and Wales (excluding 'abortion tourism') increased 4.8 per cent to 13.9 abortions per 1,000 women aged 14-49. Eighty-nine per cent of abortions were carried out at less than 13 weeks and another 10 per cent by 19 weeks. The most significant increase was among women 16-19 years old: their abortion rate rose 8.3 per cent to 26.5 abortions per 1,000 women.

In 1997, the conception rate for girls under 16 was 8.9 per 1,000, the highest rate of teenage pregnancy in Western Europe. Half of the under-16 conceptions and over one third of the 16-19 conceptions ended in abortion. There were also increases in virtually all the categories of sexually transmitted infections.

In 1993 the modern contraceptive rate for Great Britain was estimated to be 82 per cent. This figure includes a high rate (22 per cent) of male sterilization. More recently, the National Health Service reported that in 1998 an estimated 50 per cent of women aged 16-49 in England used a non-surgical method of contraception while an additional 12 per cent had been sterilized. Of those women using non-surgical contraception, 42 per cent chose the pill (down from 70 per cent in 1975) while 37 per cent used condoms (up

Source: Population Policy Data Bank maintained by the Population Division of the Department of Economic and Social Affairs of the United Nations Secretariat. For additional sources, see list of references.

from 6 per cent in 1975). The number of women attending national health clinics has remained roughly constant, although the demographic profile of attendants has changed. Under-16 attendants increased from negligible numbers in 1975 to 7 per cent in 1998-1999. Attendants aged 16-19 rose from 15 per cent in 1975 to 22 per cent in 1998-1999. These increases have been offset by a decline in attendance among women 20-34, from 21 per cent in 1975 to 12 per cent in 1998-1999.

The Abortion Act of 1967 does not apply in Northern Ireland. There the provisions of the Offences Against the Persons Act of 1861 are still in effect, as interpreted by court decision. Until 1993, however, there were no Northern Ireland court decisions specifically applying the *Rev v. Bourne* decision to Northern Ireland, although it was usually presumed that it would be applicable. In late 1993 and early 1994, two cases resolved by Northern Ireland courts confirmed this presumption. One involved a fourteen-year-old girl who had become pregnant and threatened to commit suicide if she could not obtain an abortion; the other involved a severely mentally handicapped 23-year-old woman who had been sexually assaulted and became very distressed over the resulting pregnancy. In both cases, the courts ruled that an abortion could legally be performed in Northern Ireland on serious mental health grounds, one of them specifically stating the holding of *Bourne*.

In practice, the decision to terminate a pregnancy in Northern Ireland is usually made following consultation with two physicians and with the informed consent of the pregnant woman. Although abortions are performed each year in Northern Ireland within the legal guidelines, the fear of possible accusation of acting illegally and the fact that abortion is an emotionally charged issue in Northern Ireland prevents medical staff from revealing precise data on abortions. The Department of Health and Social Services does not supply official statistics. In Northern Ireland, a woman faced with an unwanted pregnancy that does not fulfil the stated requirements can choose (a) to carry the pregnancy to term; (b) to seek an illegal abortion and risk endangering her health and life; or (c) to travel to England, where abortion is legal. Many women choose the third option.

In addition to Scotland and Northern Ireland, there are three anomalous island jurisdictions that, although under the control of the United Kingdom, are technically not part of the United Kingdom, but are considered dependencies of the British crown: the Bailiwick of Jersey and the Bailiwick of Guernsey, which are situated off the coast of Normandy and together make up the Channel Islands, and the Isle of Man (Tynwald), which lies between Ireland and Great Britain. Each has maintained a great deal of autonomy from the central Government and has its own system of law distinct from that of the United Kingdom. In all three, abortion has traditionally been largely prohibited.

In recent years, legislators in all three jurisdictions have taken steps to legalize abortion under certain circumstances, despite great opposition among certain segments of the islands' population. In 1995, the Isle of Man enacted the Termination of Pregnancy (Medical Defences) Act. Under the Act there are three grounds for the performance of legal abortions: (a) when two physicians are of the good faith opinion that it is necessary to preserve the life of the pregnant woman; examples include the situation in which the continuance of the pregnancy involves a substantial risk (other than such risk as is normally associated with pregnancy and childbirth) to the life of the pregnant woman greater than if the pregnancy is terminated and the situation in which termination of the pregnancy is necessary to prevent grave permanent injury to the physical or mental

Source: Population Policy Data Bank maintained by the Population Division of the Department of Economic and Social Affairs of the United Nations Secretariat. For additional sources, see list of references.

health of the woman (throughout pregnancy); (b) when two physicians are of the good faith opinion that the child, if carried to full term, would be unlikely to survive (throughout pregnancy) or would suffer from serious handicap (up to 24 weeks); and (c) when two physicians are of the good faith opinion, as substantiated, that the pregnancy has resulted from rape, incest or alleged assault (up to 12 weeks). In addition, an emergency abortion can be performed at any time with the approval of only one physician.

Jersey and Guernsey enacted similar legislation in 1996 and 1997, respectively. Although neither law contains special provisions for the performance of abortions in the case of pregnancies resulting from rape or incest, both laws are significantly less restrictive than the law of the Isle of Man in terms of health indications. In Guernsey an abortion can be performed during the first twelve weeks of pregnancy when the pregnancy involves a risk of injury to the physical or mental health of the pregnant woman or any existing children of her family greater than if the pregnancy were terminated. Jersey's law allows abortions during the same period if the woman's condition causes her "distress", if she then receives information from a medical practitioner other than the one performing the abortion (on medical risks connected with abortion; on entitlements for mothers, families, and children; on counselling that is available; on places where abortions can be performed; and on opportunities for adoption), and if she waits seven days until the abortion is performed.

Since abortion was legalized in Great Britain, many women from other countries have travelled to England for a safe, legal abortion. Described in the abortion statistics as "non-residents", these women come from Northern Ireland, as well as from other European countries, including France, Germany, Ireland, Italy and Spain. Others have travelled from as far away as South Africa and the United States of America. The number of women travelling to England to obtain an abortion has declined as abortion has been legalized and laws have been reformed in other countries (5,000 non-resident women had a legal abortion in England in 1969, the first full year that abortion was legal in Great Britain; the number peaked in 1973 at 53,600 non-resident abortions).

In July 1991, the United Kingdom became the second country, France being the first, to approve the use of RU-486, the abortion pill. The distribution of the pill is subject to strict controls, confining its use to National Health Service gynaecological units.

The Government of the United Kingdom considers the rates of fertility and population growth to be satisfactory. The Government has no explicit policy of intervention with respect to fertility rates, since it believes that decisions concerning fertility and childbearing should be left to the individual. The Government provides individuals with information and the necessary means for family planning and funds health programmes to improve the prevention, diagnosis and treatment of illness. The Government has also taken steps to reduce the increasing abortion rate due to unwanted fertility among young unmarried women and to encourage greater male responsibility with regard to contraception. Family planning services, including sterilization, are widely available free of charge through the National Health Service.

Source: Population Policy Data Bank maintained by the Population Division of the Department of Economic and Social Affairs of the United Nations Secretariat. For additional sources, see list of references.

United Republic of Tanzania

ABORTION POLICY

Grounds on which abortion is permitted:

To save the life of the woman	Yes
To preserve physical health	Yes
To preserve mental health	Yes
Rape or incest	No
Foetal impairment	No
Economic or social reasons	No
Available on request	No

Additional requirements:

Two physicians must certify that the abortion is necessary in order to preserve the life of the pregnant woman.

REPRODUCTIVE HEALTH CONTEXT

Government view on fertility level:	Too high
Government intervention concerning fertility level:	To lower
Government policy on contraceptive use:	Direct support provided
Percentage of currently married women using modern contraception (aged 15-49, 1996):	13
Total fertility rate (1995-2000):	5.5
Age-specific fertility rate (per 1,000 women aged 15-19, 1995-2000):	125
Government has expressed particular concern about:	
Morbidity and mortality resulting from induced abortion	..
Complications of childbearing and childbirth	Yes
Maternal mortality ratio (per 100,000 live births, 1990):	
National	770
Eastern Africa	1 060
Female life expectancy at birth (1995-2000):	49.1

Source: Population Policy Data Bank maintained by the Population Division of the Department of Economic and Social Affairs of the United Nations Secretariat. For additional sources, see list of references.

BACKGROUND

Abortion legislation in the United Republic of Tanzania is based on the English Offences Against the Person Act of 1861 and the Infant Life (Preservation) Act of 1929. Under the Revised Penal Code of Tanzania (chapter 16, sections 150-152) the performance of abortions is generally prohibited. Any person who, with intent to procure the miscarriage of a woman, whether she is pregnant or not, unlawfully uses any means upon her is subject to 14 years' imprisonment. A pregnant woman who undertakes the same act with respect to her own pregnancy or permits it to be undertaken is subject to seven years' imprisonment. Any person who supplies anything whatsoever knowing that it is intended to be unlawfully used to procure the miscarriage of a woman is subject to three years' imprisonment.

Nonetheless, an abortion may be performed to save the life of a pregnant woman. Section 230 of the Code provides that a person is not criminally responsible for performing in good faith and with reasonable care and skill a surgical operation upon an unborn child for the preservation of the mother's life if the performance of the operation is reasonable having regard to the patient's state at the time, and to all the circumstances of the case. In addition, Section 219 of the Code provides that no person shall be guilty of the offence of causing by willful act a child to die before it has an independent existence from its mother if the act was carried out in good faith for the purpose of preserving the mother's life.

Moreover, the United Republic of Tanzania, like a number of Commonwealth countries whose legal systems are based on English common law, follows the holding of the 1938 English *Rex v. Bourne* decision in determining whether an abortion performed for health reasons is lawful. In the *Bourne* decision, a physician was acquitted of the offence of performing an abortion in the case of a woman who had been raped. The court ruled that the abortion was lawful because it had been performed to prevent the woman from becoming "a physical and mental wreck", thus setting a precedent for future abortion cases performed on the grounds of preserving the pregnant woman's physical and mental health.

Although abortion is restricted by law, there is overwhelming evidence that it is widely practised in the country. The Government has expressed concern about the high incidence of illegal abortion because of its effect on maternal morbidity and mortality. Studies show that illegal abortion is one of the major causes of maternal mortality. A study conducted in the Southern Highlands in 1983 estimated that 17 per cent of maternal deaths were directly associated with abortion. Another study carried out in the Kilimanjaro region suggested that about 21 per cent of maternal deaths were related to abortion. In a study undertaken in 1987 at Muhimbili Medical Centre, the teaching hospital in Dar es Salaam, it was determined that in a random sample of 300 women admitted to the hospital for early pregnancy loss, 31 per cent had had an induced abortion.

With the adoption of a national population policy in 1992, the Government committed itself to dealing with the adverse consequences associated with high rates of population growth. Among the objectives of the Government's population programmes were to promote the improvement of maternal and child health and welfare through the prevention of illness and premature death and to establish an appropriate information, education and communication programme that would encourage the provision and use of services related to family planning and responsible parenthood.

To meet the unmet demand for family planning services, estimated to be 30 per cent of married women in 1991, a programme was established to raise the contraceptive prevalence rate. The contraceptive prevalence

Source: Population Policy Data Bank maintained by the Population Division of the Department of Economic and Social Affairs of the United Nations Secretariat. For additional sources, see list of references.

rate was estimated to be 13 per cent in 1996 for modern methods. The programme components included community-based distribution of contraceptives, family planning services in workplaces, male involvement in family planning and in-school and out-of-school family life education. The population growth rate has dropped in recent years, from 3.2 per cent for the period 1990-1995 to 2.3 per cent for 1995-2000. The population growth rate remains high, as does the current total fertility rate, estimated at 5.5 children per woman.

In the late 1990s, the cumulative impact of HIV/AIDS, the influx of Rwandan refugees, the burden of debt servicing and deteriorating socio-economic conditions resulted in a general deterioration of the sexual and reproductive health of women and adolescents. Illegal abortion and maternal mortality as a result of complications from abortion are reportedly on the rise.

Source: Population Policy Data Bank maintained by the Population Division of the Department of Economic and Social Affairs of the United Nations Secretariat. For additional sources, see list of references.

ABORTION POLICY

Grounds on which abortion is permitted:

To save the life of the woman	Yes
To preserve physical health	Yes
To preserve mental health	Yes
Rape or incest	Yes
Foetal impairment	Yes
Economic or social reasons	Yes
Available on request	Yes

Additional requirements:

Abortion is available in all states on request prior to foetal viability. After foetal viability, a state may prohibit abortion only if it provides exceptions for endangerment to the woman's life or health. Although federal law grants a woman the constitutional right to terminate her pregnancy before foetal viability, individual states are permitted to impose restrictions on abortion throughout pregnancy if they do not unduly burden a woman's right to choose.

REPRODUCTIVE HEALTH CONTEXT

Government view on fertility level:	Satisfactory
Government intervention concerning fertility level:	No intervention
Government policy on contraceptive use:	Direct support provided
Percentage of currently married women using modern contraception (aged 15-44, 1990):	67
Total fertility rate (1995-2000):	2.0
Age-specific fertility rate (per 1,000 women aged 15-19, 1995-2000):	59
Government has expressed particular concern about:	
Morbidity and mortality resulting from induced abortion	..
Complications of childbearing and childbirth	Yes
Maternal mortality ratio (per 100,000 live births, 1990):	
National	12
Developed countries	27
Female life expectancy at birth (1995-2000):	80.1

Source: Population Policy Data Bank maintained by the Population Division of the Department of Economic and Social Affairs of the United Nations Secretariat. For additional sources, see list of references.

United States of America

BACKGROUND

In the United States of America, abortions before "quickening" were permitted by traditional common law until 1845, when the first of many states passed laws prohibiting all or most abortions. By the early 1960s, 41 states permitted abortion only if the life of the pregnant woman was threatened by continuation of the pregnancy, while the remaining states permitted abortion only if the woman's life or physical health was in jeopardy. In the mid-1960s, when the pregnant woman's mental health gained acceptance as a valid justification for abortion, more legal abortions were performed, a trend that accelerated with the passage of liberalized abortion legislation in various states. In the five years leading up to the landmark Supreme Court decision of January 1973, which legalized abortion throughout the United States, 18 states had reformed or repealed their anti-abortion legislation. In the other 32 states and the District of Columbia, laws remained on the statute books that made abortion a crime unless performed to save the life or health of the woman.

In 1973, two decisions of the Supreme Court of the United States (*Roe v. Wade* and *Doe v. Bolton*) legalized abortion nationwide. In those cases, the Court ruled that a woman's decision to have an abortion in the first trimester of pregnancy should be exclusively between herself and her physician, but that individual states could regulate abortion in the second trimester in ways designed to preserve and protect the woman's health; and that after foetal viability, or the third trimester of pregnancy, the states could regulate or even proscribe abortion unless the procedure was necessary to preserve the life or health of the mother. Lastly, the Supreme Court held that a foetus was not a person and was therefore not entitled to protection guaranteed by the United States Constitution until it reached the point of viability. Viability was defined as occurring between 24 and 28 weeks of gestation.

The effect of *Roe v. Wade* on women in the United States seeking to terminate pregnancies was profound. After *Roe*, abortion procedures in the United States became widely available, legal, safe and simple. Within a few years of the decision, data indicated that the mortality rate for women undergoing legal abortions was 10 times lower than the mortality rate for women that had illegal abortions and five times lower than the rate for women undergoing childbirth.

The *Roe v. Wade* decision also had an immediate impact on the abortion debate. The right-to-life movement, which had existed in a nascent form prior to *Roe*, became very active after the ruling, and with the reversal of *Roe* as its ultimate objective. The right-to-life movement also began a campaign directed to creating as many legal barriers to abortion as possible. The abortion-rights movement was similarly engaged and campaigned to make safe and legal abortion available throughout the country.

These two opposing movements have been involved in constant legal and political battles over the abortion issue ever since, and their representatives have regularly appeared before the United States Supreme Court to argue cases concerning the nature and meaning of the constitutional protection afforded by the *Roe* decision. Over the years, the rulings of the Supreme Court have cut back on the constitutional guarantees in *Roe v. Wade*. The first of these significant decisions was the *Webster* ruling of 3 July 1989 (*Webster v. Reproductive Health Services*). By a vote of 5 to 4, the Supreme Court upheld a Missouri statute that barred the use of public funds, employees or buildings for abortions and required abortion providers to conduct tests to determine whether a foetus believed to be at least 20 weeks old was viable.

By upholding the Missouri law requiring physicians to conduct extensive viability tests on women at least 20 weeks pregnant before performing an abortion, the Webster decision weakened the trimester

Source: Population Policy Data Bank maintained by the Population Division of the Department of Economic and Social Affairs of the United Nations Secretariat. For additional sources, see list of references.

framework established in *Roe v. Wade*. Furthermore, the Court signalled its willingness to give individual states far greater latitude in placing restrictions on a woman's right to have an abortion. Following the *Webster* decision, restrictive statutes were introduced in a number of state legislatures. For example, within five months of the decision, Pennsylvania enacted a law requiring a woman to notify her husband, receive state-prepared information concerning adoption and child-support alternatives from her physician and delay the procedure for a minimum of 24 hours before obtaining an abortion. Kansas, Mississippi, North Dakota and Ohio likewise imposed similar restrictions requiring anti-abortion information to be provided and imposing mandatory delays. Louisiana, Utah and the territory of Guam went even further and enacted sweeping criminal abortion bans with exceedingly narrow exceptions. Other states, such as Connecticut, moved in the opposite direction by enacting legislation guaranteeing a woman the right to an abortion under the state law.

Abortion law in the United States is currently governed by the Supreme Court decision of 29 June 1992 (*Planned Parenthood of Southeastern Pennsylvania v. Casey*). The Supreme Court ruling in *Casey* reaffirmed the holding in *Roe v. Wade* that a woman has a constitutional right to obtain an abortion prior to foetal viability and that a state may prohibit abortion thereafter only if it provides exceptions for endangerment to the woman's life or health. Although the *Casey* ruling left no doubt that laws prohibiting abortion were unconstitutional, the Court rejected the trimester framework set forth in *Roe* and held that states have legitimate interests in protecting the health of the woman and the life of the unborn child from the outset of pregnancy.

The Supreme Court decision in *Casey* also adopted a more lenient standard for analysing the constitutionality of abortion restrictions than had been articulated in previous rulings. The Court ruled that a state may act to regulate abortion throughout pregnancy if it does not "unduly burden" a woman's right to choose. "Undue burden" was defined as a substantial obstacle in the path of a woman seeking an abortion before the foetus attains viability. In applying the "undue burden" standard, the Court in *Casey* upheld portions of the Pennsylvania abortion law that had required a woman to delay an abortion for 24 hours after hearing a state-prepared presentation on adoption and child-support alternatives and required teenagers to obtain the consent of one parent or the approval of a judge before obtaining an abortion. The only provision in the Pennsylvania statute struck down by the *Casey* decision was a husband notification requirement, which the Court found to be an "undue burden" on a married woman's right to obtain an abortion.

Following the *Casey* decision, abortion restrictions in the United States continue to vary by state. As of October 1999, forty states have laws that prevent a minor from obtaining an abortion without parental consent or notice. Thirty-six of these states provide for a judicial bypass procedure as an alternative to parental consent or notification, and eleven provide some alternative to both parental involvement and judicial bypass. In 11 of these states, these laws have been enjoined by courts from enforcement. Of the remaining states, one requires that minors receive counselling that includes discussion of the possibility of consulting her parents before obtaining an abortion and the other allows a minor to receive counselling in place of obtaining parental consent for an abortion.

Twenty-nine states have abortion-specific informed consent laws, many of which require that women be given anti-abortion information and state-prepared materials intended to discourage them from obtaining an abortion. Seventeen states have specific mandatory waiting periods of at least 24 hours between the time at which information is provided and the time at which an abortion may be performed. In five of these states, these laws have been enjoined by courts from enforcement.

Under federal law, states that accept federal Medicaid funds (matching funds provided to the states for health insurance for the poor) are required to pay for abortions sought by Medicaid recipients in cases of

---

Source: Population Policy Data Bank maintained by the Population Division of the Department of Economic and Social Affairs of the United Nations Secretariat. For additional sources, see list of references.

pregnancy that is life-endangering or the result of rape or incest. Thirty-two states have declined to use their own funds to pay for abortions for Medicaid recipients other than in these circumstances, and two states (Mississippi and South Dakota) are in violation of federal law by refusing to fund abortions except in case of pregnancy that is life-threatenting. Sixteen states use their own funds to pay for medically necessary abortions sought by Medicaid recipients.

The presidential administration that came into office in January 1993 took early action on the issue of federal limitations on abortions. On 22 January 1993, the policies of the previous administrations that were intended to discourage women from obtaining abortions were rescinded. First, the President of the United States lifted restrictions on abortion counselling at federally financed family planning clinics that had been in effect since 1988, as well as the ban on federal research using foetal tissue from aborted foetuses that was imposed in 1989. Another presidential order allowed physicians at United States military hospitals to resume performing abortions for armed services personnel and for their dependants who paid the cost. Federally financed abortions for military personnel have been barred since 1979 except in cases where the life of a pregnant woman is in danger. A fourth order cleared the way for United States funds to flow to international efforts providing abortions and other family planning services. Previously, the 1984 "Mexico City Policy" stipulated that the United States Government would not support international programmes that offered abortion services. Lastly, the President directed the Department of Health and Human Services to review the import ban on the French-made abortion pill, RU-486, and to rescind it if there were grounds for doing so.

However, congressional efforts continued to be directed at restricting the legality of abortion in the United States. One was the reinstatement of the prohibition against physicians at United States military hospitals performing abortions for armed services personnel and their dependants who paid for such abortions. Another was the enactment of legislation prohibiting federal employees' health insurance from including abortion coverage except in the case of life endangerment, rape or incest.

Perhaps the most visible area of congressional activity, though, was reflected in its efforts to restrict the performance of the dilation and extraction procedure for the performance of late-term abortions. Most recent estimates indicate that there were probably some 650 such procedures performed in 1996, accounting for about 0.03-0.05 per cent of all abortions. Legislation was introduced to prohibit the procedure entirely except when necessary to save the life of the pregnant woman. Proponents of the ban characterized the procedure as a brutal act that inflicted unnecessary suffering on the foetus and argued that there were alternative methods that could be used. Opponents of the ban contended that in a small number of cases, the procedure was both necessary to protect the health of the woman and safer than any other procedure employed to induce an abortion. Some, although opposed to the procedures, sought to include within the proposed legislation an additional exception to the ban when necessary to protect the health of the pregnant woman. The legislation was approved by Congress without this health exception by wide margins twice between 1996-1998, but the President of the United States vetoed the legislation, and Congress was unable to override the veto.

A number of states' efforts designed to prohibit the procedure were more successful. By October 1999, thirty states had enacted various versions of legislation to ban the procedure, most of them facing an immediate challenge in court. In twelve states the bans are partially or fully in effect, while in eighteen states, they have been enjoined from enforcement by courts. The great majority of the courts that have considered the validity of such laws have ruled that the laws are deficient in one of three ways: they define the procedure in terms that have no clear medical meaning; the procedures that they do define are so vague as to encompass the performance of abortions before foetal viability, which a woman has a constitutional right to have performed, and thus constitute an "undue burden" on woman's ability to obtain such a pre-viability abortion;

Source: Population Policy Data Bank maintained by the Population Division of the Department of Economic and Social Affairs of the United Nations Secretariat. For additional sources, see list of references.

and, even if precise in definition, the laws do not provide for a health exception to the prohibition as required by *Roe*, *Casey*, and other Supreme Court decisions.

On the other hand, in one area, Congress acted to protect the right of access to abortion services. In 1994, it enacted the Freedom of Access to Clinics Act (FACE) in order to counteract the more extreme activities of pro-life advocates picketing clinics where abortions are performed. The express purpose of the Act is to protect and promote public safety and health by establishing federal criminal penalties and civil remedies for certain violent, threatening, obstructive and destructive conduct that is intended to injure, intimidate or interfere with persons seeking to obtain or provide reproductive health services. To this end, the Act imposes fines and/or imprisonment on persons who contravene its provisions and authorizes persons who are "aggrieved" by conduct prohibited by the Act to sue those engaging in the conduct to obtain injunctions and compensatory and punitive damages. The Act also authorizes the federal Attorney General and states' attorneys general to institute suits on behalf of individuals and groups.

The Act was immediately criticized by some pro-choice individuals and groups as a violation of their constitutional first amendment right to freedom of speech and a violation of the Commerce Clause of the Constitution which restricts the authority of the federal Government to enact legislation unless such legislation regulates interstate activity that has a substantial effect on interstate commerce. As yet the Supreme Court has not ruled on any challenge to the Act, although lower courts have generally upheld its provisions as constitutional. In addition, courts have generally upheld the validity of similar laws enacted by thirteen individuals states to protect access to clinics.

Despite the fact that abortion has been legal in the United States since 1973, economic forces, political pressures, geography and the shortage of physicians trained and willing to perform abortions constitute a major barrier to women's access to abortion services. This problem is more acute among low-income women and women living in rural areas where there are few clinics or hospitals that provide abortion services. For many low-income women, abortion has effectively been out of reach since 1977, when Congress barred the use of federal funds to pay for abortions; and as of 1992 only 13 state governments paid for abortions for low-income women. In June 1993, the House of Representatives endorsed a continuation of the long-standing ban on federal funding of abortions for indigent women under the Medicaid programme, adding exceptions only for cases of rape or incest to the previous exception of life endangerment. Although a law went into effect in October 1993 requiring state Medicaid programmes to pay for the abortions of low-income women in cases of rape or incest, at least six states have indicated that they would flout the new law. Obstetrics-gynaecology residency programmes have made abortion an elective or have stopped offering abortion training altogether. Also, some physicians are opposed to the practice of abortion.

The United States Centres for Disease Control and Prevention reported 1,184,758 legal induced abortions in 1997, a 3 per cent decrease from 1996. These figures translate into an abortion rate of 20 abortions per 1,000 women aged 15-44. The abortion rate rose from 13 to 25 abortions per 1,000 women aged 15-44 between 1972 and 1980, and remained stable during much of the 1980s before declining in the 1990s. The 1997 rate of 20 is the lowest since 1975. In 1997, 20 per cent of women obtaining abortions were aged 19 or under, and 32 per cent were aged 20-24. In terms of gestation, 55 per cent of the 1997 abortions were performed within the first 8 weeks, and by 12 weeks that number had increased to 88 per cent. The Alan Guttmacher Institute reports that 49 per cent of pregnancies among American women are unintended and of that number, half are terminated by abortion. African-American women remain three times as likely as white women to have an abortion, and Hispanic women are roughly twice as likely. An estimated 14,000 abortions are obtained each year for rape or incest.

Source: Population Policy Data Bank maintained by the Population Division of the Department of Economic and Social Affairs of the United Nations Secretariat. For additional sources, see list of references.

ABORTION POLICY

Grounds on which abortion is permitted:

To save the life of the woman	Yes
To preserve physical health	Yes
To preserve mental health	Yes
Rape or incest	Yes
Foetal impairment	No
Economic or social reasons	No
Available on request	No

Additional requirements:

An abortion must be carried out within the first three months of pregnancy. The penalty for undergoing an abortion may be reduced or waived if the pregnancy results from rape or when there is economic hardship.

REPRODUCTIVE HEALTH CONTEXT

Government view on fertility level:	Too low
Government intervention concerning fertility level:	To raise
Government policy on contraceptive use:	Direct support provided
Percentage of currently married women using modern contraception (aged 15-49):	..
Total fertility rate (1995-2000):	2.4
Age-specific fertility rate (per 1,000 women aged 15-19, 1995-2000):	70
Government has expressed particular concern about:	
Morbidity and mortality resulting from induced abortion	No
Complications of childbearing and childbirth	No
Maternal mortality ratio (per 100,000 live births, 1990):	
National	85
South America	260
Female life expectancy at birth (1995-2000):	78.0

Source: Population Policy Data Bank maintained by the Population Division of the Department of Economic and Social Affairs of the United Nations Secretariat. For additional sources, see list of references.

BACKGROUND

Under the Criminal Code of 4 December 1933, as amended, abortion is generally illegal in Uruguay. A woman who causes her own abortion or consents to its being caused by another person is subject to three to nine months' imprisonment. Anyone who participates in the abortion of a woman with her consent in a principal or secondary manner is subject to 6-24 months' imprisonment. A person who causes the abortion of a woman without her consent is subject to two to eight years' imprisonment. Harsher penalties are imposed if, as a result of the abortion, the woman suffers serious injury or dies; or if the abortion is committed through violence or fraud, on a woman under eighteen years old deprived of her reason or senses, or by a husband.

A physician is exempt from punishment for committing the offence of abortion if the abortion is performed at any time during pregnancy with the woman's consent for serious health reasons or to save the life of the woman, whether she consents or not. A physician is also exempt from punishment if the abortion is performed during the first three months of pregnancy with the woman's consent in cases of rape. A judge may exempt a physician from punishment if the abortion is performed during the first three months of pregnancy with the woman's consent to save the honour of the woman or in cases of economic hardship.

Uruguay is believed to have a high rate of abortion; most of these abortions are illegal. In fact, abortion appears to be a major means of fertility control in the country, as well as the single most important cause of maternal mortality. Despite the lack of precise statistics on abortion, the most conservative estimates indicate that there are at least as many abortions as live births.

The total fertility rate for the period 1995-2000 was 2.4 children per woman, while the population growth rate was estimated at 0.7 per cent. The Government of Uruguay considers the rates of fertility and population growth to be too low. A number of incentives to increase fertility levels are provided, including a maternity benefit of 100 per cent of wages payable for up to 12 weeks (which can be extended up to an additional five months if confinement occurs after the expected date or in case of illness), a family allowance of not less than 8 per cent of the monthly minimum wage and nursing breaks for working mothers. The Government provides support for modern methods of contraception.

The Asociación Uruguaya de Planificación Familiar e Investigaciones sobre Reproducción Humana (AUPFIRH) was founded in 1961 as the first family planning association in South America. It cooperates with local public-health authorities in service delivery programmes to poor urban and rural areas, operating mobile clinics to reach remote areas and directing a community-based contraceptive distribution programme. AUPFIRH offers family planning services in many government health-care facilities and manages a women's programme and an adolescent centre where teenage mothers are given social, medical and legal aid. It also discusses adolescent and women's issues in the media, holds sex education training workshops and offers courses for parents, teachers and institutional and community leaders.

Unmet demand for family planning and sex education has contributed to high rates of unwanted pregnancies, adolescent pregnancies, induced abortions and infertility due to sexually transmitted diseases. Following the International Conference on Population and Development, held in Cairo in 1994, the Government inaugurated a National Programme on Reproductive Health with a family planning component that focused on information and improved access to contraception. Projects have been established in the capital and in ten regions to provide training in sex education, reproductive health and income-generating skills for women, while another project is examining adolescents' knowledge and attitudes concerning sexuality and reproduction.

Source: Population Policy Data Bank maintained by the Population Division of the Department of Economic and Social Affairs of the United Nations Secretariat. For additional sources, see list of references.

ABORTION POLICY

Grounds on which abortion is permitted:

To save the life of the woman	Yes
To preserve physical health	Yes
To preserve mental health	Yes
Rape or incest	Yes
Foetal impairment	Yes
Economic or social reasons	Yes
Available on request	Yes

Additional requirements:

An abortion requires the consent of the pregnant woman; it is authorized if performed by a licensed physician in a hospital or other recognized medical institution. Abortion is available on request during the first 12 weeks of gestation. Thereafter, induced abortion is available within 28 weeks from conception on judicial, genetic, vital, broad medical and social grounds, as well as for personal reasons with the special authorization of a commission of local physicians.

REPRODUCTIVE HEALTH CONTEXT

Government view on fertility level:	Satisfactory
Government intervention concerning fertility level:	To maintain
Government policy on contraceptive use:	Direct support provided
Percentage of currently married women using modern contraception (aged 15-49, 1996):	51
Total fertility rate (1995-2000):	3.5
Age-specific fertility rate (per 1,000 women aged 15-19, 1995-2000):	35
Government has expressed particular concern about:	
Morbidity and mortality resulting from induced abortion	Yes
Complications of childbearing and childbirth	Yes
Maternal mortality ratio (per 100,000 live births, 1990):	
National	..
South-central Asia	560
Female life expectancy at birth (1995-2000):	70.7

Source: The Population Policy Data Bank maintained by the Population Division of the Department of Economic and Social Affairs of the United Nations Secretariat. For additional sources, see list of references.

Uzbekistan

BACKGROUND

As was the case with all of the former Soviet republics, Uzbekistan, known prior to 1992 as the Uzbek Soviet Socialist Republic, observed the abortion legislation and regulations of the former Union of Soviet Socialist Republics. As a result, abortion practices in Uzbekistan were similar to those throughout the former USSR. The description given below pertains to the situation in Uzbekistan prior to independence. Since independence there has been no change in the abortion law.

The Soviet Decree of 27 June 1936 prohibited the performance of abortions except in cases of danger to life, serious threat to health, or the existence of a serious disease that could be inherited from the parents. The abortion had to be performed in a hospital or maternity home. Physicians who performed abortions outside a hospital or without the presence of one of these indications were subject to one to two years' imprisonment. If the abortion was performed under unsanitary conditions or by a person with no special medical education, the penalty was no less than three years' imprisonment. A person who induced a woman to have an abortion was subject to two years' imprisonment. A pregnant woman who underwent an abortion was subject to a reprimand and the payment of a fine of up to 300 roubles in the case of a repeat offence.

In its Decree of 23 November 1955, the Government of the former USSR repealed the general prohibition on the performance of abortions contained in the 1936 Decree. Other regulations issued in 1955 specified that abortions could be performed freely during the first 12 weeks of pregnancy if no contraindication existed and after that point when the continuance of the pregnancy and the birth would harm the mother (interpreted to include foetal handicap). The abortion had to be performed in a hospital by a physician and, unless performed in cases of threat to the mother's health, a fee was charged. Persons who performed an abortion illegally were subject to criminal penalties established by criminal laws under the Criminal Code. For example, if the abortion was not performed in a hospital, a penalty of up to one year's imprisonment could be imposed and if it was performed by a person without an advanced medical degree, a penalty of up to two years' imprisonment was possible. In the case of repeat offences or the death or serious injury of the pregnant woman, a higher penalty of up to eight years' imprisonment could be imposed. A woman who underwent an illegal abortion was not penalized.

Despite the approval of the 1955 Decree and regulations, the problem of illegal abortions did not entirely disappear in the former Soviet Union. This situation was due partly to the Government's conflicted attitude towards contraception. Although at times it manifested support for contraception, it did little to make contraception available and in 1974 effectively banned the widespread use of oral contraceptives. The situation was also due in part to a revived pronatalist approach to childbearing adopted at times by the Government, which looked unfavourably on abortion. The result was a reliance on abortion as the primary method of family planning.

Concerned with the high rate of illegal abortions, the Government in 1982 issued a decree allowing abortions for health reasons to be performed through the twenty-eighth week of pregnancy. Continuing this approach of increasing the circumstances under which legal abortions were available, on 31 December 1987 it issued an order setting out a broad range of non-medical indications for abortions performed on request through the twenty-eighth week of pregnancy. These included the death of the husband during pregnancy;

Source: The Population Policy Data Bank maintained by the Population Division of the Department of Economic and Social Affairs of the United Nations Secretariat. For additional sources, see list of references.

imprisonment of the pregnant woman or her husband; deprivation of maternity rights; multiparity (the number of children exceeds five); divorce during pregnancy; pregnancy following rape; and child disability in the family. Moreover, the order provided that, with the approval of a commission, an abortion could be performed on any other grounds.

This extension of the grounds for abortion after the first 12 weeks of pregnancy, combined with the ambivalent attitude of the Government towards contraception, led to a dramatic increase in the number of officially reported abortions. Other factors responsible for the high incidence of abortion included shortages of high-quality modern contraceptives and reliance upon less reliable traditional methods; a lack of knowledge among couples of contraception and of the detrimental health consequences of frequent abortions; and the absence of adequate training for physicians, nurses, teachers and other specialists.

The modern contraceptive prevalence rate was 51 per cent in 1996. The intrauterine device was by far the most used method of contraception. While reporting is incomplete in Uzbekistan, the abortion rate for the same year was 11.8 abortions per 1,000 women aged 15 to 44. As in other former Soviet states, abortion rates have fallen sharply in the 1990s. In Uzbekistan, the abortion rate fell from 23 per 1,000 women in 1992 to 11.8 in 1996, a drop of 51 per cent. The maternal mortality ratio in Uzbekistan deceased from an estimated 38.9 maternal deaths per 100,000 births in 1988 to 10.5 in 1997. There has also been a drop in overall fertility, from 4.4 children per woman in 1985-1990 to 3.5 in 1995-2000.

Source: The Population Policy Data Bank maintained by the Population Division of the Department of Economic and Social Affairs of the United Nations Secretariat. For additional sources, see list of references.

ABORTION POLICY

Grounds on which abortion is permitted:

To save the life of the woman	Yes
To preserve physical health	Yes
To preserve mental health	Yes
Rape or incest	No
Foetal impairment	No
Economic or social reasons	No
Available on request	No

Additional requirements:

Information is not readily available.

REPRODUCTIVE HEALTH CONTEXT

Government view on fertility level:	Satisfactory
Government intervention concerning fertility level:	No intervention
Government policy on contraceptive use:	Direct support provided
Percentage of currently married women using modern contraception (aged 15-49):	..
Total fertility rate (1995-2000):	4.3
Age-specific fertility rate (per 1,000 women aged 15-19, 1995-2000):	74
Government has expressed particular concern about:	
Morbidity and mortality resulting from induced abortion	No
Complications of childbearing and childbirth	Yes
Maternal mortality ratio (per 100,000 live births, 1990):	
National	280
Oceania	680
Female life expectancy at birth (1995-2000):	69.5

Source: Population Policy Data Bank maintained by the Population Division of the Department of Economic and Social Affairs of the United Nations Secretariat. For additional sources, see list of references.

BACKGROUND

Abortion in Vanuatu is governed by the provisions of Section 117 of the Vanuatu Penal Code, Act No. 17 of 7 August 1981. Under Section 117, the performance of abortions is generally illegal. A woman who intentionally procures her own miscarriage is subject to two years' imprisonment, as is a person who intentionally procures the miscarriage of a woman. The Code, however, allows an abortion to be performed on health grounds. Section 117 also provides that it shall be a defence to the charge of having committed the offence of abortion that the miscarriage procured constituted a termination of pregnancy for good medical reasons. The Code does not define what constitutes "good medical reasons".

Although the Code does not set a specific limit on the period during pregnancy when an abortion may be legally performed for good medical reasons, Section 113 of the Code implies that the period ends at 28 weeks. Section 113 of the Code, which is entitled "killing unborn child", provides that no person shall, when a woman is about to be delivered of a child, prevent the child from being born alive. Under English law, from which this section of the Code was derived, the term "unborn child" was usually applied to unborn children of a minimum of 28 weeks' gestation. Penalties range from 2 years for an abortion to life imprisonment for killing an unborn child.

Although the Government does not have an overall population policy, family planning has been included in the health policies of Vanuatu since it attained independence in 1980. Currently, health and family planning services are organized at the district level and are free of charge. The Family Planning Association of Vanuatu assists in the distribution of contraceptives to government centres and mission health centres. These government institutions are the only entities allowed to distribute contraceptives, with the exception of condoms, to the general population. Despite these efforts, however, the contraceptive prevalence rate is believed to be relatively low in Vanuatu. Some of the obstacles to achieving greater acceptance of family planning in Vanuatu include a cultural preference for large families, a reluctance to discuss family planning, and service delivery problems to the 14 inhabited islands.

By 1990, however, a resurgence of interest in family planning, combined with a number of health concerns, such as poor maternal health, led to the establishment of the Family Health Project. One of the objectives of the project is the improvement of family planning services by enhancing the quality of care; offering a wider range of family planning methods, including long-acting contraceptives; and facilitating access to family planning services, particularly in rural areas.

Over the period 1970-2000, the total fertility rate declined from 6.5 children per woman to 4.3, but remains high. The current population growth rate also remains high at 2.4 per cent.

Source: Population Policy Data Bank maintained by the Population Division of the Department of Economic and Social Affairs of the United Nations Secretariat. For additional sources, see list of references.

Venezuela

ABORTION POLICY

Grounds on which abortion is permitted:

To save the life of the woman	Yes
To preserve physical health	No
To preserve mental health	No
Rape or incest	No
Foetal impairment	No
Economic or social reasons	No
Available on request	No

Additional requirements:

An abortion may be performed only with the written consent of the woman, her husband or her legal representative. The procedure must be carried out in a suitable environment, using all possible scientific resources.

REPRODUCTIVE HEALTH CONTEXT

Government view on fertility level:	Satisfactory
Government intervention concerning fertility level:	To lower
Government policy on contraceptive use:	Direct support provided
Percentage of currently married women using modern contraception (aged 15-44, 1977):	38
Total fertility rate (1995-2000):	3.0
Age-specific fertility rate (per 1,000 women aged 15-19, 1995-2000):	98
Government has expressed particular concern about:	
Morbidity and mortality resulting from induced abortion	No
Complications of childbearing and childbirth	No
Maternal mortality ratio (per 100,000 live births, 1990):	
National	120
South America	260
Female life expectancy at birth (1995-2000):	75.7

Source: Population Policy Data Bank maintained by the Population Division of the Department of Economic and Social Affairs of the United Nations Secretariat. For additional sources, see list of references.

BACKGROUND

Under the Criminal Code of 2 June 1964, the performance of abortions is generally illegal in Venezuela. A person who provokes the abortion of a woman with her consent is subject to 12 to 30 months' imprisonment. If the woman does not consent, the penalty is increased to 15 months' to three years' imprisonment. A woman who intentionally performs her own abortion or consents to its performance by another person is subject to six months' to two years' imprisonment. Harsher penalties are applied if the abortion results in the death of the woman or if it is performed by the husband of the woman or by a health professional. Decreased penalties are applied if the abortion was carried out by a woman to preserve her own honour or carried out by another person to preserve the honour of a spouse, mother, descendant, sister or adoptive child.

Nonetheless, under the Criminal Code, an abortion may be legally performed by a health professional if necessary to save the life of a pregnant woman. Moreover, the Code of Medical Ethics of 1971 authorizes an abortion to be performed for "therapeutic purposes," although it does not define what therapeutic purposes are. Such an abortion may be performed only with the written consent of the woman, her husband or her legal representative. In case of emergency, however, the favourable opinion of another physician may suffice, if this can be obtained. A therapeutic abortion must be performed in a suitable environment, using all possible scientific resources. The physician selected to perform the abortion must inform the relatives if the pregnant woman is suffering from major obstetric complications and must clearly explain the procedure to be followed, with a view to obtaining their consent. In the event of a divergence of opinion, the physician must, where possible, transfer the case to another professional practitioner; otherwise, except in an emergency, the physician must request the relatives of the woman to make a written statement that they do not consent to the proposed procedure.

Proposals to reform the Venezuelan Penal Code, which were introduced in the National Congress in 1986, included recommendations to permit abortion on therapeutic grounds to preserve the physical and mental health of the mother; in cases of rape or incest; for eugenic reasons, in cases where either of the parents suffers from oligophrenia or epilepsy and a foetal injury is suspected, according to the opinion of three specialists; and in cases where the mother has suffered any sickness or exposure to radiation that might produce mental or physical defects in the foetus. These proposals, however, have not been incorporated into the Penal Code.

According to official data, complications from illegal abortions, which are often performed with unsterilized instruments by untrained persons, accounted for 24.6 per cent of all maternal deaths in Venezuela during the period 1980-1983. By 1995, that number had declined to 13.6 per cent, according to the Pan American Health Organization.

The Government of Venezuela has permitted the gradual expansion of family planning, for health-related reasons as well as to lower fertility. The total fertility rate has fallen in the period 1970-2000 from 5.9 children per woman to 3. The health-related aims of the national maternal and child health and family planning programme include providing safe and efficient contraceptives to help women avoid unwanted pregnancies; and contributing to the reduction of fertility rates among high-risk groups, such as adolescents and women with pregnancies spaced less than two years apart. A 1977 study reported a modern contraceptive prevalence rate of 38 per cent.

Source: Population Policy Data Bank maintained by the Population Division of the Department of Economic and Social Affairs of the United Nations Secretariat. For additional sources, see list of references.

Venezuela

Sterilization is permitted in Venezuela only for medical or eugenic reasons. The Government views the high incidence of illegitimate births and abortion as a social problem that can be alleviated by the increased provision of family life education and family planning services. In 1987, the Government created the Ministry of the Family, the first and only institution of its type in Latin America, to coordinate sectoral programmes dealing with youth, women and the elderly. A project promoting family life and sex education in the informal sector was begun through the Ministry of Youth in 1987. Recognizing the social and health problems associated with adolescent childbearing, the Government established the permanent Commission for the Prevention of Adolescent Pregnancy.

Source: Population Policy Data Bank maintained by the Population Division of the Department of Economic and Social Affairs of the United Nations Secretariat. For additional sources, see list of references.

ABORTION POLICY

Grounds on which abortion is permitted:

To save the life of the woman	Yes
To preserve physical health	Yes
To preserve mental health	Yes
Rape or incest	Yes
Foetal impairment	Yes
Economic or social reasons	Yes
Available on request	Yes

Additional requirements:

A legal abortion must be performed by a physician.

REPRODUCTIVE HEALTH CONTEXT

Government view on fertility level:	Too high
Government intervention concerning fertility level:	To lower
Government policy on contraceptive use:	Direct support provided
Percentage of currently married women using modern contraception (aged 15-49, 1997):	56
Total fertility rate (1995-2000):	2.6
Age-specific fertility rate (per 1,000 women aged 15-19, 1995-2000):	27
Government has expressed particular concern about:	
Morbidity and mortality resulting from induced abortion	Yes
Complications of childbearing and childbirth	Yes
Maternal mortality ratio (per 100,000 live births, 1990):	
National	160
South-eastern Asia	440
Female life expectancy at birth (1995-2000):	69.6

Source: Population Policy Data Bank maintained by the Population Division of the Department of Economic and Social Affairs of the United Nations Secretariat. For additional sources, see list of references.

Viet Nam

BACKGROUND

Limited information is available on the legal status of induced abortion in Viet Nam in early post-colonial times. What information exists suggests that abortion on request was available in the Democratic Republic of Viet Nam (North) by at least 1971 and has been available in the entire country since its unification in 1975. Previously, abortions could be performed in the Republic of Viet Nam (South) only for narrowly interpreted medical indications, owing to the existence of a 1933 decree enforcing a French law prohibiting abortion and the use of contraception.

In recent years, the Government of Viet Nam has approved a number of laws that regulate abortion in various ways. The Law on the Protection of Public Health (30 June 1989) clearly provides that "women shall be entitled to have an abortion if they so desire". Decision No. 162 of the Council of Ministers in January 1989 obligates the State to supply, free of charge, birth control devices and public-health services for abortions to eligible persons who work for the Government, to persons to whom priority is given under policy, and to poor persons who register to practice family planning. Under the regulations of 1991, which deal with pregnancy termination in the context of maternal and child health care, a medical establishment or person may not perform an abortion without the proper authorization. Decree No. 12/CP on the promulgation of Social Insurance Regulations authorizes sick leave for abortions. Most importantly, Viet Nam's Criminal Code contains no abortion provisions, evidence that the procedure has been decriminalized.

Emphasis on family planning varied greatly between the Northern and Southern Provinces of Viet Nam before unification. Beginning in 1962, in the Northern Provinces, the government planning policy was directed to reducing the rate of population growth. The use of certain relatively permanent contraceptive methods, such as the IUD, was promoted. Abortion on request (with the husband's consent) was available during the first trimester of pregnancy and was usually performed by vacuum curettage. In contrast, the family planning programme in the Southern Provinces began in the late 1960s, largely in response to concern over maternal and infant mortality and the increasing numbers of illegal abortions. However, up until the early 1970s, family planning clinics offered services only to women with at least five living children. Even when family planning services were later expanded to include women with one living child, a marriage or cohabitation certificate was required to obtain services. In the mid-1970s, the Government of the Republic of Viet Nam stated that family planning had been adopted as an official policy, but inadequate medical facilities made it impossible to implement an effective family planning programme.

Since the unification of Viet Nam, family planning has been considered a major national priority. In 1982, various family planning measures were adopted by the Government, including the use of abortion and the creation of the National Committee for Population and Family Planning. After 1983, limiting families to two children became obligatory. Incentives for contraceptive and abortion acceptors, as well as penalties for family planning violations, were further increased in 1985, in an effort to promote implementation of family planning. Viet Nam has successfully lowered its total fertility rate over the period 1970-2000 from 5.9 children per woman to 2.6.

Abortions rose six-fold between 1982 and 1994 in Viet Nam. The country had an estimated abortion rate of 83.3 abortions per 1,000 women in 1996, the highest in the world for that year according to the Alan Guttmacher Institute. The National Committee for Population and Family Planning reported 1.5 million

Source: Population Policy Data Bank maintained by the Population Division of the Department of Economic and Social Affairs of the United Nations Secretariat. For additional sources, see list of references.

abortions in 1998. These figures do not include a growing number of private-sector abortions, estimated at 500,000 or more additional abortions per year. At the same time, the maternal mortality ratio of 160 maternal deaths per 100,000 live births is low, roughly a third of the regional rate of 440.

Surveys indicate that contraceptive awareness is very high in the country, particularly in regard to IUDs, the predominant method. The use of modern contraceptives has grown steadily in the 1990s, from 38 per cent in 1988, to 44 per cent in 1994 and to 56 per cent in 1997, according to the most recent Demographic Health Survey. While the IUD remained the most widely used method, supply-based methods and the condom in particular were increasingly used. There appears to be a substantial unmet demand for family planning, given the reliance upon pregnancy termination and menstrual regulation and the significant number of women not using contraceptives that do not desire another birth. Limited contraceptive choice, erratic supply and delivery problems in a largely agrarian and mountainous State are some of the continuing obstacles to family planning in Viet Nam.

Source: Population Policy Data Bank maintained by the Population Division of the Department of Economic and Social Affairs of the United Nations Secretariat. For additional sources, see list of references.

ABORTION POLICY

Grounds on which abortion is permitted:

To save the life of the woman	Yes
To preserve physical health	No
To preserve mental health	No
Rape or incest	No
Foetal impairment	No
Economic or social reasons	No
Available on request	No

Additional requirements:

Information is not readily available.

REPRODUCTIVE HEALTH CONTEXT

Government view on fertility level:	Too high
Government intervention concerning fertility level:	To lower
Government policy on contraceptive use:	Direct support provided
Percentage of currently married women using modern contraception (aged 15-49, 1997):	10
Total fertility rate (1995-2000):	7.6
Age-specific fertility rate (per 1,000 women aged 15-19, 1995-2000):	102
Government has expressed particular concern about:	
Morbidity and mortality resulting from induced abortion	..
Complications of childbearing and childbirth	..
Maternal mortality ratio (per 100,000 live births, 1990):	
National	1 400
Western Asia	320
Female life expectancy at birth (1995-2000):	58.4

Source: Population Policy Data Bank maintained by the Population Division of the Department of Economic and Social Affairs of the United Nations Secretariat. For additional sources, see list of references.

Yemen

BACKGROUND

Abortion in Yemen is governed by the uncodified principles of Islamic law. Under Islamic law, the performance of an abortion is generally illegal except when carried out to save the life of the pregnant woman. Prior to unification of the country in May 1990, both the Yemen Arab Republic and Democratic Yemen prohibited abortion except when continuation of the pregnancy would endanger the life of the mother.

The Government of Democratic Yemen considered growth rates to be satisfactory but expressed concern about the high fertility rate. As a result of its belief that population issues should be viewed comprehensively within the framework of economic and social development, Government policy was directed to improving socio-economic conditions as a means of resolving population problems. The Government provided family planning services and population information and education.

Although the Government of the Yemen Arab Republic did not have an explicit population policy, it considered fertility reduction necessary to achieve social and economic development objectives. The Government encouraged family planning activities mainly to improve maternal and child health and family well-being. It established the Yemeni Family Care Association, which provided prenatal services and information on birth control. The Government directly supported the provision of contraceptives and the training of family planning volunteers. It also encouraged women's participation in the labour force and supported raising the educational status of women.

On 22 May 1990, the Yemen Arab Republic and Democratic Yemen united to become the Republic of Yemen. The new Government recognized that a deeper understanding of the relations between population and development, as well as the means of influencing those relations, was critical to the future development of the country. Faced with a number of serious population problems, including the negative effects of high fertility on women's health due to frequent childbearing, the Government in 1991 held its first national conference on population, adopted a National Population Strategy, and established the National Population Commission. The Government set several targets for the year 2000, including a contraceptive prevalence rate of 35 per cent and a total fertility rate of 6.0 births per woman. By 1997, the modern contraceptive rate had risen to 10 per cent from 6 per cent in 1991-1992. The total fertility rate remained high at 7.6 children per woman for the period 1995-2000, as did the population growth rate at 3.7 per cent. Maternal mortality was also very high, estimated in 1985 to be at 1,400 maternal deaths per 100,000 live births. The delivery of family planning services to remote areas remains a challenge.

Source: Population Policy Data Bank maintained by the Population Division of the Department of Economic and Social Affairs of the United Nations Secretariat. For additional sources, see list of references.

ABORTION POLICY

Grounds on which abortion is permitted:

To save the life of the woman	Yes
To preserve physical health	Yes
To preserve mental health	Yes
Rape or incest	Yes
Foetal impairment	Yes
Economic or social reasons	Yes
Available on request	Yes

Additional requirements:

An abortion must be performed in a hospital or other authorized health-care facility. If the woman is a minor, approval of her parents or guardian is required, unless she has been recognized as fully competent to earn her own living. After the first 10 weeks of pregnancy, special authorization by a commission composed of a gynaecologist/obstetrician, a general physician or a specialist in internal medicine and a social worker or a psychologist is required.

REPRODUCTIVE HEALTH CONTEXT

Government view on fertility level:	Satisfactory
Government intervention concerning fertility level:	To maintain
Government policy on contraceptive use:	Indirect support provided
Percentage of currently married women using modern contraception (under age 45, 1976):	12*
Total fertility rate (1995-2000):	1.8
Age-specific fertility rate (per 1,000 women aged 15-19, 1995-2000):	39
Government has expressed particular concern about:	
Morbidity and mortality resulting from induced abortion	Yes
Complications of childbearing and childbirth	No
Maternal mortality ratio (per 100,000 live births, 1990):	
National	..
Developed countries	27
Female life expectancy at birth (1995-2000):	75.5

Source: Population Policy Data Bank maintained by the Population Division of the Department of Economic and Social Affairs of the United Nations Secretariat. For additional sources, see list of references.

Yugoslavia

BACKGROUND

Article 191 of the Federal Constitution of Yugoslavia of 21 February 1974 provides that "it is a human right to decide on the birth of children". To implement this article, the eight territorial units of the former Socialist Federal Republic of Yugoslavia took legislative action between 1977 and 1979 concerning the legal status of abortion. Most recently, the 1995 Law on Conditions and Procedures for Induced Abortion in Health Care Institutions reiterated the basic provisions governing abortion in Yugoslavia.

Under these laws, which are all similar in nature, abortion is allowed on request during the first 10 weeks of pregnancy. The intervention must be performed in a hospital or other authorized health-care facility. If the woman is a minor, the approval of her parents or guardian is required. After the first 10 weeks of pregnancy, special authorization by a commission, composed of various health personnel, including social workers and psychologists, depending on the territorial unit, is required. The commission decides on the basis of the existence of medical, juridical, or socio-economic grounds or foetal impairment, depending on the territorial unit. The woman can appeal to the Commission of Second Instance if the Commission of First Instance rejects her request. An abortion may be performed at any time during pregnancy to save the life or health of a seriously endangered woman.

Penal provisions are imposed on medical organizations and persons who violate provisions of the law. A woman, however, is never held criminally responsible for inducing her own abortion or for cooperating in such a procedure.

Beginning in 1952, abortion legislation in the former Yugoslavia was liberalized in response to the significant increase in illegal abortions associated with high levels of morbidity and mortality. Subsequent changes in the abortion laws were adopted at the federal level and implemented at the local level. They were expressly directed to facilitating access to legal abortion in order to discourage illegal practices. For instance, a significant decline in the number of illegal abortions is attributed to the decision in 1969 to eliminate the requirement of a commission's approval for termination of pregnancies of less than 10 weeks, a requirement that had been a practical and psychological obstacle to abortion. Increased numbers of medical facilities, better access to information on abortion services and higher levels of education all facilitated the legal liberalization of abortion. Although abortion rates continued to be very high, the Government of the former Yugoslavia essentially achieved its objective: illegal abortions were practically eliminated, and the country experienced a significant decline in maternal morbidity and mortality related to abortion. For example, mortality associated with abortion declined from 180 maternal deaths per 100,000 abortions in 1960 to 11 per 100,000 in 1976.

Family planning services have been part of the regular medical services in Yugoslavia since the mid-1950s. A family planning institution was established in 1963 at the national and local levels, and the Family Planning Association, affiliated with the International Planned Parenthood Federation, has existed since 1966. However, sex education in the schools and family planning counselling have not been systematically developed, and family planning has encountered continuing resistance throughout the country. As a result, insufficient knowledge and fear of modern methods of contraception is widespread. According to official

---

Source: Population Policy Data Bank maintained by the Population Division of the Department of Economic and Social Affairs of the United Nations Secretariat. For additional sources, see list of references.

data, the percentage of married women using any method of contraception in Yugoslavia actually decreased slightly between 1970 and 1976, from 56.2 to 52.9 per cent. Withdrawal accounted for 66.7 per cent of that total. According to the same 1976 data, only 12 per cent of married women used a modern method of contraception. Sterilization is prohibited by law. Contraceptive practices were roughly similar in the 1980s.

Taken as a whole, Yugoslavia experienced declining total fertility rates and population growth rates over the period 1970-2000: the total fertility rate fell over that period from 2.4 children per woman to 1.8, while the population growth rate fell similarly from 0.9 per cent to 0.1. High rates of abortion, as well as a high rate of repeat abortions, an increase in second-trimester abortions and an increase in abortions among adolescents are problems experienced throughout the country. The estimated abortion rate for Yugoslavia in 1993 was 54.6 abortions per 1,000 women aged 15-44. Abortion continues to be relied on as a contraceptive method, with consequent increased health risks.

In the late 1980s, the former Government indicated deep concern about the high abortion rates and low rates of usage of modern contraceptive methods. In the Resolution on Population, Development and Family Planning of 1989, which set out general principles and directions with regard to population matters, special emphasis was given to fertility and family planning. The resolution, while reconfirming the right of each person to decide freely on the number and spacing of children, as established in the Constitution of 1974, was directed to attaining replacement-level fertility in all areas of the country. In part to reduce the incidence of abortion and in part to reduce fertility in some republics, specific measures to disseminate contraceptive information and supplies more widely were taken at the federal level. Social welfare measures, such as prolonged maternity leave, child allowances and childcare facilities, were also strengthened in areas of the country where fertility was below replacement level.

In the former Yugoslavia, the republics and autonomous provinces were responsible for implementing within their borders the general principles of population policy adopted by the Federal Assembly. However, the republics and autonomous provinces often abstained from executing federally adopted policies. Implementation of population policies, in particular, was often hampered by the sensitivity of demographic issues in maintaining the fragile equilibrium between individual republics and the national minorities.

Throughout the 1990s, the dissolution of the former Yugoslavia involved armed conflict in Croatia, Bosnia and Herzegovina, and Kosovo and has led to the largest movement of war victims and internally displaced persons in Europe since the Second World War. The dissolution of the former Yugoslavia also reinforced the sensitivity of regional demographic issues in the successor State of Yugoslavia. Given the persistence of wide regional differences in fertility, the Government of Yugoslavia reiterated in 1998 that it sought to harmonize rates of fertility throughout the country and to achieve a net reproduction rate of approximately 1.0 in order to perpetuate the demographic status quo. Measures have been designed with the goal of encouraging the three-child family, while discouraging higher order births. Family allowances for the third child are not subject to an income test and maternity allowances are provided for the third child in areas of the country experiencing negative population growth.

Source: Population Policy Data Bank maintained by the Population Division of the Department of Economic and Social Affairs of the United Nations Secretariat. For additional sources, see list of references.

Zambia

ABORTION POLICY

Grounds on which abortion is permitted:

To save the life of the woman	Yes
To preserve physical health	Yes
To preserve mental health	Yes
Rape or incest	No
Foetal impairment	Yes
Economic or social reasons	Yes
Available on request	No

Additional requirements:

An abortion requires the consent of three physicians, one of whom must be a specialist in the branch of medicine related to the woman's reason for seeking an abortion. However, the requirement may be waived if the abortion is immediately necessary to save the life or prevent grave permanent injury to the physical or mental health of the woman. A legal abortion must be performed by a registered physician in a government hospital or other approved institution unless the patient's life is in danger.

REPRODUCTIVE HEALTH CONTEXT

Government view on fertility level:	Too high
Government intervention concerning fertility level:	To lower
Government policy on contraceptive use:	Direct support provided
Percentage of currently married women using modern contraception (aged 15-49, 1996):	14
Total fertility rate (1995-2000):	5.6
Age-specific fertility rate (per 1,000 women aged 15-19, 1995-2000):	134
Government has expressed particular concern about:	
Morbidity and mortality resulting from induced abortion	Yes
Complications of childbearing and childbirth	Yes
Maternal mortality ratio (per 100,000 live births, 1990):	
National	940
Eastern Africa	1 060
Female life expectancy at birth (1995-2000):	40.6

Source: Population Policy Data Bank maintained by the Population Division of the Department of Economic and Social Affairs of the United Nations Secretariat. For additional sources, see list of references.

Zambia

BACKGROUND

Zambia has one of the most liberal abortion laws in sub-Saharan Africa, allowing abortions to be carried out on broad health, as well as socioeconomic grounds. The Termination of Pregnancy Act of 1972 permits an abortion to be performed if three registered medical practitioners are of the opinion formed in good faith that (a) continuation of the pregnancy would involve risk to the life or of injury to the physical or mental health of the pregnant woman, or of injury to the physical or mental health of any existing children of the pregnant woman, greater than if the pregnancy were terminated; or (b) that there is substantial risk that if the child should be born, it would suffer from such physical or mental abnormalities as to be severely handicapped. In determining whether (a) above exists, account may be taken of the pregnant woman's actual or reasonably foreseeable environment or age.

A person who performs an abortion in violation of the provisions of the Act is subject to the punishments prescribed in the Penal Code of 1 November 1931 for the performance of an illegal abortion. The penalty is fourteen years' imprisonment for a person who, with intent to procure a miscarriage, unlawfully administers a noxious thing or uses any means. A woman who undertakes the same act with respect to herself or consents to such an act is subject to seven years' imprisonment.

A legal abortion must be performed by a registered medical practitioner in a hospital. One of the three physicians consenting to an abortion must be a specialist in the branch of medicine in which the patient is specifically required to be examined. Thus, a woman seeking an abortion for mental health reasons must be examined by a psychiatrist, while one with a specific medical condition must be examined by a specialist in that area of medicine. In the case of an emergency, an abortion need not be performed in a hospital and only one physician need consent to its performance.

Complicated procedural requirements and inadequate services limit the number of legal abortions performed in Zambia. Thus, despite the liberal nature of its abortion law, there are continuing obstacles to obtaining a legal abortion and therefore a continued reliance on illegal abortion. For example, the University Teaching Hospital is the only facility at Lusaka where a legal abortion can be obtained. Moreover, such facilities are almost non-existent in the rest of the country because of a scarcity of gynaecologists at provincial hospitals. The requirement that three physicians consent to the abortion is also difficult to satisfy because many hospitals do not have three physicians. Moreover, some physicians are reluctant to sign the forms for religious and personal reasons, and crowded hospitals make it difficult to obtain timely appointments with physicians. These obstacles force many women to induce their own abortion and then proceed to a hospital for emergency medical treatment. In 1976, a total of 173 legal abortions were performed at the University Teaching Hospital at Lusaka, whereas 1,000 cases of illegally induced abortions were admitted to the same hospital.

The Government has expressed concern about the high incidence of illegal abortion in Zambia. Many studies have also shown that illegal abortion is one of the major causes of the high rate of maternal mortality in the country (940 deaths per 100,000 live births in 1990). A study conducted at the University Teaching Hospital between 1982 and 1983 found that 18 per cent of all maternal deaths were due to complications from incomplete induced abortions. Zambia also has one of the highest proportions of orphaned children in the world, with 23 per cent of children under 15 missing one or both parents.

Source: Population Policy Data Bank maintained by the Population Division of the Department of Economic and Social Affairs of the United Nations Secretariat. For additional sources, see list of references.

Zambia

Attitudes towards population growth rates and fertility among Zambian leaders have ranged until recently from pronatalist to laissez-faire. While knowledge of contraception is high in Zambia, the use of modern methods of contraception is low but increasing from 9 per cent of women in 1992 to 14 per cent in 1996. The formulation of a population policy was not a priority in the decade following independence because it was felt that the country was relatively large (about 750,000 square kilometres) in relation to its population size (8.4 million in 1990). In the mid-1980s, however, two major developments forced the Government to change its attitude towards population policy. The first was the release of the 1980 census, which provided evidence of high fertility and rapid population growth. The other factor was a stagnating economy. Although Zambia had been experiencing a series of economic problems since the mid-1970s, they became more severe during the 1980s. Indeed, per capita income in the 1980s was lower than it had been at the time of independence in 1964. Following these developments, the National Commission for Development Planning drafted a national population policy in 1986, which was ultimately adopted in 1989.

The overall objective of the Government's population policy was to improve the health and quality of life of all Zambians as well as slow the rate of population growth. The policy called for sustained measures to reduce the total fertility rate from 7.2 in 1975 to 4.0 by the year 2015 and to reduce the population growth rate from 3.7 to 2.5 per cent per annum during the same period. The Government sought to provide family planning services to at least 30 per cent of all adults in need of them by the end of the century. The total fertility rate did indeed drop to 5.6 children per woman by 2000. The population growth rate for the period 1995-2000 was estimated at 2.3 per cent.

Source: Population Policy Data Bank maintained by the Population Division of the Department of Economic and Social Affairs of the United Nations Secretariat. For additional sources, see list of references.

ABORTION POLICY

Grounds on which abortion is permitted:

To save the life of the woman	Yes
To preserve physical health	Yes
To preserve mental health	No
Rape or incest	Yes
Foetal impairment	Yes
Economic or social reasons	No
Available on request	No

Additional requirements:

A legal abortion must be performed by a physician in a designated institution with the permission of the superintendent of the institution . If the pregnancy resulted from unlawful intercourse, a magistrate of a court in the jurisdiction where the abortion will be performed must certify that the alleged intercourse was reported to the police and that pregnancy may have resulted from it. When the abortion is requested because the pregnancy poses a threat to the life or physical health of the pregnant woman, or on grounds of foetal impairment, two physicians that are not members of the same practice must certify to the relevant hospital superintendent that one of these conditions exists. However, if the woman's life is in danger, a physician can perform the abortion in a place other than a designated institution and without a second medical opinion.

REPRODUCTIVE HEALTH CONTEXT

Government view on fertility level:	Too high
Government intervention concerning fertility level:	To lower
Government policy on contraceptive use:	Direct support provided
Percentage of currently married women using modern contraception (aged 15-49, 1994):	42
Total fertility rate (1995-2000):	3.8
Age-specific fertility rate (per 1,000 women aged 15-19, 1995-2000):	89
Government has expressed particular concern about:	
Morbidity and mortality resulting from induced abortion	Yes
Complications of childbearing and childbirth	Yes
Maternal mortality ratio (per 100,000 live births, 1990):	
National	570
Eastern Africa	1 060
Female life expectancy at birth (1995-2000):	44.7

Source: Population Policy Data Bank maintained by the Population Division of the Department of Economic and Social Affairs of the United Nations Secretariat. For additional sources, see list of references.

Zimbabwe

BACKGROUND

Prior to the enactment of the Termination of Pregnancy Act of 1977, abortion legislation in Zimbabwe was governed by Roman-Dutch common law, which permitted an abortion to be performed only to save the life of the pregnant woman. The Termination of Pregnancy Act (No. 29 of 1977) extended the grounds under which a legal abortion could be obtained in Zimbabwe. The Act permits the performance of an abortion if continuation of the pregnancy so endangers the life of the woman or so constitutes a serious threat or permanent impairment to her physical health that the termination of the pregnancy is necessary to ensure her life or physical health, or where there is a serious risk that if the child to be born would suffer from a physical or mental defect of such a nature as to be severely handicapped, or where there is a reasonable possibility that the foetus is conceived as a result of unlawful intercourse. "Unlawful intercourse" is defined by the Act as rape, incest or intercourse with a mentally handicapped woman.

A legal abortion must be performed by a medical practitioner in a designated institution with the written permission of the superintendent of the institution. If the pregnancy resulted from unlawful intercourse, the superintendent is not to provide written permission unless a magistrate of a court in the jurisdiction where the abortion will be performed has furnished a certification of satisfaction that a complaint about the alleged intercourse was lodged with the police; that, on the balance of probabilities the unlawful intercourse has taken place; and that the pregnancy is the result of such intercourse (in the case of incest, that the prohibited degree of relationship exists between the complainant and the alleged perpetrator). When the abortion is requested because the pregnancy poses a threat to the life or the physical health of the woman, or on grounds of foetal deformity, the superintendent of the institution is not to provide written permission unless he or she is satisfied that two physicians who are not members of the same practice have certified that the grounds for the abortion exist and that, in the case of foetal deformity, any prescribed investigation has been carried out. In the case of an emergency involving a threat to life or physical health, a medical practitioner may terminate a pregnancy outside a designated institution without the permission of the superintendent, provided that a report on the intervention is submitted to the Secretary of Health within the following 48 hours.

Under the Act, no medical practitioner or nurse or person employed in any other capacity at a designated institution is obliged to participate or assist in the termination of a pregnancy.

Any person who performs an abortion in violation of the provisions of the Act, provides a false certificate or grants permission for an abortion on the basis of a certificate known to be false is guilty of an offence and liable to a fine not exceeding 5,000 Zimbabwe dollars and/or to imprisonment for a period not exceeding five years.

While there are no reliable figures readily available, the Government has expressed concern about the high level of induced abortion in Zimbabwe. Studies indicate that complications from unsafe, illegal abortions are a major and growing public health concern. While there are no national estimates, records obtained from Harare Hospital do show that the number of admissions for abortion complications have increased over time and have resulted in high rates of maternal mortality. The maternal mortality ratio in 1990 was estimated to be 570 deaths per 100,000 live births. The demand for abortion is fueled by the erosion of traditional cultural values in the wake of rural-urban migration, the increased need to limit family size, delay in the age at marriage owing to increased educational opportunities for women and the fact that contraceptives are not readily available to women under 18 years of age.

Source: Population Policy Data Bank maintained by the Population Division of the Department of Economic and Social Affairs of the United Nations Secretariat. For additional sources, see list of references.

Zimbabwe has one of the most successful family planning programmes in sub-Saharan Africa. Its modern contraceptive prevalence rate is one of the highest in the region, estimated in 1994 at 42 per cent of married women. Zimbabwe was also the first sub-Saharan African country to experience a fertility decline; the total fertility rate declined from 6.5 to 3.8 births per woman between 1984 and 2000. The population growth rate has recorded a similar decline and is estimated at 1.4 per cent for the period 1995-2000. Following the International Conference on Population and Development, held in Cairo in 1994, the Government of Zimbabwe incorporated family planning and reproductive health into its rolling three-year national development plans.

Source: Population Policy Data Bank maintained by the Population Division of the Department of Economic and Social Affairs of the United Nations Secretariat. For additional sources, see list of references.

References

The references for this volume are divided into two sections: the first contains the general references used for the introductory chapters as well as for background information throughout the volume; the second contains the references used in the individual country profiles. The latter references are presented by country. Unless otherwise indicated, data used in the country profiles were taken from replies to the Seventh and Eighth United Nations Population Inquiry among Governments; *World Population Prospects: The 1998 Revision; World Contraceptive Use 1998* (see complete references below); and from other materials in the Population Policy Data Bank and the Population Projections Database (Demobase) maintained by the Population Division, Department of Economic and Social Affairs, United Nations Secretariat. Data on maternal mortality come from the World Health Organization, 1990 (revised) estimates.

A. For the introduction and background text

Bankole, Akinrinola, Susheela Singh and Taylor Haas (1999). Characteristics of women who obtain induced abortion: A worldwide review. *International Family Planning Perspectives* (New York), vol. 25, No. 2 (June), pp. 68-77.

Boland, Reed (1992). Selected legal developments in reproductive health in 1991. *Family Planning Perspectives* (New York), vol. 24, No. 4 (July/August), pp. 178-185.

Cairns, Gail (1984). Law and the status of women in Latin America: a survey. Development Law and Policy Program Working Paper, No. 13. New York: Columbia University, Centre for Population and Family Health.

Cook, Rebecca J. (1989). Abortion laws and policies: challenges and opportunities. In "Women's health in the third-world: the impact of unwanted pregnancy", A. Rosenfield and others, eds. *International Journal of Gynecology and Obstetrics* (Limerick, Ireland), Supplement No. 3, pp. 61-87.

Cook, Rebecca J., and Bernard M. Dickens (1979). Abortion laws in Commonwealth countries. *International Digest of Health Legislation* (Geneva), vol. 30, No. 3, pp. 395-502.

__________ (1982). *Emerging Issues in Commonwealth Abortion Laws, 1982.* London: Commonwealth Secretariat.

__________ (1986). *Issues in Reproductive Health Law in the Commonwealth.* London: Commonwealth Secretariat.

David, Henry P. (1983). Abortion: its prevalence, correlates, and costs. In *Determinants of Fertility in Developing Countries,* Rodolfo A. Bulatao and Ronald D. Lee, eds., with Paula E. Hollerbach and John Bongaarts, vol. 2. New York: Academic Press.

David, René, and John E. C. Brierley (1978). *Major Legal Systems in the World Today.* London: Stevens & Sons.

El-Kammash, Magdi M. (1971). Islamic countries. In *Population and Law*, Luke T. Lee and Arthur Larson, eds. Leiden, Netherlands: A. W. Sijthoff; and Durham, North Carolina: Rule of Law Press.

El-Moiz Nigm, Abd (1986). *Human Rights and Health Care.* Cairo, Egypt: Assiut University Faculty of Law.

Francome, Colin (1988). United Kingdom. In *International Handbook on Abortion*, Paul Sachdev, ed. New York: Westport, Connecticut; and London: Greenwood Press.

Glendon, Mary Ann (1987). *Abortion and Divorce in Western Law.* Cambridge, Massachusetts: Harvard University Press.

Guilbert, Edith (1991). *Les femmes et l'avortement: revue de littérature.* Groupe de recherche multidisciplinaire féministe, cahier 44. Québec: Université Laval.

Hecht, Jacqueline (1987). La législation de l'avortement en Europe de l'Est et en Union Soviétique. *Politiques de population: études et documents* (Louvain-la-Neuve, Belgium), vol. III, No. 1 (juin), pp. 89-105.

Henshaw, Stanley K. (1993). Recent trends in the legal status of induced abortion. Paper prepared for the Annual Meeting of the Population Association of America, Cincinnati, Ohio, 1-3 May.

Henshaw, Stanley K., and Evelyn Morrow (1990). *Induced Abortion: A World Review, 1990 Supplement.* New York: The Alan Guttmacher Institute.

Henshaw, Stanley K., Susheela Singh and Taylor Haas (1999). The incidence of abortion worldwide. *International Family Planning Perspectives* (New York), vol. 25 (January), Supplement, pp. S30-S38.

__________(1999). Recent Trends in Abortion Rates Worldwide. *International Family Planning Perspectives* (New York), vol. 25, No. 1 (January), pp. 44-48.

International Planned Parenthood Federation (1986). *Family Planning in Five Continents,* London.

__________(1993). Unsafe Abortion: Dialogue, Overview, Responses, Action. *Planned Parenthood Challenges,* No. 1993/1. London.

__________(2000). Country Profiles. [http://www.ippf.org/regions/index.htm]

Ketting, Evert (1993). Abortion in Europe: current status and major issues. *Planned Parenthood in Europe* (London), vol. 22, No. 3 (October), pp. 4-7.

Kloss, Diana M., and Bertram L. Raisbeck (1973). *Law and Population Growth in the United Kingdom.* Law and Population Monograph Series, No. 11. Medford, Massachusetts: Tufts University, The Fletcher School of Law and Diplomacy.

Knoppers, Bartha Maria, and Isabel Brault (1989). *La loi et l'avortement dans les pays francophones.* Montreal, Canada: Les Editions Thémis.

Lee, Luke T., and Arthur Larson, eds. (1971). *Population and Law.* Leiden, Netherlands: A. W. Sijthoff; and Durham, North Carolina: Rule of Law Press.

Lee, Sun-Hee (1995), Reproductive Health and family planning in the Pacific: current situation and the way forward. Discussion Paper No. 14. Suva: UNFPA, Country Support Team, Office for the South Pacific.

Liskin, Laurie S. (1980). *Complications of Abortion in Developing Countries.* Population Reports, Series F, No. 7. Baltimore, Maryland: Johns Hopkins University, Population Information Program.

Moore-Čavar, Emily Campbell (1974). *International Inventory on Information on Induced Abortion.* New York: Columbia University, International Institute for the Study of Human Reproduction.

Newman, Karen (1993). *Progress Postponed, Abortion in Europe in the 1990s.* London: International Planned Parenthood Federation Europe Region.

Omran, Abdel R., and others, eds. (1992). *Reproductive Health in the Americas.* Washington, D.C.: Pan American Health Organization.

Pan American Health Organization (1990). *Health Conditions in the Americas: 1990 Edition,* vol. I. Scientific Publication, No. 524, Washington, D.C.

Rahman, Anika, Laura Katzive and Stanley K. Henshaw (1998). A global review of laws on induced abortion, 1985-1997. *International Family Planning Perspectives* (New York), vol. 24, No. 2 (June), pp. 56-64.

Royston, Erica, and Sue Armstrong, eds. (1989). *Preventing Maternal Deaths.* Geneva: World Health Organization.

Sachdev, Paul, ed. (1988). *International Handbook on Abortion.* New York; Westport, Connecticut; and London: Greenwood Press.

Tietze, Christopher, and Stanley K. Henshaw (1986). *Induced Abortion: A World Review, 1986.* New York: The Alan Guttmacher Institute.

United Nations (1987). *World Population Policies*, vol. I, *Afghanistan to France*. Population Studies, No. 102. Sales No. E.87.XIII.4.

__________ (1989a). *Adolescent Reproductive Behaviour*, vol. II, *Evidence from Developing Countries.* Population Studies, No. 109A. Sales No. E.89.XIII.10.

__________ (1989b). *World Population Policies,* vol. II, *Gabon to Norway.* Population Studies, No. 102/Add.1. Sales No. E.89.XIII.3.

__________ (1990). *World Population Policies*, vol. III, *Oman to Zimbabwe.* Population Studies, No. 102/Add.2. Sales No. E.90.XIII.2.

__________ (1992a). *World Population Monitoring, 1991: With Special Emphasis on Age Structure.* Population Studies, No. 126. Sales No. E .92.XIII.2.

__________ (1992b). *Global Population Policy Database, 1991.* ST/ESA/SER.R/118.

__________ (1993). *World Population Prospects: The 1992 Revision.* Sales No. E.93.XIII.7.

__________ (1995). *World Population Prospects: The 1994 Revision.* Sales No. E.95.XIII.16.

__________(1998a). *World Population Monitoring, 1996: Selected Aspects of Reproductive Rights and Reproductive Health.* Sales No. E .97.XIII.5.

__________(1998b). *National Population Policies.* Sales No. E.99.XIII.3.

__________(1998c). *Global Population Policy Database 1997.* Sales No. E.98.XIII.11.

__________ (1999a). *World Population Prospects: the 1998 Revision,* vol. I*: Comprehensive Tables.* Sales No. E.99.XIII.9.

__________(1999b). *Levels and Trends of Contraceptive Use as Assessed in 1998.* Sales No. E.01.XIII.4

__________(forthcoming). *World Population Monitoring, 2000: Population, Gender and Development* ST/ESA/SER.A/192.

United Nations Children's Fund (1999). *The State of the World's Children, 1999.* Oxford, United Kingdom: Oxford University Press.

United Nations Fund for Population Activities (1979). *Survey of Laws on Fertility Control.* New York.

__________ (various years). Country reports of the Mission on Needs Assessment for Population Assistance. New York: UNFPA.

United Nations Population Fund, and Harvard Law School Library (various years). *Annual Review of Population Law.* New York: UNFPA.

World Bank (2000). Reproductive health and other indicators. *World Development Indicators 2000.* Washington D.C: World Bank.

World Health Organization (1975). *International Classification of Diseases,* vol. 1, Ninth Revision. Geneva: WHO.

__________ (1991a). *Maternal Mortality: A Global Factbook.* Compiled by Carla Abou Zahr and Erica Royston. Geneva: WHO.

__________ (1991b). *Maternal Mortality Ratios and Rates: A Tabulation of Available Information.* Geneva: WHO.

__________ (1994a). *Abortion: A Tabulation of Available Data on the Frequency and Mortality of Unsafe Abortion, 2nd edition.* Geneva: WHO.

__________ (1994b). *Constitution of the World Health Organization.* In *Basic Documents,* (40th edition, vol. 7. Geneva: WHO

__________ (2000). *World Health Report 2000.* Geneva: WHO.

__________ (various years). *International Digest of Health Legislation.* Geneva: WHO.

B. For country profiles*

Oman

United Nations Fund for Population Activities (1979). *Survey of Laws on Fertility Control.* New York.

World Health Organization (1987). *Evolution of the Strategy for Health for All by the Year 2000, Seventh Report on the World Health Situation*, vol. 6, *Eastern Mediterranean Region.* Alexandria, Egypt.

Pakistan

Anonymous (1992). Pakistan 1990/91: results from the Demographic and Health Survey. *Studies in Family Planning* (New York), vol. 23, No. 4 (July/August), pp. 274-278.

Aslam, Abid (1991). Pakistan's renewed commitment to family planning. *Populi* (New York), vol. 18, No. 4 (December), pp. 28-35.

Boland, Reed (1992). Selected legal developments in reproductive health in 1991. *Family Planning Perspectives* (New York), vol. 24, No. 4 (July-August), pp. 178-185.

__________ (1992). New abortion laws run into problems. *People* (London), vol. 19, No. 1, pp. 41-42.

Hakim, Abdul (1993). Women in Pakistan. *ANU Development Bulletin* (Canberra), vol. 26 (January).

Harrison, Frances C. S. (1989). The family planning programme in Pakistan. *Contemporary Review* (London), vol. 255, No. 1487 (December), pp. 288-295.

Hashmi, Makhdoom Muhammad Javed (1999). Statement by the Representative of Pakistan to the General Assembly at its twenty-first special session for the review and appraisal of implementation of the Programme of Action of the International Conference on Population and Development. New York, July 2, 1999.

Henshaw, Stanley K. (1990). Induced abortion: a world review. *Family Planning Perspectives* (New York), vol. 22, No. 2 (March-April) pp. 76-89.

International Planned Parenthood Federation (1992). *Pakistan.* IPPF Country Profiles, 1992. London.

Macro International Inc. (1991). *Pakistan Demographic and Health Survey 1991.* Calverton, Maryland: Macro International.

Moore-Čavar, Emily Campbell (1974). *International Inventory of Information on Induced Abortion.* New York: Columbia University, International Institute for the Study of Human Reproduction.

Pakistan (1991). Criminal Law (Second Amendment) Ordinance, 1990. Ordinance VII of 1990. In *The All-Pakistan Legal Decisions*, vol. 43, Central Statutes.

Ranchhoddas, R. (1982). *Law of Crimes.* Lahore, India: Mansoor Book House.

Ross, John A. (1992). Sterilization: past, present, future. *Studies in Family Planning* (New York), vol. 23, No. 3 (May/June), pp. 187-198.

Sher, Farida (1992). Enough confusion about women's needs. *Populi* (New York), vol. 19, No. 3 (September), p. 12.

* All countries covered in chapters II and III are listed alphabetically in the reference list.

United Nations, Economic and Social Commission for Asia and Pacific (1993). Pakistan's contraceptive use rate remains low despite high growth, *Population Headliners* (Bangkok) (July), p. 5.

United Nations Fund for Population Activities (1979). *Survey of Laws on Fertility Control.* New York.

United Nations Population Fund (1989). *South Asia Study of Population Policy and Programmes: Pakistan.* Islamabad.

United Nations Population Fund, and Harvard Law School Library (1992). *Annual Review of Population Law, 1989*, vol. 16. New York: UNFPA.

__________ (1993). *Annual Review of Population Law, 1990*, vol. 17. New York: UNFPA.

World Health Organization (1990). Safe motherhood: abortion. A tabulation of available data on the frequency and mortality of unsafe abortion. Geneva. Unpublished report.

Palau

United Nations Children's Fund (1999). UNICEF Country Statistics – Palau. http://www.unicef.org/statis/Country_1Page133.html].

Panama

International Planned Parenthood Federation (1992). Panamanian FPA supporting 10,000 adolescents. IPPF Open File: a news digest of the International Planned Parenthood Federation (London) (November), p. 13.

__________ (1988). *Family Planning in Latin America and the Caribbean.* Country Fact Sheets. New York.

Panama, Contraloria General de la República (1990). Tabulaciones no publicadas elaborado por la Oficina de Población y de Planificación Social del Ministerio de Planificación y Política Económica. Panama: Dirección de Estadística y Censo, Sección de Estadísticas Vitales.

Patriquin, Wendy (1988). Spotlight: Panama. *Population Today* (Washington, D.C.), vol. 16, No. 9 (September), p. 12.

United Nations Fund for Population Activities (1979). *Survey of Laws on Fertility Control.* New York.

United Nations Population Fund, and Harvard Law School Library (1991). *Annual Review of Population Law, 1988*, vol. 15. New York: UNFPA.

__________ (1992). *Annual Review of Population Law, 1989*, vol. 16. New York: UNFPA.

Papua New Guinea

Cook, Rebecca J., and Bernard M. Dickens (1979). Abortion laws in Commonwealth countries. *International Digest of Health Legislation* (Geneva), vol. 30, No. 3, pp. 395-502.

Demas, Joseph (1999). Statement by the Representative of Papua New Guinea to the General Assembly at its twenty-first special session on the International Conference on Population and Development. New York, 1 July 1999.

McGoldrick, I. A. (1981). Termination of pregnancy in Papua New Guinea: the traditional and contemporary position. *Papua New Guinea Medical Journal* (Goroka, Papua New Guinea), vol. 24, No. 2 (June), pp. 113-120.

Mola, G., and I. Aitken (1984). Maternal mortality in Papua New Guinea, 1976-1983. *Papua New Guinea Medical Journal* (Goroka, Papua New Guinea), vol. 27, No. 2 (June), pp. 65-71.

Osborn, M. (1986). Family planning in Papua New Guinea. *New Zealand Nursing Journal* (Wellington, New Zealand), vol. 79, No. 11 (November), pp. 20-21.

United Nations, Economic and Social Commission for Asia and the Pacific (1977). Papua New Guinea launches its population policy. *Asian Population Programme News* (Bangkok), vol. 6, No. 2, pp. 26-28.

__________ (1982). *Population of Papua New Guinea*. South Pacific Commission Country Monograph Series, No. 7. New York; and Noumea, New Caledonia.

United Nations Fund for Population Activities (1979). *Survey of Laws on Fertility Control*. New York.

United Nations Population Fund, and Harvard Law School Library (1989). *Annual Review of Population Law, 1986*, vol. 13. New York: UNFPA.

Paraguay

Anonymous (1981). El aborto en el Paraguay: algunos datos inquietantes. *Temas de Población* (Asunción), vol. 7, No. 2 (Mayo), pp. 14-15.

Castagnino, D., J. M. Carron and M. M. Melian (1986). *Aborto: Transfondo social de un drama humano*. Estudios de población, No. 37. Asunción, Paraguay: Centro Paraguayo de Estudios de Población.

International Planned Parenthood Federation (1992). DHS results on Paraguay. IPPF Open File: a news digest of the International Planned Parenthood Federation (London) (July), p. 14.

Jones, Maggie (1992). Paraguay: getting on the right track. *People* (London), vol. 19, No. 1, pp. 28-31.

__________ (1988). *Family Planning in Latin America and the Caribbean*. Country Fact Sheets. New York.

Macro International Inc. (1990). *Paraguay Demographic and Health Survey 1990*. Calverton, Maryland: Macro International.

Saguier, Miguel Abdon. Statement by the Representative of Paraguay to the General Assembly at its twenty-first special session on implementing the Programme of Action of the International Conference on Population and Development. New York, 1 July 1999.

__________ (1979). *Survey of Laws on Fertility Control*. New York.

United Nations Fund for Population Activities, and Harvard Law School Library (1981). *Annual Review of Population Law, 1981*, vol. 8. New York: UNFPA.

Viel, Benjamin (1988). Latin America. In *International Handbook on Abortion,* Paul Sachdev, ed. New York; Westport, Connecticut; and London: Greenwood Press.

World Health Organization (1981). *International Digest of Health Legislation* (Geneva), vol. 32, No. 4, pp. 624-625.

Peru

Boland, Reed (1992). Selected legal developments in reproductive health in 1991. *Family Planning Perspectives* (New York), vol. 24, No. 4 (July/August), pp. 178-185.

International Planned Parenthood Federation, Western Hemisphere Region (1988). *Family Planning in Latin America and the Caribbean.* Country Fact Sheets. New York.

Macro International Inc. (1996). *Peru Demographic and Health Survey 1996.* Calverton, Maryland: Macro International.

Peru, Consejo Nacional de Población (1986). *Ley de Política Nacional de Población.* Decreto Legislativo No. 346. Lima, Peru.

Singh, Susheela, and Deirdre Wulf (1991). Estimating abortion levels in Brazil, Colombia and Peru, using hospital admissions and fertility survey data. *International Family Planning Perspectives* (New York), vol. 17, No. 1 (March), pp. 8-24.

United Nations Fund for Population Activities (1979). *Annual Review of Population Law, 1978.* New York.

__________ (1979). *Survey of Laws on Fertility Control.* New York.

United Nations Population Fund, and Harvard Law School Library (1982). *Annual Review of Population Law, 1981*, vol. 8. New York.

__________ (1988). *Annual Review of Population Law, 1985*, vol. 12. New York: UNFPA.

World Health Organization (1970). *International Digest of Health Legislation* (Geneva), vol. 21, No. 1, pp. 140-141.

__________ (1981). *International Digest of Health Legislation* (Geneva), vol. 32, No. 2, pp. 255-256.

__________ (1983). *International Digest of Health Legislation* (Geneva), vol. 34, No. 1, pp. 76-77.

__________ (1990). Safe motherhood: abortion. A tabulation of available data on the frequency and mortality of unsafe abortion. Geneva. Unpublished report.

Philippines

Aslam, Abid (1993). Beyond the Holy War. *Populi* (New York) vol. 20, No. 3 (September), pp. 7-9.

Flavier, Juan M., and Charles H. C. Chen (1980). Induced abortion in rural villages of Cavite, the Philippines: knowledge, attitudes and practice. *Studies in Family Planning* (New York), vol. 11, No. 2 (February), pp. 67-71.

Gallen, Moira (1982). Abortion in the Philippines: a study of clients and practitioners. *Studies in Family Planning* (New York), vol. 13, No. 2 (February), pp. 35-44.

Henshaw, Stanley K., and Evelyn Morrow (1990). *Induced Abortion: A World Review, 1990 Supplement.* New York: The Alan Guttmacher Institute.

International Planned Parenthood Federation (2000). Country Profiles: Philippines. [http://ippfnet.ippf.org/pub/IPPF_Regions/IPPF_CountryProfile.asp?ISOCode=PH].

Macro International Inc. (1998). *Philippines Demographic and Health Survey 1998.* Calverton, Maryland: Macro International.

Medalla, Felipe M. (1999). Statement by the Representative of the Philippines to the General Assembly at its twenty-first special session on implementing the Programme of Action of the International Conference on Population and Development. New York, 1 July 1999.

Ross, John A., and others (1992). *Family Planning and Child Survival Programmes as Assessed in 1991.* New York: The Population Council.

Tadiar, Alfredo Flores (1989). Commentary on the law and abortion in the Philippines. *International Journal of Gynaecology and Obstetrics* (Limerick, Ireland), vol. 3, Supplement, pp. 89-92.

United Nations, Economic and Social Commission for Asia and the Pacific (1978). *Population of the Philippines.* ESCAP Country Monograph Series, No. 5. Bangkok, Thailand.

__________ (1993). Philippines launches new bid to slow population. *Population Headliners* (Bangkok), No. 222 (September), p. 1.

United Nations Fund for Population Activities (1979). *Survey of Laws on Fertility Control.* New York: UNFPA.

United Nations Population Fund (1989). *The Philippines: Report of Third Mission on Needs Assessment for Population Activities.* No. 100. New York: UNFPA.

United Nations Population Fund, and Harvard Law School Library (1990). *Annual Review of Population Law, 1987*, vol. 14. New York: UNFPA.

__________ (1991). *Annual Review of Population Law, 1988,* vol. 15. New York: UNFPA.

World Health Organization (1973). *International Digest of Health Legislation* (Geneva), vol. 24, No. 4, p. 897.

Poland

Anonymous (1993). Walesa signs law sharply restricting abortions. *The New York Times* (New York), 16 February.

David, Henry P. (1992). Abortion in Europe, 1920-91: a public health perspective. *Studies in Family Planning* (New York), vol. 23, No. 1 (January/February), pp. 1-22.

Frejka, Tomas (1983). Induced abortion and fertility: a quarter century of experience in Eastern Europe. *Population and Development Review* (New York), vol. 9, No. 3 (September), pp. 494-520.

de Guibert-Lantoine, Catherine, and Alain Monnier (1992). La conjoncture démographique: l'Europe et les pays développés d'Outre-Mer. *Population* (Paris), vol. 47, No. 4 (septembre-octobre), pp. 1017-1036.

Henshaw, Stanley K. (1990). Induced abortion: a world review, 1990. In *Induced Abortion: A World Review, 1990 Supplement*, Stanley K. Henshaw and Evelyn Morrow, eds. New York: The Alan Guttmacher Institute.

International Planned Parenthood Federation (1993). *Unsafe Abortion: Dialogue, Overview, Responses, Action.* Planned Parenthood Challenges, No. 1993/1. London.

Nowicka, Wanda (1996). The effects of the 1993 Anti-Abortion Law in Poland. *Entre Nous,* the European magazine on sexual and reproductive of the WHO Regional Office for Europe, (Geneva), No. 34-35 (December), pp. 12-15.

Okólski, Marek (1983). Abortion and contraception in Poland. *Studies in Family Planning* (New York), vol. 14, No. 11 (November), pp. 263-274.

__________ (1988). Poland. In *International Handbook on Abortion,* Paul Sachdev, ed. New York; Westport, Connecticut; and London: Greenwood Press.

Rivero, Miguel, and Anne Olson (1993). Poland: Polish women cross to Czech Republic in abortion search. *Inter Press Service* (New York), 1 April.

United Nations Fund for Population Activities (1979). *Survey of Laws on Fertility Control.* New York: UNFPA.

World Health Organization (1958). *International Digest of Health Legislation* (Geneva), vol. 9, pp. 319-323.

__________ (1962). *International Digest of Health Legislation* (Geneva), vol. 13, No. 1, pp. 140-142.

__________ (1991). *International Digest of Health Legislation* (Geneva), vol. 42, No. 3, pp. 463-466.

Portugal

Amado, Luis Felipe Marques (1999). Statement by the Secretary of State for Foreign Affairs and Development Cooperation of Portugal to the General Assembly twenty-first special session devoted to the overall review and appraisal of the implementation of the Programme of Action of the International Conference on Population and Development. New York, 2 July 1999.

Glendon, Mary Ann (1987). *Abortion and Divorce in Western Law.* Cambridge, Massachusetts: Harvard University Press.

Hamand, Jeremy (1981). Rapid progress in Portugal. *People* (London), vol. 8, No. 3, p. 25.

Hatton, Barry (1997). Portugal rejects abortion bill. *Associated Press*, 20 February 1997

International Planned Parenthood Federation (2000). Country Profiles: Portugal. [http://ippfnet.ippf.org/pub/IPPF_Regions/IPPF_CountryProfile.asp?ISOCode=PT].

United Nations Fund for Population Activities (1979). *Survey of Laws on Fertility Control.* New York: UNFPA.

United Nations Population Fund, and Harvard Law School Library (1987). *Annual Review of Population Law, 1984*, vol. 11. New York.

Qatar

World Health Organization (1983). Qatar. *International Digest of Health Legislation* (Geneva), vol. 34, No. 4, pp. 738-739.

__________ (1987). *Evolution of the Strategy for Health for All by the Year 2000: Seventh Report on the World Health Situation, vol. 6, Eastern Mediterranean Region.* Alexandria, Egypt.

Republic of Korea

Cha, Heung-Bong (1999). Statement by the Minister of Health and Welfare of the Republic of Korea to the General Assembly at its twenty-first special session devoted to the overall review and appraisal of the implementation of the Programme of Action of the International Conference on Population and Development. New York, 1 July 1999.

Haub, Carl (1991). South Korea's low fertility raises European-style issues. *Population Today* (Washington, D.C.), vol. 19, No. 10 (October), p. 3.

Henshaw, Stanley K., and Evelyn Morrow (1990). *Induced Abortion: A World Review, 1990 Supplement.* New York: The Alan Guttmacher Institute.

Henshaw, Stanley K., Susheela Singh and Taylor Haas (1999). The incidence of abortion worldwide. *International Family Planning Perspectives* (New York), vol. 25 (January), Supplement, pp. S30-S38.

__________(1999). Recent trends in abortion rates worldwide. *International Family Planning Perspectives* (New York), vol. 25 no. 1 (January), pp. 44-48.

Hong, Sung-bong. (1988). South Korea. In *International Handbook on Abortion*, Paul Sachdev, ed. New York; Westport, Connecticut; and London: Greenwood Press.

Hong, Sung-bong, and W. B. Watson (1976). *The Increasing Utilization of Induced Abortion in Korea.* Seoul: Korea University Press.

Hopper, R. F. (1975). Abortion in Korea: before and after the law. *Journal of Family Planning Studies* (Seoul), vol. 2 (June), pp. 192-202.

International Planned Parenthood Federation (1992). South Korea legalizes abortion. IPPF Open File: a news digest of the International Planned Parenthood Federation (London) (October), pp. 17-18.

International Planned Parenthood Federation (2000). Country Profiles – Korea (Republic of) [http://ippfnet.ippf.org/pub/IPPF_Regions/IPPF_CountryProfile.asp?ISOCode=KR].

Kim, Taek, and Nam Hoon Cho (1980). Republic of Korea. In "East Asia review, 1978-79", J. Jarrett Clinton and Jean Baker, eds. *Studies in Family Planning* (New York), vol. II, No. 11 (November), pp. 324-330.

Lee, S. J. (1975). Republic of Korea. In *Psychological Aspects of Abortion in Asia*, H. P. David and B. Shashi, eds. Proceedings of Asian Regional Research Seminar on Psychological Aspects of Abortion, Kathmandu, Nepal, 26-29 November 1974.

Lim, Jong-Kwon (1988). A review on induced abortion in Korea. *Journal of Population and Health Studies* (Seoul), vol. 8, No. 2 (December), pp. 57-95.

Nam-Hoon Cho, Moon-Hee Seo and Boon-Ann Tan (1990). Recent changes in the population control policy and its future directions in Korea. *Journal of Population, Health and Social Welfare* (Seoul), vol. 10, No. 2 (December), pp. 152-175.

Park, Y. W., and S. K. Kong (1985). A review on repeat induced abortions in Korea: 1974-1982. *Journal of Population and Health Studies* (Seoul), vol. 5, No. 2 (December), pp. 101-114.

Ross, John A., and others (1992). *Family Planning and Child Survival Programmes as Assessed in 1991.* New York: The Population Council.

Tietze, Christopher, and Stanley K. Henshaw (1986). *Induced Abortion: A World Review, 1986.* New York: The Alan Guttmacher Institute.

United Nations Fund for Population Activities (1979). *Survey of Laws on Fertility Control.* New York: UNFPA.

World Health Organization (1973). *International Digest of Health Legislation* (Geneva), vol. 24, No. 4 (January), pp. 900-902.

Borisov, V. A., compiler (1989). *Naselenie Mira: Demographichesky Spravochnik* (World population: demographic reference book). Moscow: Mysl'.

David, Henry P., and Robert I. McIntyre (1981). *Reproductive Behavior: Central and Eastern European Experience.* New York: Springer Publishing.

Henshaw, Stanley K., Susheela Singh and Taylor Haas (1999). The incidence of abortion worldwide. *International Family Planning Perspectives* (New York), vol. 25 (January), Supplement, pp. S30-S38.

__________(1999). Recent Trends in Abortion Rates Worldwide. *International Family Planning Perspectives* (New York), vol. 25 no. 1 (January), pp. 44-48.

Hotineanu, Vladimir (1999). Statement by the Vice Minister of Health of Moldova to the General Assembly at its twenty-first special session of the devoted to the overall review and appraisal of the implementation of the Programme of Action of the International Conference on Population and Development. New York, 1 July 1999.

International Planned Parenthood Federation (2000). Country Profiles: Moldova. [http://ippfnet.ippf.org/pub/IPPF_Regions/IPPF_CountryProfile.asp?ISOCode=MD].

Popov, Andrei A. (1991). Family planning and induced abortion in the USSR: basic health and demographic characteristics. *Studies in Family Planning* (New York), vol. 22, No. 6 (November/December), pp. 368-377.

Russian Soviet Federative Socialist Republic, People's Commissariat of Public Health, People's Comissariat of Justice (1920). Ob iskusstvennom preryvanii beremennosti (On the artificial interruption of pregnancy). Decree of 16 November. In *Postanovleniya KPSS i Sovetskogo Pravitel'stva ob Okhrane Zdorov'ya* (Decrees of CPSU and the Soviet Government on public health care). Moscow: Medgiz, 1958.

Union of Soviet Socialist Republics, Central Executive Committee and Council of People's Commissars (1936). *O zapreshchenii abortov, uvelichenii material'noi pomoshchi zhenshchinam, ustanovlenii gosudarstvennoi pomoshchi bol'shim sem'yam, rasshirenii seti rodil'nykh domov, detskikh yaslei i detskikh domov, usilenii ugolovnogo nakazaniya za neplatezh alimentov i o nekotorykh izmeneniyakh v zakonodatel''stve o razvodakh* (On prohibition of abortions, increase of financial help to women, establishment of state assistance for large families; broadening network of maternity wards, crêches and day care centres, strengthening of judicial punishment for non-payment of alimonies and some changes in legislation on divorces). In *Postanovleniya KPSS i Sovetskogo Pravitel'stva ob Okhrane Zdorov'ya* (Decrees of CPSU and the Soviet Government on public health care). Moscow: Medgiz, 1958.

Union of Soviet Socialist Republics, Ministry of Public Health (1974). *O Pobochnom Deistvii i Oslozhneniyakh pri Primenenii Oral'nykh Kontratseptivov: Informatsionnoe Pis'mo* (On the side-effects and complications of oral contraceptives: information letter). Compiled by E. A. Babaian, A. S. Lopatin and I. G. Lavretskii. Moscow.

__________ (1982). *O Poryadke Provedeniya Operatsii Iskusstvennogo Preryvaniya Beremennosti* (On the artificial interruption of pregnancies). Decree No. 234, 16 March. Moscow.

__________ (1987). *O Poryadke Provedeniya Operatsii Iskusstvennogo Preryvaniya Beremennosti Rannikh Srokov Metodom Vacuum-aspiratsii* (On the artificial interruption of early-stage pregnancies by vacuum aspiration). Decree No. 757, 5 June. Moscow.

__________ (1987). *O Poryadke Provedeniya Operatsii Iskusstvennogo Preryvaniya Beremennosti Po Nemeditsinskim Pokazaniyam* (On the artificial interruption of pregnancies for non-medical reasons). Decree No. 1342, 31 December. Moscow.

__________ (1989). *Zdorov'e Naseleniya SSSR i Deyatelnost' Uchrezhdenii Zdravookhraneniya v 1988* (Health of the population of the USSR and activities of public-health services in 1988). Moscow.

__________ (1990). *Zdravookhraneniye v SSSR v 1989. Statisticheskie Materialy* (Public health care in the USSR in 1989; statistical data). Moscow.

Union of Soviet Socialist Republics, Moscow State University (1985). *Demografichesky Entsiclopedichesky Slovar'* (Demographic encyclopedic dictionary). Moscow: Sovetskaya Entsiclopediya.

Union of Soviet Socialist Republics, Presidium of the Supreme Soviet (1955). Ob otmene zapreshcheniya abortov (On repeal of the prohibition of abortions). Decree of 23 November. In *Postanovleniya KPSS i Sovetskogo Pravitel'stva ob Okhrane Zdorov'ya Naroda* (Decrees of CPSU and the Soviet Government on public health care). Moscow: Medgiz, 1958.

Union of Soviet Socialist Republics, State Committee on Statistics (1988, 1989). *Naselenie SSSR, 1987* and *1988*. Moscow: Finance and Statistics.

__________ (1990). *Demografichesky Ezhegodnik SSSR, 1990* (Demographic yearbook of the USSR, 1990). Moscow: Finance and Statistics.

__________ (1991). Problemy sem'i, okhrany materinstva i detstva (Problems of family, maternal and child care). *Vestnik Statistiki* (Moscow), No. 8, pp. 60-61.

United Nations (1992). Demographic estimates for the newly independent States of the former USSR. *Population Newsletter* (New York), No. 53 (June), p. 22.

United Nations Children's Fund/World Health Organization (1992). Moldova; transition and independence: urgent human needs. Report of a joint UNICEF/WHO/UNFPA/UNDP and WFP mission to Moldova, 23-24 February. Unpublished.

__________ (1992). The looming crisis in health and the need for international support: overview of the reports on the Commonwealth of Independent States and the Baltic countries. Prepared by the UNICEF/WHO Collaborative Missions with the participation of UNFPA, WFP and UNDP, 17 February - 2 March 1992. Unpublished.

United States Agency for International Development (1998). The USAID FY 1998 Congressional Presentation: Moldova: FY 1998, Assistance to the NIS Request. [http://www.usaid.gov/pubs/cp98/eni/countries/md.htm].

Romania

Boland, Reed (1990). Recent developments in abortion law in industrialized countries. *Law, Medicine and Health Care* (Boston), vol. 18, No. 4 (Winter), pp. 404-418.

Cook, Rebecca J., and Bernard M. Dickens (1988). International developments in abortion laws: 1977-1988. *American Journal of Public Health* (Washington, D.C.), vol. 78, No. 10, pp. 1305-1311.

David, Henry P. (1992). Abortion in Europe, 1920-91: a public health perspective. *Studies in Family Planning* (New York), vol. 23, No. 1 (January/February), pp. 1-22.

Frejka, Tomas (1983). Induced abortion and fertility: a quarter century of experience in Eastern Europe. *Population and Development Review* (New York), vol. 9, No. 3 (September), pp. 494-520.

de Guibert-Lantoine, Catherine, and Alain Monnier (1992). La conjoncture démographique: l'Europe et les pays développés d'Outre-Mer. *Population* (Paris), vol. 47, No. 4 (septembre-octobre), pp. 1017-1036.

Henshaw, Stanley K. (1990). Induced abortion: a world review, 1990. In *Induced Abortion: A World Review, 1990 Supplement*, by Stanley K. Henshaw and Evelyn Morrow. New York: The Alan Guttmacher Institute.

Henshaw, Stanley K., Susheela Singh and Taylor Haas (1999). The incidence of abortion worldwide. *International Family Planning Perspectives* (New York), vol. 25 (January), Supplement, pp. S30-S38.

__________(1999). Recent Trends in Abortion Rates Worldwide. *International Family Planning Perspectives* (New York), vol. 25 no. 1 (January), pp. 44-48.

Hord, Charlotte, and others (1991). Reproductive health in Romania: reversing the Ceausescu legacy. *Studies in Family Planning* (New York), vol. 22, No. 4 (July/August), pp. 231-240.

United Nations Fund for Population Activities (1979). *Survey of Laws on Fertility Control*. New York: UNFPA.

World Health Organization (1967). *International Digest of Health Legislation* (Geneva), vol. 18, No. 4, pp. 822-827.

__________ (1974). *International Digest of Health Legislation* (Geneva), vol. 25, No. 2, p. 433.

Russian Federation

Alan Guttmacher Institute (1992). Russian fertility is low, despite early age at first birth and lack of effective contraceptive methods. *Family Planning Perspectives* (New York), vol. 24, No. 5 (September/October), pp. 236-237.

Babin, E. B., and A. A. Popov (1984). *Mediko-demograficheskoe izuchenie ispol'zovaniya zhenshchinami goroda Moskvy metodov i sredstv kontratseptsii* (Medical and demographic study of contraception use by women of Moscow). In *Sem'ya i obshchestvo. Ukreplenie sem'i i okhrana zdorov'ya naseleniya v sisteme mer demograficheskoi politiki. Tezisy nauchno-prakticheskoi konferentsii* (Family and society: family protection and public health services in the system of measures of demographic policy: theses of research and practical conference). Moscow and Rostov-na-Don: Ministry of Public Health of the RSFSR.

Borisov, V. A., compiler (1989). *Naselenie Mira: Demographichesky Spravochnik* (World population: demographic reference book). Moscow: Mysl'.

David, Henry P., and Robert I. McIntyre (1981). *Reproductive Behavior: Central and Eastern European Experience*. New York: Springer Publishing.

Henshaw, Stanley K. (1990). Induced abortion: a world review, 1990. *International Family Planning Perspectives* (New York), vol. 12, No. 2 (June), pp. 59-65.

Henshaw, Stanley K., and Evelyn Morrow (1990). *Induced Abortion: A World Review, 1990 Supplement*. New York: The Alan Guttmacher Institute.

Henshaw, Stanley K., Susheela Singh and Taylor Haas (1999). The incidence of abortion worldwide. *International Family Planning Perspectives* (New York), vol. 25 (January), Supplement, pp. S30-S38.

__________(1999). Recent Trends in Abortion Rates Worldwide. *International Family Planning Perspectives* (New York), vol. 25 no. 1 (January), pp. 44-48.

International Planned Parenthood Federation (1992). Family planning in the Russian Federation. *Planned Parenthood in Europe* (London), vol. 21, No. 2 (May).

International Planned Parenthood Federation (2000). Country Profiles: Russian Federation. [[http://ippfnet.ippf.org/pub/IPPF_Regions/IPPF_CountryProfile.asp?ISOCode=RU].

Kuznetsov, V. K., and E. V. Baranova (1982). Abort kak problema meditsinskoi demografii: obzor. (Abortion as a problem of medical demography: review). *Novosti meditsiny i meditsinskoi tekhniki* (News of medicine and medical technique) (Moscow), No. 1.

Matvienko, Valentina (1999). Statement by the Representative of the Russian Federation to the General Assembly at its twenty-first special session for the review and appraisal of the implementation of the Programme of Action of the International Conference on Population and Development. New York, 20 June 1999.

Popov, Andrei A. (1996). Family planning and induced abortion in post-Soviet Russia of the early 1990s: unmet needs in information supply. Paper prepared for a conference sponsored by the RANDCentre for Russia and Eurasia. In the *Conference Report: Russia's Demographic "Crisis"*, Chapter 3, Julie DaVanzo, ed. (No. CF-124-CRES). Santa Monica, California: RAND

__________. (1991). Family planning and induced abortion in the USSR: basic health and demographic characteristics. *Studies in Family Planning* (New York), vol. 22, No. 6 (November/December), pp. 368-377.

__________ (1990). Sky-high abortion rates reflect dire lack of choice. *Entre Nous: The European Family Planning Magazine* (Copenhagen), No. 16 (September), pp. 5-7.

Russian Soviet Federative Socialist Republic, People's Commissariat of Public Health, People's Comissariat of Justice (1920). Ob iskusstvennom preryvanii beremennosti (On the artificial interruption of pregnancy). Decree of 16 November. In *Postanovleniya KPSS i Sovetskogo Pravitel'stva ob Okhrane Zdorov'ya* (Decrees of CPSU and the Soviet Government on public health care). Moscow: Medgiz, 1958.

Sadvokasova, E. A. (1969). *Sotsial'no-gigienicheskie aspekty regulirovaniya razmerov sem'i* (Social and hygienic aspects of birth control). Moscow: Meditsina.

Union of Soviet Socialist Republics, Central Executive Committee and Council of People's Commissars (1936). *O zapreshchenii abortov, uvelichenii material'noi pomoshchi zhenshchinam, ustanovlenii gosudarstvennoi pomoshchi bol'shim sem'yam, rasshirenii seti rodil'nykh domov, detskikh yaslei i detskikh domov, usilenii ugolovnogo nakazaniya za neplatezh alimentov i o nekotorykh izmeneniyakh v zakonodatel'stve o razvodakh* (On prohibition of abortions, increase of financial help to women, establishment of state assistance for large families; broadening network of maternity wards, crêches and day-care centres, strengthening of judicial punishment for non-payment of alimonies and some changes in legislation on divorces). In *Postanovleniya KPSS i Sovetskogo Pravitel'stva ob Okhrane Zdorov'ya* (Decrees of CPSU and the Soviet Government on public health care). Moscow: Medgiz, 1958.

Union of Soviet Socialist Republics, Ministry of Public Health (1962). *O Merakh po Usileniyu Bor'by s Abortami* (On measures of adjusting the fight against abortion). Decree No. 377. Moscow.

__________, Ministry of Public Health (1974). *O Pobochnom Deistvii i Oslozhneniyakh pri Primenenii Oral'nykh Kontratseptivov: Informatsionnoe Pis'mo* (On the side-effects and complications of oral contraceptives: information letter). Compiled by E. A. Babaian, A. S. Lopatin and I. G. Lavretskii. Moscow.

__________ (1975). *Propaganda mer Preduprezhdeniya Aborta v Sovremennykh Usloviyakh: Metodicheskie Rekomendatsii* (Propaganda for measures to prevent abortion in modern conditions: methodological recommendations). Compiled by S. L. Polchanova. Moscow.

__________ (1982). *O Poryadke Provedeniya Operatsii Iskusstvennogo Preryvaniya Beremennosti* (On the artificial interruption of pregnancies). Decree No. 234, 16 March. Moscow.

__________ (1987). *O Poryadke Provedeniya Operatsii Iskusstvennogo Preryvaniya Beremennosti Rannikh Srokov Metodom Vacuum-aspiratsii* (On the artificial interruption of early-stage pregnancies by vacuum aspiration). Decree No. 757, 5 June. Moscow.

__________ (1987). *O Poryadke Provedeniya Operatsii Iskusstvennogo Preryvaniya Beremennosti po Nemeditsinskim Pokazaniyam* (On the artificial interruption of pregnancies for non-medical reasons). Decree No. 1342, 31 December. Moscow.

__________ (1989). *Zdorov'e Naseleniya SSSR i Deyatelnost' Uchrezhdenii Zdravookhraneniya v 1988* (Health of the population of the USSR and activities of public-health services in 1988). Moscow.

__________ (1990). *Zdravookhraneniye v SSSR v 1989: Statisticheskie Materialy* (Public health care in the USSR in 1989: statistical data). Moscow.

__________ (1983). *Metody Preduprezhdeniya Beremennosti: Metodicheskie Rekomendatsii.* (Methods of birth control: recommendations). Compiled by I. A. Manuilova and others. Moscow.

Union of Soviet Socialist Republics, Moscow State University (1985). *Demografichesky Entsiclopedichesky Slovar'* (Demographic encyclopedic dictionary). Moscow: Sovetskaya Entsiclopediya.

Union of Soviet Socialist Republics, Presidium of the Supreme Soviet (1955). Ob otmene zapreshcheniya abortov (On repeal of the prohibition of abortions). Decree of 23 November. In *Postanovleniya KPSS i Sovetskogo Pravitel'stva ob Okhrane Zdorov'ya Naroda* (Decrees of CPSU and the Soviet Government on public health care). Moscow: Medgiz, 1958.

__________ (1981). O merakh po usileniyu gosudarstvennoi pomoshchi sem'iam, imeyushchim detei (On the measures of improving of State financial help for families with children). Decree of 2 September. *Sovetskaya Yustitsiya* (Moscow), No. 22, p. 28.

Union of Soviet Socialist Republics, State Committee on Statistics (1988, 1989). *Naselenie SSSR, 1987* and *1988*. Moscow: Finance and Statistics.

__________ (1990). *Demografichesky Ezhegodnik SSSR, 1990* (Demographic yearbook of the USSR, 1990). Moscow: Finance and Statistics.

__________ (1991). Problemy sem'i, okhrany materinstva i detstva (Problems of family, maternal and child care). *Vestnik Statistiki* (Moscow), No. 8, pp. 60-61.

United Nations (1992). Demographic estimates for the newly independent States of the former USSR. *Population Newsletter* (New York), No. 53 (June), p. 22.

United Nations Children's Fund/World Health Organization (1992). Immediate and growing needs for help to a fragile new democracy: health in the Russian Federation with emphasis on children and women. Report of a joint UNICEF/WHO/UNFPA/UNDP and WFP mission to the Russian Federation, 17 February - 2 March. Unpublished.

__________ (1992). The looming crisis and fresh opportunity: health in Kazakhstan, Kyrgyzstan, Tadjikistan, Turkmenistan and Uzbekistan with emphasis on women and children. Report of a joint UNICEF/WHO/UNFPA/UNDP and WFP mission, 17 February - 2 March. Unpublished.

__________ (1992). The looming crisis in health and the need for international support: overview of the reports on the Commonwealth of Independent States and the Baltic countries. Prepared by the UNICEF/WHO Collaborative Missions with the participation of UNFPA, WFP and UNDP, 17 February - 2 March 1992. Unpublished.

Vasilevskii, L. A., and L. M. Vasilevskii (1924). Abort kak Sotsial'noe Yavlenie: Sotsial'no-gigienicheskii Ocherk (Abortion as a social phenomena: social and hygienic essay). Moscow-Leningrad: Frenkelia.

Rwanda

Henshaw, Stanley K., and Evelyn Morrow (1990). *Induced Abortion: A World Review, 1990 Supplement*. New York: The Alan Guttmacher Institute.

Human Rights Watch (1996). *Shattered Lives: Sexual Violence During the Rwandan Genocide and its Aftermath.* (New York) [http://www.hrw.org/hrw/summaries/s.rwanda969.html].

International Planned Parenthood Federation (2000). Country Profiles: Rwanda. [http://ippfnet.ippf.org/pub/IPPF_Regions/IPPF_CountryProfile.asp?ISOCode=RW].

Knoppers, Bartha Maria, and Isabel Brault (1989). *La loi et l'avortement dans les pays francophones*. Montreal, Canada: Les Editions Thémis.

Knoppers, Bartha Maria, and Isabel Brault and Elizabeth Sloss (1990). Abortion law in francophone countries. *American Journal of Comparative Law* (Berkeley, California), vol. 38, No. 4 (Fall), pp. 889-922.

Macro International Inc. (1992). *Rwanda Demographic and Health Survey 1992.* Calverton, Maryland: Macro International.

Royston, Erica, and Sue Armstrong, eds. (1989). *Preventing Maternal Deaths.* Geneva: World Health Organization.

Tietze, Christopher, and Stanley K. Henshaw (1986). *Induced Abortion: A World Review, 1986*. New York: The Alan Guttmacher Institute.

United Nations Fund for Population Activities (1976). *Survey of Contraceptive Laws*. New York: UNFPA.

__________ (1979). *Survey of Laws on Fertility Control*. New York: UNFPA.

United Nations Fund for Population Activities, and Harvard Law School Library (1980). *Annual Review of Population Law, 1980*. New York: UNFPA.

World Health Organization (1970). Comparative health legislation: abortion laws. *International Digest of Health Legislation* (Geneva), vol. 21, No. 3, pp. 437-512.

Saint Kitts and Nevis

Cook, Rebecca J., and Bernard M. Dickens (1979). Abortion laws in Commonwealth countries. *International Digest of Health Legislation* (Geneva), vol. 30, No. 3, pp. 395-502.

International Planned Parenthood Federation (1988). *Family Planning in Latin America and the Caribbean.* Country Fact Sheets New York.

Martin, Earl. A (1999). Statement by the Representative of Saint Kitts and Nevis to the General Assembly at its twenty-first special session on implementing the Programme of Action of the International Conference on Population and Development New York, 2 July 1999.

Saint Lucia

Barbados Family Planning Association (1983). *A Comparative Study of Contraceptive Prevalence in Antigua, Dominica, St. Lucia and St. Vincent*. Bridgetown, Barbados: Barbados Family Planning Association; and Columbia, Maryland: Westinghouse Health Systems.

International Planned Parenthood Federation (1990). Population: a priority for St. Lucia. *Forum* (New York), vol. 6, No. 2 (July), p. 21.

Cook, Rebecca J., and Bernard M. Dickens (1979). Abortion laws in Commonwealth countries. *International Digest of Health Legislation* (Geneva), vol. 30, No. 3, pp. 395-502.

Ebanks, G. Edward (1985). *Mortality, Fertility and Family Planning: Dominica and St. Lucia.* CELADE Series A, No. 171. Santiago, Chile: Centro Latinoamericano de Demografía.

Flood-Beaubrun, Sarah (1999). Statement by the Representative of the Saint Lucia to the General Assembly at its twenty-first special session on implementing the Programme of Action of the International Conference on Population and Development. New York, 2 July 1999.

International Planned Parenthood Federation (2000). Country Profiles: Saint Lucia [http://ippfnet.ippf.org/pub/IPPF_Regions/IPPF_CountryProfile.asp?ISOCode=LC].

Saint Lucia Planned Parenthood (1988). *Annual Report, 1987.* Catries, Saint Lucia.

Saint Vincent and the Grenadines

Cook, Rebecca J., and Bernard M. Dickens (1979). Abortion laws in Commonwealth countries. International Digest of Health Legislation (Geneva), vol. 30, No. 3, pp. 395-502.

__________ (1986). *Issues in Reproductive Health Law in the Commonwealth.* London: Commonwealth Secretariat.

International Planned Parenthood Federation (1988). *Family Planning in Latin America and the Caribbean.* Country Fact Sheets. New York.

United Nations Population Fund, and Harvard Law School Library (1991). *Annual Review of Population Law, 1988*, vol. 15. New York: UNFPA.

Samoa

Annandale, V. E. (1985). Traditional control of fertility in Western Samoa. *British Journal of Family Planning* (London), vol. 11, No. 2, pp. 63-66.

Cook, Rebecca J., and Bernard M. Dickens (1977). Abortion laws in Commonwealth countries. *International Digest of Health Legislation* (Geneva), vol. 30, No. 3, pp. 395-502.

Lavea, L. (1983). Health care in Samoa. *World Health Forum* (Geneva), vol. 4, No. 4, p. 315.

Samoa, Department of Statistics, (1984). *Vital Statistics Sample Survey, Report 1983.* Apia.

Stanley, S., and T. Me (1979). *Measurement of the Impact of Family Planning, Suva, 2-20 July 1979.* Apia. Department of Statistics.

Sun, T. H. (1973). *A Report on Knowledge, Attitudes and Practice on Fertility and Family Planning in Western Samoa, 15 November 1971 - 31 January 1972.* Western Samoa 9601-E. New York: World Health Organization.

United Nations Fund for Population Activities (1983). *Samoa: Report of Mission on Needs Assessment for Population Assistance.* Report No. 52. New York: UNFPA.

United Nations Population Fund, and Harvard Law School Library (1989). *Annual Review of Population Law, 1986*, vol. 13. New York: UNFPA.

San Marino

Segreteria di Stato per gli Affari Interni. *Codice Penale della Repubblica di San Marino.* Law No. 17 of 25 February 1974. San Marino.

Sao Tome and Principe

Royston, Erica, and Sue Armstrong, eds. (1989). *Preventing Maternal Deaths.* Geneva: World Health Organization.

United Nations Fund for Population Activities (1988). *Sao Tomé-et-Principe: rapport de mission sur l'évaluation des besoins d'aide en matière de population.* Report No. 94. New York: UNFPA.

Saudi Arabia

International Planned Parenthood Federation (1973). *Saudi Arabia.* IPPF Situation Report. London.

__________ (1975). *People* (London), vol. 2, No. 3. p. 37.

Population Reference Bureau (1975). *Intercom* (Washington, D.C.), vol. 2, No. 3 (July), p. 9.

The New York Times (1992). Saudi census counts 16.9 million people. *The New York Times* (16 December), p. A-8.

United Nations Fund for Population Activities (1976). *Survey of Contraceptive Laws: Country Profiles, Checklists and Summaries.* New York: UNFPA.

World Health Organization (1993). Saudi Arabia. *International Digest of Health Legislation* (Geneva), vol. 43, No. 1, p. 26.

Senegal

Anonymous (1977). "Epidemic" of teenage pregnancy. *Science News* (Washington, D.C.), vol. III, No. 6 (5 February), p. 86.

Charbit, Yves, and others (1989). Nuptialité et fécondité au Sénégal. *Annales de l'Institut de formation et de recherche démographiques (IFORD)* (Yaoundé), vol. 13, No. 2 (December), pp. 37-74.

Gomis, Emilie (1986). L'avortement clandestin au Sénégal. *Afrique médicale* (Dakar), vol. 25, No. 244 (September), pp. 489-490.

Gueye, F. (1986). *Place de la communication dans un projet de santé maternelle et infantile y compris la planification familiale: cas du Centre Santiba de Ziguinchor.* Dakar: Ministère de l'Education et de l'Enseignement Superieur, Ecole nationale d'économie appliquée.

Hardee, Karen, and others (1999). Reproductive health policies and programmes in eight countries: progress since Cairo. *International Family Planning Perspectives.* New York, vol. 25, Supplement (January), pp. S2-S9.

Henshaw, Stanley K., and Evelyn Morrow (1990). *Induced Abortion: A World Review, 1990 Supplement.* New York: The Alan Guttmacher Institute.

International Planned Parenthood Federation (1988). Senegal adopts population policy. IPPF Open File: a news digest of the world's largest voluntary family planning organization (two weeks ending 20 May), p. 29. London. Mimeographed.

__________ (1989a). Men's attitude about family planning in Senegal. IPPF Open File: a news digest of the world's largest voluntary family planning organization (week ending 7 July), p. 7. London. Mimeographed.

__________ (1989b). Only 11 per cent of Senegalese women practice birth control. IPPF Open File: a news digest of the world's largest voluntary family planning organization (week ending 7 July), p. 7. London. Mimeographed.

__________ (1992). New vigour for family planning in Senegal. IPPF Open File: a news digest of the world's largest voluntary family planning organization (London) (January), p. 12.

Jean-Bart, Anne (1985). "Running wild" in Dakar. *People* (London), vol. 12, No. 1, pp. 18-19.

Knoppers, Bartha M., and Isabel Brault (1989). *La loi et l'avortement dans les pays francophones.* Montreal, Canada: Les Editions Thémis.

Knoppers, Bartha M., Isabel Braul, and Elizabeth Sloss (1990). Abortion law in francophone countries. *American Journal of Comparative Law* (Berkeley, California), vol. 38, No. 4 (Fall), pp. 889-922.

Macro International Inc. (1997). *Senegal Demographic and Health Survey 1997.* Calverton, Maryland: Macro International.

Ndiaye, M. (1977). View from Africa: Senegal. In *Adolescent Fertility*, Donald J. Bogue and others, eds. Chicago: University of Chicago, Community and Family Study Center.

Royston, Erica, and Sue Armstrong, eds. (1989). *Preventing Maternal Deaths.* Geneva: World Health Organization.

Tietze, Christopher, and Stanley K. Henshaw (1986). *Induced Abortion: A World Review, 1986.* New York: The Alan Guttmacher Institute.

United Nations Fund for Population Activities (1976). *Survey of Contraceptive Laws: Country Profiles, Checklists and Summaries.* New York.

__________ (1979). *Survey of Laws on Fertility Control.* New York: UNFPA.

__________ (1986). *Sénégal: rapport de mission sur l'évaluation des besoins d'aide en matière de population.* Report No. 96. New York.

United Nations Fund for Population Activities, and Harvard Law School Library (1982). *Annual Review of Population Law, 1981,* vol. 8. New York: UNFPA.

World Health Organization (1983). *International Digest of Health Legislation* (Geneva), vol. 34, No. 1, p. 77.

Seychelles

Cook, Rebecca J., and Bernard M. Dickens (1979). *Issues in Reproductive Health in the Commonwealth.* London: Commonwealth Secretariat.

Pierotti, D. (1991). Family Planning in Seychelles. *Entre Nous: The European Family Planning Magazine* (Copenhagen), No. 18 (August), p. 16.

Rogers, M. (1985). *A Decade of Women and the Law in the Commonwealth.* London: Commonwealth Secretariat.

United Nations Fund for Population Activities, and Harvard Law School Library (1982). *Annual Review of Population Law, 1981*, vol. 8. New York.

Sierra Leone

Cook, Rebecca J., and Bernard M. Dickens (1979). Abortion laws in Commonwealth countries. *International Digest of Health Legislation* (Geneva), vol. 30, No. 3, pp. 395-502.

Gyepi-Garbrah, Benjamin (1985). *Adolescent Fertility in Sierra Leone.* Boston, Massachusetts: The Pathfinder Fund.

Sierra Leone (1960). *The Laws of Sierra Leone in Force on the 1st Day of January, 1960,* vol 1. Freetown, Sierra Leone: Government Printer.

United Nations Fund for Population Activities (1979). *Survey of Laws on Fertility Control.* New York: UNFPA.

United Nations Population Fund, and Harvard Law School Library (1992). *Annual Review of Population Law*, vol. 15, pp. 37-38. New York: UNFPA.

Singapore

Chen, A. J., S. C. Emmanuel and S. B. Kina (1985). Legalized abortion: the Singapore experience. *Studies in Family Planning* (New York), vol. 16, No. 3 (May/June), pp. 170-178.

Cook, Rebecca J., and Bernard M. Dickens (1979). Abortion laws in Commonwealth countries. *International Digest of Health Legislation* (Geneva), vol. 30, No. 3, pp. 395-502.

Henshaw, Stanley K., Susheela Singh and Taylor Haas (1999). The incidence of abortion worldwide. *International Family Planning Perspectives* (New York), vol. 25 (January), Supplement, pp. S30-S38.

__________(1999). Recent Trends in Abortion Rates Worldwide. *International Family Planning Perspectives* (New York), vol. 25 no. 1 (January), pp. 44-48.

Saw, Swee-Hock (1988). Seventeen years of legalized abortion in Singapore. *Biology and Society* (London), vol. 5, No. 2 (June), pp. 63-72.

__________ (1990). *Changes in the Fertility Policy of Singapore.* Singapore: Institute of Policy Studies.

United Nations Fund for Population Activities (1979). *Survey of Laws on Fertility Control.* New York.

World Health Organization (1970). *International Digest of Health Legislation* (Geneva), vol. 21, No. 4, pp. 843-851.

__________ (1975). *International Digest of Health Legislation* (Geneva), vol. 26, No. 3, pp. 587-593.

Slovakia

Boland, Reed (1992). Selected legal developments in reproductive health in 1991. *Family Planning Perspectives* (New York), vol. 24, No. 4 (July/August), pp. 178-185.

Buresová, Alexandra (1991). Czechoslovakia 1991: abortion and contraception. *Planned Parenthood in Europe* (London), vol. 20, No. 2 (September), p. 6.

Czechoslovakia, Federal Statistical Office (various years). *Statistiká Roenka CSSR* (Statistical yearbook). Prague.

Government of Slovakia (1997). The National Action Plan for Women in the Slovak Republic. [http://www.un.org/womenwatch/confer/beijing/national/slovakia.htm].

Government of Slovakia, Slovakia Statistical Office (various years). *Statistiká Roenka Slovenske* (Statistical Yearbook of Slovakia). Bratislava.

Henshaw, Stanley K., and Evelyn Morrow (1990). *Induced Abortion: A World Review, 1990 Supplement.* New York: The Alan Guttmacher Institute.

Henshaw, Stanley K., Susheela Singh and Taylor Haas (1999). The incidence of abortion worldwide. *International Family Planning Perspectives* (New York), vol. 25 (January), Supplement, pp. S30-S38.

__________(1999). Recent Trends in Abortion Rates Worldwide. *International Family Planning Perspectives* (New York), vol. 25 no. 1 (January), pp. 44-48.

International Dateline News of World Population and Development, a service for Mass Media (1993). Population Communication International (New York), April.

International Planned Parenthood Federation (1989). Abortion laws in Europe. *Planned Parenthood in Europe* (London), vol. 18, No. 1 (Spring), Supplement, pp. 1-10.

__________ (1993). Czech Republic closes doors to Poles seeking abortion. IPPF Open File: a news digest of the International Planned Parenthood Federation (London) (May), p. 13.

__________ (1993). Unmet need for education in Eastern Europe. IPPF Open File: a news digest of the International Planned Parenthood Federation (London) (April), p. 6.

__________ (2000). Country Profiles: Slovakia. [http://ippfnet.ippf.org/pub/IPPF_Regions/IPPF_CountryProfile.asp?ISOCode=SK].

Magvasi, Peter (1999). Statement by the Minister of Labour, Social Affairs and Family of the Slovak Republic to the General Assembly at its twenty-first special session devoted to the overall review and appraisal of the implementation of the Programme of Action of the International Conference on Population and Development. New York, 2 July 1999.

Tietze, Christopher, and Stanley K. Henshaw (1986). *Induced Abortion: A World Review, 1986.* New York: The Alan Guttmacher Institute.

United Nations Fund for Population Activities (1976). *Survey of Contraceptive Laws: Country Profiles, Checklists and Summaries.* New York: UNFPA.

_________ (1979). *Survey of Laws on Fertility Control.* New York: UNFPA.

United Nations Fund for Population Activities, and Harvard Law School Library (1988). *Annual Review of Population Law, 1986.* vol. 12. New York: UNFPA.

Slovenia

Andolšek, Lidija (1988). Yugoslavia. In *International Handbook on Abortion*, Paul Sachdev, ed. New York; Westport, Connecticut; and London: Greenwood Press.

Cook, Rebecca J. (1989). Abortion laws and policies: challenges and opportunities. In "Women's health in the third world: the impact of unwanted pregnancy", A. Rosenfield and others, eds. *International Journal of Gynecology and Obstetrics* (Limerick, Ireland), Supplement No. 3, pp. 61-87.

Cook, Rebecca J., and Bernard M. Dickens (1988). International developments in abortion laws: 1977-88. *American Journal of Public Health* (Washington, D.C.), vol. 78, No. 10 (October), pp. 1305-1311.

David, Henry P., and Robert J. McIntyre (1981). *Reproductive Behavior: Central and Eastern European Experience.* New York: Springer Publishing Company.

Henshaw, Stanley K., Susheela Singh and Taylor Haas (1999). The incidence of abortion worldwide. *International Family Planning Perspectives* (New York), vol. 25 (January), Supplement, pp. S30-S38.

__________(1999). Recent Trends in Abortion Rates Worldwide. *International Family Planning Perspectives* (New York), vol. 25 no. 1 (January), pp. 44-48.

Kapor-Stanulovic, Nila (1989). Liberal approach for a patchwork population. *People* (London), vol. 16, No. 3, pp. 16-18.

Malacic, Janez (1989). Family planning, population policy and declining birth rates in Yugoslavia. *Planned Parenthood in Europe* (London), vol. 18, No. 2 (September).

__________ (1990). Political changes in Yugoslavia and family planning. *Planned Parenthood in Europe* (London), vol. 19, No. 2 (September).

Rop, Anton (1999). Statement by the Minister of Labour, Family and Social Affairs of Slovenia to the General Assembly at its twenty-first special session of the devoted to the overall review and appraisal of the implementation of the Programme of Action of the International Conference on Population and Development. New York, 2 July 1999.

Royston, Erica, and Sue Armstrong, eds. (1989). *Preventing Maternal Deaths.* Geneva: World Health Organization.

United Nations Fund for Population Activities (1976). *Survey of Contraceptive Laws: Country Profiles, Checklists and Summaries.* New York: UNFPA.

__________ (1979). *Survey of Laws on Fertility Control.* New York: UNFPA.

United Nations Fund for Population Activities, and Harvard Law School Library (1978). *Annual Review of Population Law, 1977.* New York.

World Health Organization (1970). Comparative health legislation: abortion laws. *International Digest of Health Legislation* (Geneva), vol. 21, No. 3, pp. 437-512.

__________ (1979). Slovenia. *International Digest of Health Legislation* (Geneva), vol. 28, p. 1112.

World Health Organization, Regional Office for Europe (1990). Yugoslavia. *Entre nous: The European Family Planning Magazine* (Copenhagen), No. 16 (September), pp. 11-12.

Solomon Islands

Cook, Rebecca J., and Bernard M. Dickens (1979). Abortion laws in Commonwealth countries. *International Digest of Health Legislation* (Geneva), vol. 30, No. 3, pp. 395-502.

International Planned Parenthood Federation (1988). Family planning commitment increases in Solomon Islands. IPPF Open File: a news digest of the world's largest voluntary family planning organization (two weeks ending 15 September), p. 29. London. Mimeographed.

Pulea, Mere (1986). *The Family, Law and Population in the Pacific Islands.* Suva: University of South Pacific, Institute of Pacific Studies.

United Nations Funds for Population Activities (1981). *Solomon Islands: Report of Mission on Needs Assessment for Population Assistance.* Report No. 43. New York: UNFPA.

United Nations Population Fund (1992). *The South Pacific Programme.* Programme Review and Strategy Development Report. New York: UNFPA.

Somalia

Ganzglass, Martin R. (1971). *The Penal Code of the Somali Democratic Republic.* New Brunswick, New Jersey: Rutgers University Press.

Henshaw, Stanley K. (1990). Induced abortion: a world review, 1990. In *Induced Abortion: A World Review, 1990 Supplement*, by Stanley Henshaw and Evelyn Morrow. New York: The Alan Guttmacher Institute.

United Nations Fund for Population Activities (1979). *Survey of Laws on Fertility Control.* New York: UNFPA.

South Africa

Henshaw, Stanley K., and Evelyn Morrow (1990). *Induced Abortion: A World Review, 1990 Supplement.* New York: The Alan Guttmacher Institute.

Henshaw, Stanley K., Susheela Singh and Taylor Haas (1999). The incidence of abortion worldwide. *International Family Planning Perspectives* (New York), vol. 25 (January), Supplement, pp. S30-S38.

__________(1999). Recent Trends in Abortion Rates Worldwide. *International Family Planning Perspectives* (New York), vol. 25 no. 1 (January), pp. 44-48.

Nash, E. S. (1990). Teenage pregnancy: need a child bear a child? *South African Medical Journal* (Pinelands, South Africa), vol. 77, No. 3, pp. 147-151.

Tietze, Christopher, and Stanley K. Henshaw (1986). *Induced Abortion: A World Review, 1986.* New York: The Alan Guttmacher Institute.

United Nations Fund for Population Activities (1979). *Survey of Laws on Fertility Control.* New York: UNFPA.

van Oosten, F. F. W., and Monica Ferreira (1988). Republic of South Africa. In *International Handbook on Abortion,* Paul Sachdev, ed. New York; Westport, Connecticut; and London: Greenwood Press.

Varkey, Sanjani Jane (2000). Abortion services in South Africa: available yet not accessible to all. *International Family Planning Perspectives*, vol. 26, No. 2 (June), pp 87-89.

World Health Organization (1975). *International Digest of Health Legislation* (Geneva), vol. 26. No. 4.

Spain

Anonymous (1979). Notes from Spain and Portugal. *Abortion Research News* (Bethesda, Maryland), vol. 8, Nos. 3 and 4 (December), p. 1.

Boland, Reed (1992). Selected legal developments in reproductive health in 1991. *Family Planning Perspectives* (New York), vol. 24, No. 4, (July/August), pp. 179-180.

Council of Europe (1993). *Recent Demographic Developments in Europe and North America, 1992.* Strasbourg: Council of Europe Press.

Glendon, Mary Ann (1987). *Abortion and Divorce in Western Law.* Cambridge, Massachusetts: Harvard University Press.

Henshaw, Stanley K. (1990). Induced abortion: a world review, 1990. *Family Planning Perspectives* (New York), vol. 22, No. 2, (March/April), pp. 78-79.

Henshaw, Stanley K., and Evelyn Morrow (1990). *Induced Abortion: A World Review, 1990 Supplement.* New York: The Alan Guttmacher Institute.

Henshaw, Stanley K., Susheela Singh and Taylor Haas (1999). The incidence of abortion worldwide. *International Family Planning Perspectives* (New York), vol. 25 (January), Supplement, pp. S30-S38.

__________(1999). Recent Trends in Abortion Rates Worldwide. *International Family Planning Perspectives* (New York), vol. 25 no. 1 (January), pp. 44-48.

International Planned Parenthood Federation (1991). Spain still in need of good abortion law. *Planned Parenthood Federation in Europe* (London), vol. 20, No. 2.

Ruiz, Magdalena (1989). Spain. *British Medical Journal* (London), vol. 299 (30 September), p. 816.

United Nations Fund for Population Activities (1979). *Survey of Laws on Fertility Control.* New York: UNFPA.

United Nations Fund for Population Activities, and Harvard Law School Libraryy (1985). *Annual Review of Population Law, 1983*, vol. 10. New York: UNFPA.

__________(1987). *Annual Review of Population Law, 1984,* vol. 11. New York: UNFPA.

__________(1988). *Annual Review of Population Law, 1985*, vol. 12. New York: UNFPA.

__________(1989). *Annual Review of Population Law, 1986*, vol. 13. New York: UNFPA.

World Health Organization (1987). *International Digest of Health Legislation* (Geneva), vol. 38. No. 2, pp. 262-265.

__________(1985). *International Digest of Health Legislation* (Geneva), vol. 36, No. 3, pp. 614-615.

Sri Lanka

International Planned Parenthood Federation (1992). *Sri Lanka: South Asia Region.* IPPF Country Profiles, 1992. London.

Jayasuriya, D. C. (1976). *Law and Population Growth in Sri Lanka*. Law and Population Monograph Series, No. 40. Medford, Massachusetts: Tufts University, The Fletcher School of Law and Diplomacy.

Kodagoda, N., and Pramilla Senanayake (1988). Sri Lanka. In *International Handbook on Abortion*, Paul Sachdev, ed. New York; Westport, Connecticut; and London: Greenwood Press.

Sri Lanka Peacenet (1999). INFORM: January 1999 Situation Report – Abortion. Colombo.

United Nations Fund for Population Activities (1979). *Survey of Laws on Fertility Control*. New York. UNFPA.

Sudan

Bradshaw, L.E. (1986). Local initiative to provide family planning in Juba Town, Southern Sudan. Paper prepared for the 14th Annual Meeting of the American Public Health Association, Las Vegas, Nevada, 28 September-3 October 1986.

Gledhill, Alan (1963). *The Penal Codes of Northern Nigeria and the Sudan*. London: Seet Maxwell; and Lagos: African Universities Press.

Government of Sudan, Ministry of Economic and National Planning (1981). *The Sudan Fertility Survey, 1979: Principal Report*, vol. 2. Khartoum.

Government of Sudan, and Institute for Resource Development/Macro International (1991). *Sudan Demographic and Health Survey, 1989/1990*. Khartoum, Sudan; and Columbia, Maryland.

Rushwan, H. (1981). Health issues of abortion. In *Health Needs of the World's Poor Women*, Patricia W. Blair, ed. Washington, D.C.: Equity Policy Center.

Rushwan, H., A. A. Farah and S. H. Ishaq (1988). Towards safe motherhood: policies and strategies. In *Population and Development in the Sudan: The Quest for a National Population Policy*, Atif A. Rahman Saghayroun and others, eds. Khartoum, Sudan: National Population Committee.

United Nations Fund for Population Activities (1979). *Survey of Laws on Fertility Control*. New York: UNFPA.

Suriname

Adhin, J. H. (1986). The criminal law aspects of planned parenthood. In *Seminar on the Influence of Planned Parenthood on the Health and Development of the People*. Paramaribo, Suriname: Stichting Lobi.

David, Henry, and Susan Pick de Weiss (1992). Abortion in the Americas. In *Reproductive Health in the Americas*, Abdel R. Omran and others, eds. Washington, D. C.: Pan American Health Organization.

International Planned Parenthood Federation (1988). *Family Planning in Latin America and the Caribbean*. Country Fact Sheets. New York.

__________ (1986). *Family Planning in Five Continents*. London.

International Planned Parenthood Federation (2000). Country Profiles: Suriname. [http://ippfnet.ippf.org/pub/IPPF Regions/IPPF CountryProfile.asp?ISOCode=SR].

United Nations Population Fund and Harvard Law School Library (1990). *Annual Review of Population Law, 1987*, vol 14. New York: UNFPA.

Swaziland

Amoah, P. K. A., and others (1982). *Law, Population and Development in Swaziland.* Law and Population Project. Kwaluseni, Swaziland: University College of Swaziland, Department of Law.

Armstrong, Alice K. (1987). Access to health care and family planning in Swaziland: Law and practice. *Studies in Family Planning* (New York), vol. 18, No. 6 (November/December), pp. 371-382.

Armstrong, Alice K., and Ronald T. Nhlapo (1985). *Law and the Other Sex: The Legal Position of Women in Swaziland.* Mbabone: Webster's.

Dlamini, Moses M. (1999). Statement by the Permanent Representative of Swaziland to the General Assembly at its twenty-first session for the review and appraisal of the implementation of the Programme of Action of the International Conference on Population and Development. New York, 30 June 1999.

Swaziland, Ministry of Health (1990). *Swaziland: 1988 Family Health Survey.* Atlanta, Georgia: United States Centres for Disease Control and Prevention.

United Nations Fund for Population Activities (1979). *Survey of Laws on Fertility Control.* New York: UNFPA.

Sweden

Glendon, Mary Ann (1987). *Abortion and Divorce in Western Law.* Cambridge, Massachusetts: Harvard University Press.

Government of Sweden (1993). Country statement submitted by the Government of Sweden at the European Population Conference, Geneva, 23-26 March.

de Guibert-Lantoine, Catherine, and Alain Monnier (1992). La conjoncture démographique: l'Europe et les pays développés d'Outre-Mer. *Population* (Paris), vol. 47, No. 4 (septembre-octobre), pp. 1017-1036.

Henshaw, Stanley K., and Evelyn Morrow (1990). *Induced Abortion: A World Review, 1990 Supplement.* New York: The Alan Guttmacher Institute.

Henshaw, Stanley K., Susheela Singh and Taylor Haas (1999). The incidence of abortion worldwide. *International Family Planning Perspectives* (New York), vol. 25 (January), Supplement, pp. S30-S38.

________(1999). Recent trends in abortion rates worldwide. *International Family Planning Perspectives* (New York), vol. 25 no. 1 (January), pp. 44-48.

Holmgren, Kristina (1989). Sweden: an open society. *Planned Parenthood in Europe* (London), vol. 18, No. 1 (Spring), pp. 15-17.

Santow, Gigi, and Michael Bracher (1999). Explaining trends in teenage childbearing in Sweden. *Studies in Family Planning* (New York) vol. 30, No. 3 (September), pp. 27-35.

Sundström-Feigenberg, Kajsa (1988). Sweden. In *International Handbook on Abortion*, Paul Sachdev, ed. New York; Westport, Connecticut; and London: Greenwood Press.

United Nations Fund for Population Activities (1979). *Survey of Laws on Fertility Control.* New York: UNFPA.

Switzerland

L'Association suisse pour le droit à l'avortment et à la contraception (1991). *Interruption de grossesse en Suisse: loi, pratiques et prevention.* Lausanne.

Glendon, Mary Ann (1987). *Abortion and Divorce in Western Law.* Cambridge, Massachusetts: Harvard University Press.

Henshaw, Stanley K., and Evelyn Morrow (1990). *Induced Abortion: A World Review, 1990 Supplement.* New York: Alan Guttmacher Institute.

Henshaw, Stanley K., Susheela Singh and Taylor Haas (1999). The incidence of abortion worldwide. *International Family Planning Perspectives* (New York), vol. 25 (January), Supplement, pp. S30-S38.

__________(1999). Recent trends in abortion rates worldwide. *International Family Planning Perspectives* (New York), vol. 25 no. 1 (January), pp. 44-48.

International Planned Parenthood Federation (2000). News archive: Women in Switzerland may soon obtain the right to decide for themselves whether or not to have an abortion. Swiss Union for Decriminalizing Abortion, 12 April 2000.

Office fédéral de la statistique suisse (1997). La contraception est largement pratiquée, les avortements sont en diminution. Communiqué de presse No. 28, 14 Avril 1997, Berne.

Rey, Anne-Marie (1992). Abortion in Switzerland. Unpublished.

United Nations Fund for Population Activities (1979). *Survey of Laws on Fertility Control.* New York: UNFPA.

United Nations Population Fund, and Harvard Law School Library (1988). *Annual Review of Population Law, 1985*, vol. 12. New York: UNFPA.

United States Census Bureau (1998). *World Population Profile 1998,* Washington D.C.

Syrian Arab Republic

Ghebe, G., N. Hallak and A. R. Omran (1981). Family formation and pregnancy outcome: Syrian Arab Republic. In *Family Formation Patterns and Health-Further Studies: An International Collaborative Study in Colombia, Egypt, Pakistan and the Syrian Arab Republic*, A. R. Omran and C. C. Standley, eds. Geneva: World Health Organization.

International Planned Parenthood Federation (1974). *Syria.* IPPF Situation Report. London (May).

Moore-Čavar, Emily Campbell (1974). *International Inventory of Information on Induced Abortion.* New York: Columbia University, International Institute for the Study of Human Reproduction.

United Nations Fund for Population Activities (1976). *Survey of Contraceptive Laws: Country Profiles, Checklists and Summaries.* New York: UNFPA.

__________ (1979). *Survey of Laws on Fertility Control.* New York: UNFPA.

__________ (1987). *Population* (New York), vol. 13, No. 11 (November).

United Nations Population Fund (1990). *Syrian Arab Republic.* Programme Review and Strategy Development Report. New York.

World Health Organization (1972). *International Digest of Health Legislation* (Geneva), vol. 23, No. 4, p. 855.

Tajikistan

Borisov, V. A., compiler (1989). *Naselenie Mira: Demographichesky Spravochnik* (World population: demographic reference book). Moscow: Mysl'.

David, Henry P., and Robert I. McIntyre (1981). *Reproductive Behavior: Central and Eastern European Experience*. New York: Springer Publishing.

Henshaw, Stanley K., Susheela Singh and Taylor Haas (1999). The incidence of abortion worldwide. *International Family Planning Perspectives* (New York), vol. 25 (January), Supplement, pp. S30-S38.

__________(1999). Recent trends in abortion rates worldwide. *International Family Planning Perspectives* (New York), vol. 25 no. 1 (January), pp. 44-48.

Maltseva, Valentina A. (1995). Tajikistan: Succeeding against the odds. *Entre Nous*, the European magazine on sexual and reproductive health of the WHO Regional Office for Europe (Geneva), No. 28-29 (May), p. 11.

Popov, Andrei A. (1991). Family planning and induced abortion in the USSR: basic health and demographic characteristics. *Studies in Family Planning* (New York), vol. 22, No. 6 (November/December), pp. 368-377.

Union of Soviet Socialist Republics, Central Executive Committee and Council of People's Commissars (1936). *O zapreshchenii abortov, uvelichenii material'noi pomoshchi zhenshchinam, ustanovlenii gosudarstvennoi pomoshchi bol'shim sem'yam, rasshirenii seti rodil'nykh domov, detskikh yaslei i detskikh domov, usilenii ugolovnogo nakazaniya za neplatezh alimentov i o nekotorykh izmeneniyakh v zakonodatel'stve o razvodakh* (On prohibition of abortions, increase of financial help to women, establishment of state assistance for large families, broadening network of maternity wards, crêches and day care centres, strengthening of judicial punishment for non-payment of alimonies and some changes in legislation on divorces). In *Postanovleniya KPSS i Sovetskogo Pravitel'stva ob Okhrane Zdorov'ya* (Decrees of CPSU and the Soviet Government on public health care). Moscow: Medgiz, 1958.

Union of Soviet Socialist Republics, Ministry of Public Health (1974). *O Pobochnom Deistvii i Oslozhneniyakh pri Primenenii Oral'nykh Kontratseptivov: Informatsionnoe Pis'mo* (On the side-effects and complications of oral contraceptives: information letter). Compiled by E. A. Babaian, A. S. Lopatin and I. G. Lavretskii. Moscow.

__________ (1982). *O Poryadke Provedeniya Operatsii Iskusstvennogo Preryvaniya Beremennosti* (On the artificial interruption of pregnancies). Decree No. 234, 16 March. Moscow.

__________ (1987). *O Poryadke Provedeniya Operatsii Iskusstvennogo Preryvaniya Beremennosti Rannikh Srokov Metodom Vacuum-aspiratsii* (On the artificial interruption of early-stage pregnancies by vacuum aspiration). Decree No. 757, 5 June. Moscow.

__________ (1987). *O Poryadke Provedeniya Operatsii Iskusstvennogo Preryvaniya Beremennosti Po Nemeditsinskim Pokazaniyam* (On the artificial interruption of pregnancies for non-medical reasons). Decree No. 1342, 31 December. Moscow.

__________ (1989). *Zdorov'e Naseleniya SSSR i Deyatelnost' Uchrezhdenii Zdravookhraneniya v 1988* (Health of the population of the USSR and activities of public-health services in 1988). Moscow.

__________ (1990). *Zdravookhraneniye v SSSR v 1989. Statisticheskie Materialy* (Public health care in the USSR in 1989; statistical data). Moscow.

Union of Soviet Socialist Republics, Moscow State University (1985). *Demografichesky Entsiclopedichesky Slovar'* (Demographic encyclopedic dictionary). Moscow: Sovetskaya Entsiclopediya.

Union of Soviet Socialist Republics, Presidium of the Supreme Soviet (1955). Ob otmene zapreshcheniya abortov (On repeal of the prohibition of abortions). Decree of 23 November. In *Postanovleniya KPSS i Sovetskogo Pravitel'stva ob Okhrane Zdorov'ya Naroda* (Decrees of CPSU and the Soviet Government on public health care). Moscow: Medgiz, 1958.

Union of Soviet Socialist Republics, State Committee on Statistics (1988, 1989). *Naselenie SSSR, 1987* and *1988*. Moscow: Finance and Statistics.

__________(1990). *Demografichesky Ezhegodnik SSSR, 1990* (Demographic yearbook of the USSR, 1990). Moscow: Finance and Statistics.

__________ (1991). Problemy sem'i, okhrany materinstva i detstva (Problems of family, maternal and child care). *Vestnik Statistiki* (Moscow). No. 8, pp. 60-61.

United Nations (1992). Demographic estimates for the newly independent States of the former USSR. *Population Newsletter* (New York), No. 53 (June), p. 22.

United Nations Children's Fund/World Health Organization (1992). The invisible emergency: a crisis of children and women in Tadjikistan. Report of a joint UNICEF/WHO/UNFPA/UNDP and WFP mission to Tadjikistan, 17-21 February. Unpublished.

__________ (1992). The looming crisis and fresh opportunity: health in Kazakhstan, Kyrgyzstan, Tadjikistan, Turkmenistan and Uzbekistan with emphasis on women and children. Report of a joint UNICEF/WHO/UNFPA/UNDP and WFP mission, 17 February - 2 March. Unpublished.

__________ (1992). The looming crisis in health and the need for international support: overview of the reports on the Commonwealth of Independent States and the Baltic countries. Prepared by the UNICEF/WHO Collaborative Missions with the participation of UNFPA, WFP and UNDP, 17 February - 2 March 1992. Unpublished.

Thailand

Anonymous (1988). *Why Thai Fertility Has Fallen: Are There Lessons for Other Countries?* Asia-Pacific Population and Policy, No. 7. Honolulu, Hawaii: Population Institute, East-West Center.

Chaturachinda, Kamheang, and others (1981). Abortion: an epidemiologic study at Ramathibodi Hospital, Bangkok. *Studies in Family Planning* (New York), vol. 12, No. 6/7 (June/July), pp. 257-262.

Government of Thailand, National Economic and Social Development Board (1981). *Population Plan, 1982-1986.* Bangkok: Office of the Prime Minister.

Institute of Population Studies (1982). *Knowledge and Attitudes Concerning Abortion Practices in Urban and Rural Areas of Thailand.* Paper No. 43. Bangkok: Chulalongkorn University.

International Planned Parenthood Federation (1986). *Proceedings of the ESEAOR Seminar on Women's Rights and Productive Health, Singapore, 12-15 August 1986.*

__________ (2000). Country Profiles – Thailand [http://ippfnet.ippf.org/pub/IPPF_Regions/IPPF_CountryProfile.asp?ISOCode=TH].

Narkavonnakit, Tongplaew (1979). Abortion in rural Thailand: a survey of practitioners. *Studies in Family Planning* (New York), vol. 10, No. 8/9 (August/September), pp. 223-229.

Narkavonnakit, Tongplaew, and Tony Bennett (1981). Health consequences on induced abortion in rural northeast Thailand. *Studies in Family Planning* (New York), vol. 12, No. 2 (February), pp. 59-65.

Plukspongsawalee, M (1982). Women and the law. *Women in Development: Implications for Population Dynamics in Thailand*, S. Prasithrathsint and S. Piampiti. eds. Bangkok, Thailand: National Institute of Development Administration.

Ross, John A., and others (1992). *Family Planning and Child Survival Programmes as Assessed in 1991.* New York: The Population Council.

Siriboon, Siriwan (1987). *The Impact of Education on Attitudes Towards Abortion among Women in Rural-Urban Thailand.* Bangkok: Chulalongkorn University, Institute of Population Studies.

United Nations Fund for Population Activities (1979). *Survey of Laws on Fertility Control.* New York: UNFPA.

__________ (1988). *Thailand: Report of Third Mission on Needs Assessment for Population Assistance.* Report No. 92. New York.

Wirasamban, Voravee (1999). Statement by the Representative of Thailand to the General Assembly at its twenty-first special session devoted to the overall review and appraisal of the implementation of the Programme of Action of the International Conference on Population and Development. New York, 2 July 1999.

Wongpanich, Malinee (1980). Health development of women in Thailand. In "*Aspects of Thai Women Today*". Background document prepared by the Thailand National Commission on Women's Affairs for the World Conference of the United Nations Decade for Women, Copenhagen, 14-30 July.

World Health Organization (1990). Safe motherhood: abortion. A tabulation of available data on the frequency and mortality of unsafe abortion. Geneva. Unpublished report.

The former Yugoslav Republic of Macedonia

Andolšek Lidija (1988). Yugoslavia. In *International Handbook on Abortion*, Paul Sachdev, ed. New York; Westport, Connecticut; and London: Greenwood Press.

Cook, Rebecca J. (1989). Abortion laws and policies: challenges and opportunities. In "Women's health in the third world: the impact of unwanted pregnancy", A. Rosenfield and others, eds. *International Journal of Gynecology and Obstetrics* (Limerick, Ireland), Supplement No. 3, pp. 61-87.

Cook, Rebecca J., and Bernard M. Dickens (1988). International developments in abortion laws: 1977-88. *American Journal of Public Health* (Washington, D.C.), vol. 78, No. 10 (October), pp. 1305-1311.

David, Henry P., and Robert J. McIntyre (1982). *Reproductive Behaviour, Central and Eastern European Experience.* New York: Springer Publishing Company.

Henshaw, Stanley K., Susheela Singh and Taylor Haas (1999). The incidence of abortion worldwide. *International Family Planning Perspectives* (New York), vol. 25 (January), Supplement, pp. S30-S38.

__________(1999). Recent trends in abortion rates worldwide. *International Family Planning Perspectives* (New York), vol. 25 no. 1 (January), pp. 44-48.

Kapor-Stanulovic, Nila (1989). Liberal approach for a patchwork population. *People* (London), vol. 16, No. 3, pp. 16-18.

Malacic, Janez (1989). Family planning, population policy and declining birth rates in Yugoslavia. *Planned Parenthood in Europe* (London), vol. 18, No. 2 (September).

__________ (1990). Political changes in Yugoslavia and family planning. *Planned Parenthood in Europe* (London), vol. 19, No. 2 (September).

Royston, Erica, and Sue Armstrong, eds. (1989). *Preventing Maternal Deaths*. Geneva: World Health Organization.

United Nations Fund for Population Activities (1976). *Survey of Contraceptive Laws: Country Profiles, Checklists and Summaries*. New York.

__________ (1979). *Survey of Laws on Fertility Control*. New York: UNFPA.

United Nations Fund for Population Activities, and Harvard Law School Library (1980). *Annual Review of Population Law, 1979*. New York: UNFPA.

World Health Organization (1970). Comparative health legislation: abortion laws. *International Digest of Health Legislation* (Geneva), vol. 21, No. 3, pp. 437-512.

World Health Organization, Regional Office for Europe (1990). Yugoslavia. *Entre nous: The European Family Planning Magazine* (Copenhagen), No. 16 (September), pp. 11-12.

Togo

Agounké, Akoua, Mensan Assogba and Kodjo Anipah (1989). *Enquête démographique et de santé au Togo, 1988*. Lomé, Togo: Direction générale de la santé, Direction de la statistique; and Columbia, Maryland: Institute for Resource Development/Macro Systems, Inc.

Ekouevi, Koffi (1994). *Family and Reproductive Behaviour in Urban Togo*. Summary Report No. 7 (March) for the UAPS Small Grants Programme on Population and Development. Dakar: African Institute for Economic Development and Planning (IDEP).

Henshaw, Stanley K., and Evelyn Morrow (1990). *Induced Abortion: A World Review, 1990 Supplement*. New York: The Alan Guttmacher Institute.

International Planned Parenthood Federation (2000). Country Profiles – Togo. [http://ippfnet.ippf.org/pub/IPPF_Regions/IPPF_CountryProfile.asp?ISOCode=TG]

Knoppers, Bartha Maria, and Isabel Brault (1989). *La loi et l'avortement dans les pays francophones*. Montreal, Canada: Les Editions Thémis.

Knoppers, Bartha Maria, and Isabel Brault and Elizabeth Sloss (1990). Abortion law in francophone countries. *American Journal of Comparative Law* (Berkeley, California), vol. 38, No. 4 (Fall), pp. 889-922.

Kumekpor, Tom (1975). Togo. *Population Growth and Socioeconomic Change in West Africa*, John Caldwell and others, eds. New York and London: Columbia University Press.

Macro International Inc. (1998). *Togo Demographic and Health Survey 1998*. Calverton, Maryland: Macro International.

Pre, Simfeitcheou (1999). Statement by the Minister of Planning and Development of Togo to the General Assembly at its twenty-first special session devoted to the overall review and appraisal of the implementation of the Programme of Action of the International Conference on Population and Development. New York, 2 July 1999.

Royston, Erica, and Sue Armstrong, eds. (1989). *Preventing Maternal Deaths*. Geneva: World Health Organization.

Tietze, Christopher, and Stanley K. Henshaw (1986). *Induced Abortion: A World Review, 1986*. New York: The Alan Guttmacher Institute.

United Nations Fund for Population Activities (1976). *Survey of Contraceptive Laws: Country Profiles, Checklists and Summaries*. New York.: UNFPA

__________ (1979). *Survey of Laws on Fertility Control*. New York: UNFPA.

United Nations Fund for Population Activities, and Harvard Law School Library (1982). *Annual Review of Population Law, 1981*, vol. 8. New York: UNFPA.

__________ (1985). *Annual Review of Population Law, 1983*, vol. 10. New York: UNFPA.

__________ (1989). *Annual Review of Population Law, 1986*, vol. 13. New York: UNFPA.

World Health Organization (2000). *World Health Report 2000*. Geneva, Switzerland: World Health Organization.

Tonga

Cook, Rebecca J., and Bernard M. Dickens (1979). Abortion laws in Commonwealth countries. *International Digest of Health Legislation* (Geneva), vol. 30, No. 3, pp. 395-502.

International Planned Parenthood Federation (2000). Country Profiles – Tonga [http://ippfnet.ippf.org/pub/IPPF_Regions/IPPF_CountryProfile.asp?ISOCode=TO]

Pacific population policies hamstrung by lack of resources: Tonga Prime Minister Baron Vaea. Pacific Islands Report, 10 February 1999. Pacific Islands Development Programmes/East-West Centre/Centre for Pacific Islands Studies, University of Hawaii at Manoa. [http://166.122.164 43/archive/1999/February/02-10-02.html].

United Nations Fund for Population Activities (1979). *Survey of Laws on Fertility Control*. New York: UNFPA.

__________ (1982). *Tonga. Report of Mission on Needs Assessment for Population Assistance*. Report No. 51. New York: UNFPA.

United Nations Population Fund, and Harvard Law School Library (1989). *Annual Review of Population Law, 1986*, vol. 13. New York: UNFPA.

Trinidad and Tobago

Daly, S. (1975). *The Legal Status of Women in Trinidad and Tobago, 1975*. Port-of-Spain, Trinidad: National Commission on the Status of Women.

International Planned Parenthood Federation (1978). Clarification in Trinidad and Tobago. *People* (London), vol. 5, No. 2, p. 35.

__________ (1988). *Family Planning in Latin America and the Caribbean*. Country Fact Sheets. New York.

International Planned Parenthood Federation, Western Hemisphere Region. (1988). Trinidad and Tobago: a recent decline in fertility. *Forum* (New York), vol. 4, No. 1 (April), pp. 5-6.

__________ (1990). Trinidad and Tobago. Family Planning Association on the move. *Forum* (New York), vol. 5 (January).

__________ (2000). Country Profiles – Trinidad and Tobago. [http://ippfnet.ippf.org/pub/IPPF_Regions/IPPF_CountryProfile.asp?ISOCode=TT]

Maynard, Glenda (1988). Case study on Trinidad and Tobago. Paper presented at the Expert Group Meeting on Social Support Measures for the Advancement of Women, Vienna, 14-18 November. EGM/SSMAW/1988/CS.14.

Pan-American Health Organization (PAHO) (1999). Trinidad and Tobago health overview.

Ramsaran, Manomar (1999). Statement by the Minister of Social and Community Development of Trinidad and Tobago to the General Assembly at its twenty-first special session of the devoted to the overall review and appraisal of the implementation of the Programme of Action of the International Conference on Population and Development. New York, 1 July 1999.

United Nations Fund for Population Activities (1979). *Survey of Laws on Fertility Control*. New York: UNFPA.

World Health Organization (1990). Safe motherhood: abortion. A tabulation of available data on the frequency and mortality of unsafe abortion. Geneva. Unpublished report.

Tunisia

Ben Aissa, Rim (2000). Population policy in Tunisia. Paper presented at the International Policy Dialogue: Population and Sustainable Development, Expo 2000, Hanover, Germany, 22-24 November 1999. Berlin: Development Policy Forum/German Foundation for International Development (DSE). [http://www.dse.de/ef/populat/aissa.htm]

Ben Cheikh, T., and M. Laribi (1972). The Tunisian experience of induced abortion. In *Induced Abortion: A Hazard to Public Health?* Isam R. Nazer, ed. Proceedings of the 1st Conference of the IPPF Middle East and North Africa Region, Beirut, Lebanon, February. Beirut: International Planned Parenthood Federation.

Boukhris, Mohamed (1992). *La population en Tunisie: réalitiés et perspectives*. Tunis: Office national de la famille et de la population.

Charfeddine, Abdelmalek (1980). Evolution récente du programme national de planning familial. *Revue tunisienne des études de population* (Tunis), vol. 1, No. 1, pp. 105-130.

Curtis, Richard (1996). Tunisia's family planning success underlies its economic progress. *Washington Report on Middle East Affairs* (November-December), pp.72-76.

Henshaw, Stanley K., and Evelyn Morrow (1990). *Induced Abortion: A World Review, 1990 Supplement*. New York: The Alan Guttmacher Institute.

Henshaw, Stanley K., Susheela Singh and Taylor Haas (1999). The incidence of abortion worldwide. *International Family Planning Perspectives* (New York), vol. 25 (January), Supplement, pp. S30-S38.

__________(1999). Recent trends in abortion rates worldwide. *International Family Planning Perspectives* (New York), vol. 25 no. 1 (January), pp. 44-48.

International Planned Parenthood Federation (2000). Country Profiles – Tunisia. [http://ippfnet.ippf.org/pub/IPPF_Regions/IPPF_CountryProfile.asp?ISOCode=TN]

Knoppers, Bartha M., and Isabel Brault (1989). *La loi et l'avortement dans les pays francophones*. Montreal, Canada: Les Editions Thémis.

Labidi, Lilia, ed. (1988). *Médecine, santé des femmes*. Tunis, Tunisia: Hospital d'enfants, Unité de pédiatrie préventive et sociale.

Tietze, Christopher, and Stanley K. Henshaw (1986). *Induced Abortion: A World Review, 1986*. New York: The Alan Guttmacher Institute.

United Nations Fund for Population Activities (1976). *Survey of Contraceptive Laws: Country Profiles, Checklists and Summaries*. New York.

United Nations Fund for Population Activities, and Harvard Law School Library (1979). *Survey of Laws on Fertility Control*. New York: UNFPA.

World Health Organization (1968). *International Digest of Health Legislation* (Geneva), vol. 19, p. 217.

__________ (1974) *International Digest of Health Legislation* (Geneva), vol. 25, p. 184.

Turkey

Akadli, Bana (1985). A cross-sectional study of abortions. *Turkish Journal of Population Studies* (Izmir, Turkey), vol. 7, pp. 27-41.

Cook, Rebecca, J., and Bernard M. Dickens (1988). International developments in abortion laws: 1977-88. *American Journal of Public Health* (Washington, D.C.), vol. 78, No. 10 (October), pp. 1305-1311.

Council of Europe (1993). *Recent Demographic Developments in Europe and North America, 1992*. Strasbourg: Council of Europe Press.

Dervisoglu, Ayse Akin and Mehmet Ali Biliker (1995). Turkey: fertility continues to decline. *Entre Nous*, the European magazine on sexual and reproductive health of the WHO Regional Office for Europe (Geneva), No. 30-31 (December).

Durmus, Osman (1999). Statement by the Minister of Health of Turkey to the General Assembly at its twenty-first special session of the devoted to the overall review and appraisal of the implementation of the Programme of Action of the International Conference on Population and Development. New York, 1 July 1999.

Government of Turkey, Ministry of Health (1997). Health Services: Reproductive Health. See Ministry of Health of Turkey website: [http://www.saglik.gov.tr/. In Turkish.

Henshaw, Stanley K., Susheela Singh and Taylor Haas (1999). The incidence of abortion worldwide. *International Family Planning Perspectives* (New York), vol. 25 (January), Supplement, pp. S30-S38.

__________(1999). Recent trends in abortion rates worldwide. *International Family Planning Perspectives* (New York), vol. 25 no. 1 (January), pp. 44-48.

Institute of Population Studies (1987). *1983 Turkish Population and Health Survey*. Ankara, Turkey: Haceteppe University.

International Planned Parenthood Federation (1998). Turkey provides contraceptive information and supplies to post-abortion patients. *International Family Planning Perspectives*, vol. 24, No. 4. (December).

International Planned Parenthood Federation (2000). Country Profiles – Turkey. [http://ippfnet.ippf.org/pub/IPPF_Regions/IPPF_CountryProfile.asp?ISOCode=TR]

Macro International Inc. (1998). *Turkey Demographic and Health Survey 1998.* Calverton, Maryland: Macro International.

McLaurin, Katie E., Charlotte E. Hord and Merrill Wolf (1990). Health systems' role in abortion care: the need for a pro-active approach. Paper prepared for the meeting From Abortion to Contraception, Tbilisi, USSR, 10-13 October.

Shane, B. C. (1990). Survey report: Turkey. *Population Today* (Washington, D.C.), vol. 18, No. 12, pp. 5.

Tietze, Christopher, and Stanley K. Henshaw (1986). *Induced Abortion: A World Review, 1986.* New York: The Alan Guttmacher Institute.

United Nations Fund for Population Activities (1979). *Survey of Laws on Fertility Control.* New York: UNFPA.

World Health Organization (1966). *International Digest of Health Legislation* (Geneva), vol. 17, No. 4, pp. 985-987.

__________ (1983). *International Digest of Health Legislation* (Geneva), vol. 34, No. 4, pp. 759-762.

Turkmenistan

Ataeva, Aksoltan (1999). Statement by the Permanent Representative of Turkmenistan to the General Assembly at its twenty-first special session devoted to the overall review and appraisal of the implementation of the Programme of Action of the International Conference on Population and Development. New York, 2 July 1999.

Borisov, V. A., compiler (1989). *Naselenie Mira: Demographichesky Spravochnik* (World population: demographic reference book). Moscow: Mysl'.

David, Henry P., and Robert I. McIntyre (1981). *Reproductive Behavior: Central and Eastern European Experience.* New York: Springer Publishing.

Henshaw, Stanley K., Susheela Singh and Taylor Haas (1999). The incidence of abortion worldwide. *International Family Planning Perspectives* (New York), vol. 25 (January), Supplement, pp. S30-S38.

__________(1999). Recent trends in abortion rates worldwide. *International Family Planning Perspectives* (New York), vol. 25 no. 1 (January), pp. 44-48.

Mamedov, Khangeldi (1995). Turkmenistan: abortion rate declines. *Entre Nous*, the reproductive health magazine of the WHO Regional Office for Europe (Geneva), No. 28-29 (May).

Popov, Andrei A. (1991). Family planning and induced abortion in the USSR: basic health and demographic characteristics. *Studies in Family Planning* (New York), vol. 22, No. 6 (November/December), pp. 368-377.

Russian Soviet Federative Socialist Republic, People's Commissariat of Public Health, People's Comissariat of Justice (1920). Ob iskusstvennom preryvanii beremennosti (On the artificial interruption of pregnancy). Decree of 16 November. In *Postanovleniya KPSS i Sovetskogo Pravitel'stva ob Okhrane Zdorov'ya* (Decrees of CPSU and the Soviet Government on public health). Moscow: Medgiz, 1958.

Union of Soviet Socialist Republics, Central Executive Committee and Council of People's Commissars (1936). *O zapreshchenii abortov, uvelichenii material'noi pomoshchi zhenshchinam, ustanovlenii gosudarstvennoi pomoshchi bol'shim sem'yam, rasshirenii seti rodil'nykh domov, detskikh yaslei i detskikh domov, usilenii ugolovnogo nakazaniya za neplatezh alimentov i o nekotorykh izmeneniyakh v zakonodatel'stve o razvodakh* (On prohibition of abortions, increase of financial help to women, establishment of state assistance for large families, broadening network of maternity wards, crêches and day-care centres, strengthening of judicial punishment for non-payment of alimonies and some changes in legislation on divorces). *In Postanovleniya KPSS i Sovetskogo Pravitel'stva ob Okhrane Zdorov'ya* (Decrees of CPSU and the Soviet Government on public health care). Moscow: Medgiz, 1958.

Union of Soviet Socialist Republics, Ministry of Public Health (1974). *O Pobochnom Deistvii i Oslozhneniyakh pri Primenenii Oral'nykh Kontratseptivov: Informatsionnoe Pis'mo* (On the side-effects and complications of oral contraceptives: information letter). Compiled by E. A. Babaian, A. S. Lopatin and I. G. Lavretskii. Moscow.

__________ (1982). *O Poryadke Provedeniya Operatsii Iskusstvennogo Preryvaniya Beremennosti* (On the artificial interruption of pregnancies). Decree No. 234, 16 March. Moscow.

__________ (1987). *O Poryadke Provedeniya Operatsii Iskusstvennogo Preryvaniya Beremennosti Rannikh Srokov Metodom Vacuum-aspiratsii* (On the artificial interruption of early-stage pregnancies by vacuum aspiration). Decree No. 757, 5 June. Moscow.

__________ (1987). *O Poryadke Provedeniya Operatsii Iskusstvennogo Preryvaniya Beremennosti Po Nemeditsinskim Pokazaniyam* (On the artificial interruption of pregnancies for non-medical reasons). Decree No. 1342, 31 December. Moscow.

__________ (1989). *Zdorov'e Naseleniya SSSR i Deyatelnost' Uchrezhdenii Zdravookhraneniya v 1988* (Health of the population of the USSR and activities of public-health services in 1988). Moscow.

__________ (1990). *Zdravookhraneniye v SSSR v 1989. Statisticheskie Materialy* (Public health care in the USSR in 1989; statistical data). Moscow.

Union of Soviet Socialist Republics, Moscow State University (1985). *Demografichesky Entsiclopedichesky Slovar'* (Demographic encyclopedic dictionary). Moscow: Sovetskaya Entsiclopediya.

Union of Soviet Socialist Republics, Presidium of the Supreme Soviet (1955). Ob otmene zapreshcheniya abortov (On repeal of the prohibition of abortions). Decree of 23 November. In *Postanovleniya KPSS i Sovetskogo Pravitel'stva ob Okhrane Zdorov'ya Naroda* (Decrees of CPSU and the Soviet Government on public health care). Moscow: Medgiz, 1958.

Union of Soviet Socialist Republics, State Committee on Statistics (1988, 1989). *Naselenie SSSR, 1987* and *1988.* Moscow: Finance and Statistics.

__________(1990). *Demografichesky Ezhegodnik SSSR, 1990* (Demographic yearbook of the USSR, 1990). Moscow: Finance and Statistics.

__________ (1991). Problemy sem'i, okhrany materinstva i detstva (Problems of family, maternal and child care). *Vestnik Statistiki* (Moscow), No. 8, pp. 60-61.

United Nations (1992). Demographic estimates for the newly independent States of the former USSR. *Population Newsletter* (New York), No. 53 (June), p. 22.

United Nations Children's Fund/World Health Organization (1992). Republic of Turkmenistan. Report of a joint UNICEF/WHO/UNFPA/UNDP and WFP mission to Turkmenistan, 17-21 February. Unpublished.

__________ (1992). The looming crisis and fresh opportunity: health in Kazakhstan, Kyrgyzstan, Tadjikistan, Turkmenistan and Uzbekistan with emphasis on women and children. Report of a joint UNICEF/WHO/UNFPA/UNDP and WFP mission, 17 February - 2 March. Unpublished.

__________ (1992). The looming crisis in health and the need for international support: overview of the reports on the Commonwealth of Independent States and the Baltic countries. Prepared by the UNICEF/WHO Collaborative Missions with the participation of UNFPA, WFP and UNDP, 17 February - 2 March 1992. Unpublished.

United Nations Population Fund (1997). Turkmenistan Country Programme: Introduction and Background. [http://www.unfpa.org/regions/apd/countries/turkmenistan.htm].

Tuvalu

Chee, Stephen, William J. House and Laurie Lewis (1999). Population policies and programmes in the post-ICPD era: can the pacific island countries meet the challenge?" *Asia-Pacific Population Journal*, vol. 14, No. 1, pp. 3-20.

International Planned Parenthood Federation (1974). *Gilbert and Ellice Islands* (*Family Planning*). IPPF Situation Report. London.

_________ (2000). Country Profiles – Tuvalu. [http://ippfnet.ippf.org/pub/IPPF_Regions/IPPF_CountryProfile.asp?ISOCode=TV]

Tuvalu (1986). Tuvalu Third Development Plan, 1984-1987.

United Nations Population Fund (1998). Programme of Assistance to Pacific Island Countries. [http://www.undp.org.fj/un/UNFPA/unfpa_pic.htm].

World Health Organization (2000). Country Profiles: Tuvalu. [http://www.wpro.who.int/themes_focuses/theme2/focus3/country_profiles/tuvalu.htm].

Uganda

World Health Organization (1990). Safe motherhood: abortion. A tabulation of available data on the frequency and mortality of unsafe abortion. Geneva. Unpublished report.

International Planned Parenthood Federation (2000). Country Profiles – Uganda [http://ippfnet.ippf.org/pub/IPPF_Regions/IPPF_CountryProfile.asp?ISOCode=UG]

Macro International Inc. (1995). *Uganda Demographic and Health Survey 1995.* Calverton, Maryland: Macro International.

Uganda physicians and church leaders clash over abortion. *Marathana Christian Journal*, 21 April 2000. [http//:www.mcjonline.com/news/00/20000421d.htm]

Ssendaula, Gerald (1999). Statement by the Minister of Finance, Planning, and Economic Development of Uganda to the General Assembly at its twenty-first special session devoted to the overall review and appraisal of the implementation of the Programme of Action of the International Conference on Population and Development. New York, 30 June 1999.

Turyasingura, G. (1986). Case records and commentary presented for the degree of Master of Medecine (Obstetrics and Gynaecology) at Mulago Hospital, Kampala, Uganda.

Ukraine

Borisov, V. A., compiler (1989). *Naselenie Mira: Demographichesky Spravochnik* (World population: demographic reference book). Moscow: Mysl'.

Chalyi, Olexander (1999). Statement by the Permanent Representative of Ukraine to the General Assembly at its twenty-first special session devoted to the overall review and appraisal of the implementation of the Programme of Action of the International Conference on Population and Development. New York, 30 June 1999.

David, Henry P., and Robert I. McIntyre (1981). *Reproductive Behavior: Central and Eastern European Experience*. New York: Springer Publishing.

Henshaw, Stanley K., Susheela Singh and Taylor Haas (1999). The incidence of abortion worldwide. *International Family Planning Perspectives* (New York), vol. 25 (January), Supplement, pp. S30-S38.

________(1999). Recent trends in abortion rates worldwide. *International Family Planning Perspectives* (New York), vol. 25 no. 1 (January), pp. 44-48.

Popov, Andrei A. (1991). Family planning and induced abortion in the USSR: basic health and demographic characteristics. *Studies in Family Planning* (New York), vol. 22, No. 6 (November/December), pp. 368-377.

Population Action International (1997). Contraception reduces reliance on abortion. http://www.populationaction.org/programs/reliance.htm]

Russian Soviet Federative Socialist Republic, People's Commissariat of Public Health, People's Comissariat of Justice (1920). Ob iskusstvennom preryvanii beremennosti (On the artificial interruption of pregnancy). Decree of 16 November. In *Postanovleniya KPSS i Sovetskogo Pravitel'stva ob Okhrane Zdorov'ya* (Decrees of CPSU and the Soviet Government on public health care). Moscow: Medgiz, 1958.

Ukraine, Ministry of Statistics (1990). *Narodne Hozyaistvo Ukrainskoi SSR v 1989 godu* (National economy of the Ukrainian SSR, 1989). Kiev.

________(1992). *Narodne Gospodarstvo Ukraini u 1991 rotsi* (National economy of Ukraine, 1991). Kiev.

Union of Soviet Socialist Republics, Central Executive Committee and Council of People's Commissars (1936). *O zapreshchenii abortov, uvelichenii material'noi pomoshchi zhenshchinam, ustanovlenii gosudarstvennoi pomoshchi bol'shim sem'yam, rasshirenii seti rodil'nykh domov, detskikh yaslei i detskikh domov, usilenii ugolovnogo nakazaniya za neplatezh alimentov i o nekotorykh izmeneniyakh v zakonodatel'stve o razvodakh (On prohibition of abortions, increase of financial help to women, establishment of state assistance for large families, broadening network of maternity wards, crêches and day-care centres, strengthening of judicial punishment for non-payment of alimonies, and some changes in legislation on divorces). In Postanovleniya KPSS i Sovetskogo Pravitel'stva ob Okhrane Zdorov'ya* (Decrees of CPSU and the Soviet Government on public health care). Moscow: Medgiz, 1958.

Union of Soviet Socialist Republics, Ministry of Public Health (1974). *O Pobochnom Deistvii i Oslozhneniyakh pri Primenenii Oral'nykh Kontratseptivov: Informatsionnoe Pis'mo* (On the side-effects and complications of oral contraceptives: information letter). Compiled by E. A. Babaian, A. S. Lopatin and I. G. Lavretskii. Moscow.

__________ (1982). *O Poryadke Provedeniya Operatsii Iskusstvennogo Preryvaniya Beremennosti* (On the artificial interruption of pregnancies). Decree No. 234, 16 March. Moscow.

__________ (1987). *O Poryadke Provedeniya Operatsii Iskusstvennogo Preryvaniya Beremennosti Rannikh Srokov Metodom Vacuum-aspiratsii* (On the artificial interruption of early-stage pregnancies by vacuum aspiration). Decree No. 757, 5 June. Moscow.

__________ (1987). *O Poryadke Provedeniya Operatsii Iskusstvennogo Preryvaniya Beremennosti Po Nemeditsinskim Pokazaniyam* (On the artificial interruption of pregnancies for non-medical reasons). Decree No. 1342, 31 December. Moscow.

__________ (1989). *Zdorov'e Naseleniya SSSR i Deyatelnost' Uchrezhdenii Zdravookhraneniya v 1988* (Health of the population of the USSR and activities of public-health services in 1988). Moscow.

__________ (1990). *Zdravookhraneniye v SSSR v 1989. Statisticheskie Materialy* (Public health care in the USSR in 1989: statistical data). Moscow.

Union of Soviet Socialist Republics, Moscow State University (1985). *Demografichesky Entsiclopedichesky Slovar'* (Demographic encyclopedic dictionary). Moscow: Sovetskaya Entsiclopediya.

Union of Soviet Socialist Republics, Presidium of the Supreme Soviet (1955). Ob otmene zapreshcheniya abortov (On repeal of the prohibition of abortions). Decree of 23 November. In *Postanovleniya KPSS i Sovetskogo Pravitel'stva ob Okhrane Zdorov'ya Naroda* (Decrees of CPSU and the Soviet Government on public health care). Moscow: Medgiz, 1958.

Union of Soviet Socialist Republics, State Committee on Statistics (1988, 1989). *Naselenie SSSR, 1987* and *1988.* Moscow: Finance and Statistics.

__________(1990). *Demografichesky Ezhegodnik SSSR, 1990* (Demographic yearbook of the USSR, 1990). Moscow: Finance and Statistics.

__________ (1991). Problemy sem'i, okhrany materinstva i detstva (Problems of family, maternal and child care). *Vestnik Statistiki* (Moscow), No. 8, pp. 60-61.

United Nations (1992). Demographic estimates for the newly independent States of the former USSR. *Population Newsletter* (New York), No. 53 (June), p. 22.

United Nations Children's Fund/World Health Organization (1992). Ukraine. Crisis and transition: meeting human needs. Report of a joint UNICEF/WHO/UNFPA/UNDP and WFP mission to Ukraine, 25-28 February. Unpublished.

__________ (1992). The looming crisis in health and the need for international support: overview of the reports on the Commonwealth of Independent States and the Baltic countries. Prepared by the UNICEF/WHO Collaborative Missions with the participation of UNFPA, WFP and UNDP, 17 February - 2 March 1992. Unpublished.

United Arab Emirates

Henshaw, Stanley K., and Evelyn Morrow (1990). *Induced Abortion: A World Review, 1990 Supplement.* New York: The Alan Guttmacher Institute.

Tietze, Christopher, and Stanley K. Henshaw (1986). *Induced Abortion: A World Review*, 1986. New York: The Alan Guttmacher Institute.

World Health Organization (1976). *International Digest of Health Legislation* (Geneva), vol. 27, No. 4, pp. 893-895.

__________ (1988). *International Digest of Health Legislation* (Geneva), vol. 39, No. 2, p. 388.

Population Action International (1997). Ten countries making the mostpProgress in access to contraception, 1982 to 1994. [http://www.populationaction.org/programs/ten.htm].

United Kingdom of Great Britain and Northern Ireland

Alan Guttmacher Institute (1992). Pregnancy and abortion increase among single women in Great Britain. *Family Planning Perspectives* (New York), vol. 24, No. 2 (March/April), pp. 92-93.

British Broadcasting Corporation (BBC) (2000). Health: Abortion rate jumps (Thursday, 30 September 1999). [http://news.bbc.co.uk/hi/english/health/newsid_461000/461648.stm]

Cossey, Dilys (1989). England and Wales, meeting the needs of European women. *Planned Parenthood in Europe* (London), vol. 8, No. 1 (Spring), pp. 10-12.

Francome, Colin (1988). United Kingdom. In *International Handbook on Abortion*, Paul Sachdev, ed. New York; Westport, Connecticut; and London: Greenwood Press, pp. 458-472.

Glendon, Mary Ann (1987). *Abortion and Divorce in Western Law.* Cambridge, Massachusetts: Harvard University Press.

Henshaw, Stanley K., and Evelyn Morrow (1990). *Induced Abortion: A World Review, 1990 Supplement.* New York: The Alan Guttmacher Institute.

Kloss, Diana M., and Bertram L. Raisbeck (1973). *Laws and Population Growth in the United Kingdom.* Law and Population Monograph Series, No. 11. Medford, Massachusetts: Tufts University, The Fletcher School of Law and Diplomacy.

Simpson, Audrey (1989). Northern Ireland, an anomaly. *Planned Parenthood in Europe* (London), vol. 18, No. 1 (Spring), pp. 8-10.

United Kingdom, Department of Health (1999). *NHS Contraceptive Services, England: 1998-1999.* Bulletin No. 1999/30 (November). [can also be found at http:www.doh.gov.uk/public/sb9930.htm].

United Kingdom, Department of Health (2000). National strategy on sexual health and HIV. [http://www.doh.gov.uk/nshs./index.htm or http://www.doh.gov.uk/nshs/strategy.htm].

United Kingdom, Office of Population Censuses and Surveys (1988). *Abortion Statistics. Legal Abortions Carried Out Under the 1967 Abortion Act in England and Wales.* 1987 Series AB, No. 14. London: Her Majesty's Stationery Office.

United Nations Fund for Population Activities (1979). *Survey of Laws on Fertility Control.* New York: UNFPA.

United Republic of Tanzania

Armon, P. J. (1979). Maternal deaths in the Kilimanjaro region of Tanzania. *Transactions of the Royal Society of Tropical Medicine and Hygiene* (London), vol. 73, No. 3, pp. 284-288.

Cook, Rebecca J., and Bernard M. Dickens (1979). Abortion laws in Commonwealth countries. *International Digest of Health Legislation* (Geneva), vol. 30, No. 3, pp. 395-502.

Justesen, Aafke, Saidi H. Kapiga and Henri A. G. A. van Asten (1992). Abortion in a hospital setting: hidden realities in Dar es Salaam, Tanzania. *Studies in Family Planning* (New York), vol. 23, No. 5 (September/October), pp. 325-329.

Macro International Inc. (1996). *Tanzania Demographic and Health Survey 1996.* Calverton, Maryland: Macro International.

Price, T. G. (1984). Preliminary report on maternal deaths in the Southern Highlands of Tanzania in 1983. *Journal of Obstetrics and Gynecology of Eastern and Central Africa (Nairobi, Kenya)*, vol. 3, No. 3, pp. 103-110.

Uche, U. U. (1978). Report of the African Regional Law Panel field trips with special reference to abortion laws. Paper prepared for A Strategy for Abortion Management in Africa: African Regional Workshop, Nairobi, Kenya. 20-23 March.

United Nations (1989). *Case Studies in Population Policy: United Republic of Tanzania.* Sales No. E.90.XIII.29.

United Nations Fund for Population Activities (1979). *Survey of Laws on Fertility Control.* New York: UNFPA.

United Nations Population Fund, and Harvard Law School Library (1991). *Annual Review of Population Law, 1991*, vol. 15. New York: UNFPA.

World Health Organization (1990). Safe motherhood: abortion. A tabulation of available data on the frequency and mortality of unsafe abortion. Geneva. Unpublished report.

United States of America

Alan Guttmacher Institute (2000). Facts in Brief: Induced abortion (February). [http://www.agi-usa.org/pubs/fb_induced_abortion.html]

Anonymous (1992). Court reaffirms Roe but upholds restrictions. *Family Planning Perspectives* (New York), vol. 24, No. 4 (July/August), pp. 174-177.

Boland, Reed (1990). Abortion law in industrialized countries. *Law, Medicine and Health Care* (Boston, Massachusetts), vol. 18, No. 4 (Winter), pp. 404-418.

Centres for Disease Contro and Preventionl (2000). Abortion surveillance: preliminary analysis – United States, 1997. *Morbidity and Mortality Weekly Report*, vol. 48, Nos. 51-52 (7 January 2000), pp.1171-1174, 1191.

de Guibert-Lantoine, Catherine, and Alain Monnier (1992). La conjoncture démographique: l'Europe et les pays développés d'Outre-Mer. *Population* (Paris), vol. 47, No. 4 (septembre-octobre), pp. 1017-1036.

Henshaw, Stanley K. (1990). Induced abortion: a world review, 1990. In *Induced Abortion: A World Review, 1990 Supplement,* by Stanley K. Henshaw and Evelyn Morrow. New York: The Alan Guttmacher Institute.

__________ (1992). Abortion trends in 1987 and 1988: age and race. *Family Planning Perspectives* (New York), vol. 24, No. 2 (March/April), pp. 85-86, 96.

Henshaw, Stanley K., and Jennifer Van Vort (1990). Abortion services in the United States, 1987 and 1988. *Family Planning Perspectives* (New York), vol. 22, No. 3 (May/June), pp. 102-108, 142.

Henshaw, Stanley K., Susheela Singh and Taylor Haas (1999). The incidence of abortion worldwide. *International Family Planning Perspectives* (New York), vol. 25 (January), Supplement, pp. S30-S38.

__________(1999). Recent trends in abortion rates worldwide. *International Family Planning Perspectives* (New York), vol. 25 no. 1 (January), pp. 44-48.

International Planned Parenthood Federation (2000). Country Profiles: United States [http://ippfnet.ippf.org/pub/IPPF_Regions/IPPF_CountryProfile.asp?ISOCode=US]

Legge, Jerome S., Jr. (1985). *Abortion Policy: An Evaluation of the Consequences for Maternal and Infant Health.* Albany, New York: State University of New York Press.

Lewin, Tamar (1992). Hurdles increase for many women seeking abortion. *The New York Times* (15 March), p. I-1.

National Abortion Action League (NARAL Foundation) (1992). *Facing a Future Without Choice: A Report of Reproductive Liberty in America.* Washington, D.C.: The NARAL Foundation.

__________ (1993). *Who Decides? A State-by-State of Abortion Rights.* Washington, D.C.: The NARAL Foundation.

Susser, Mervyn (1992). Induced abortion and health as a value. *American Journal of Public Health* (Washington, D.C.), vol. 82, No. 10 (October), pp. 1323-1324.

Torres, Silverman, and Aida Torres (1989). *Pregnancy, Contraception, and Family Planning Services in Industrialized Countries.* New Haven: Yale University Press.

Tribe, Laurence H. (1991). *Abortion: The Clash of Absolutes.* New York: W. W. Norton and Co.

United Nations Fund for Population Activities (1979). *Survey of Laws on Fertility Control.* New York: UNFPA.

Ventura, Stephanie J., and others (1992). *Trends in Pregnancies and Pregnancy Rates, United States, 1980-88.* Monthly Vital Statistics Report, vol. 41, No. 6, Supplement. Hyattsville, Maryland: United States Department of Health and Human Services, National Center for Health Statistics.

Uruguay

International Planned Parenthood Federation (1974). Abortion: changing attitudes in Latin America. *People* (London), vol. 1, No. 2 (January), pp. 26-27.

__________ (1988). *Family Planning in Latin America and the Caribbean.* Country Fact Sheets. New York.

Pan American Health Organization (1990). *Health Conditions in the Americas: 1990 Edition*, vol. II. Scientific Publication, No. 524. Washington, D.C.

Perez-Otermin, Jorge (1999). Statement by the Permanent Representative of Uruguay to the General Assembly at its twenty-first special session devoted to the overall review and appraisal of the implementation of the Programme of Action of the International Conference on Population and Development. New York, 1 July 1999.

Population Crisis Committee (1979). *World Abortion Trends.* Population: Briefing Papers on Issues of National and International Importance in the Population Field, No. 9 (April). Washington, D.C.

Thevenet, Emilio F. (1978). Aborto en el Uruguay. Montevideo: Impresora Cordon. Abstract in English.

United Nations Fund for Population Activities (1979). *Survey of Laws on Fertility Control.* New York: UNFPA.

United Nations Population Fund (1993). *Latin America and the Caribbean.* New York: UNFPA.

Uzbekistan

Borisov, V. A., compiler (1989). *Naselenie Mira: Demographichesky Spravochnik* (World population: demographic reference book). Moscow: Mysl'.

David, Henry P., and Robert I. McIntyre (1981). *Reproductive Behavior: Central and Eastern European Experience.* New York: Springer Publishing.

Henshaw, Stanley K., Susheela Singh and Taylor Haas (1999). The incidence of abortion worldwide. *International Family Planning Perspectives* (New York), vol. 25 (January), Supplement, pp. S30-S38.

__________(1999). Recent trends in abortion rates worldwide. *International Family Planning Perspectives* (New York), vol. 25 no. 1 (January), pp. 44-48.

Kuptsova, L. Iu. (1975). *Izuchenie aborta v sotsial'no - gigienicheskom aspekte v gorode Tashkente. Avtoreferat dissertatsii* (Studies of abortion in the city of Tashkent). Synopsis of doctoral dissertation. Tashkent.

Macro International Inc. (1996). *Uzbekistan Demographic and Health Survey 1996.* Calverton, Maryland: Macro International.

Popov, Andrei A. (1991). Family planning and induced abortion in the USSR: basic health and demographic characteristics. *Studies in Family Planning* (New York), vol. 22, No. 6 (November/December), pp. 368-377.

Union of Soviet Socialist Republics, Central Executive Committee and Council of People's Commissars (1936). *O zapreshchenii abortov, uvelichenii material'noi pomoshchi zhenshchinam, ustanovlenii gosudarstvennoi pomoshchi bol'shim sem'yam, rasshirenii seti rodil'nykh domov, detskikh yaslei i detskikh domov, usilenii ugolovnogo nakazaniya za neplatezh alimentov i o nekotorykh izmeneniyakh v zakonodatel'stve o razvodakh* (On prohibition of abortions, increase of financial help to women, establishment of state assistance for large families, broadening network of maternity wards, crêches and day-care centres, strengthening of judicial punishment for non-payment of alimonies and some changes in legislation on divorces). *In Postanovleniya KPSS i Sovetskogo Pravitel'stva ob Okhrane Zdorov'ya* (Decrees of CPSU and the Soviet Government on public health care). Moscow: Medgiz, 1958.

Union of Soviet Socialist Republics, Ministry of Public Health (1974). *O Pobochnom Deistvii i Oslozhneniyakh pri Primenenii Oral'nykh Kontratseptivov: Informatsionnoe Pis'mo* (On the side-effects and complications of oral contraceptives: information letter). Compiled by E. A. Babaian, A. S. Lopatin and I. G. Lavretskii. Moscow.

__________ (1982). *O Poryadke Provedeniya Operatsii Iskusstvennogo Preryvaniya Beremennosti* (On the artificial interruption of pregnancies). Decree No. 234, 16 March. Moscow.

__________ (1987). *O Poryadke Provedeniya Operatsii Iskusstvennogo Preryvaniya Beremennosti Rannikh Srokov Metodom Vacuum-aspiratsii* (On the artificial interruption of early-stage pregnancies by vacuum aspiration). Decree No. 757, 5 June. Moscow.

__________ (1987). *O Poryadke Provedeniya Operatsii Iskusstvennogo Preryvaniya Beremennosti Po Nemeditsinskim Pokazaniyam* (On the artificial interruption of pregnancies for non-medical reasons). Decree No. 1342, 31 December. Moscow.

__________ (1989). *Zdorov'e Naseleniya SSSR i Deyatelnost' Uchrezhdenii Zdravookhraneniya v 1988* (Health of the population of the USSR and activities of public-health services in 1988). Moscow.

__________ (1990). *Zdravookhraneniye v SSSR v 1989: Statisticheskie Materialy* (Public health care in the USSR in 1989: statistical data). Moscow.

Union of Soviet Socialist Republics, Moscow State University (1985). *Demografichesky Entsiclopedichesky Slovar'* (Demographic encyclopedic dictionary). Moscow: Sovetskaya Entsiclopediya.

Union of Soviet Socialist Republics, Presidium of the Supreme Soviet (1955). Ob otmene zapreshcheniya abortov (On repeal of the prohibition of abortions). Decree of 23 November. In *Postanovleniya KPSS i Sovetskogo Pravitel'stva ob Okhrane Zdorov'ya Naroda* (Decrees of CPSU and the Soviet Government on public health care). Moscow: Medgiz, 1958.

Union of Soviet Socialist Republics, State Committee on Statistics (1988, 1989). *Naselenie SSSR, 1987* and *1988*. Moscow: Finance and Statistics.

__________(1990). *Demografichesky Ezhegodnik SSSR, 1990* (Demographic yearbook of the USSR, 1990). Moscow: Finance and Statistics.

__________ (1991). Problemy sem'i, okhrany materinstva i detstva (Problems of family, maternal and child care). *Vestnik Statistiki* (Moscow), No. 8, pp. 60-61.

United Nations (1992). Demographic estimates for the newly independent States of the former USSR. *Population Newsletter* (New York), No. 53 (June), p. 22.

United Nations Children's Fund/World Health Organization (1992). Republic of Uzbekistan. Report of a joint UNICEF/WHO/UNFPA/UNDP and WFP mission, 21 February - 2 March. Unpublished.

__________ (1992). The looming crisis and fresh opportunity: health in Kazakhstan, Kyrgyzstan, Tadjikistan, Turkmenistan and Uzbekistan with emphasis on women and children. Report of a joint UNICEF/WHO/UNFPA/UNDP and WFP mission, 17 February - 2 March. Unpublished.

__________ (1992). The looming crisis in health and the need for international support: overview of the reports on the Commonwealth of Independent States and the Baltic countries. Prepared by the UNICEF/WHO Collaborative Missions with the participation of UNFPA, WFP and UNDP, 17 February - 2 March 1992. Unpublished.

Vanuatu

Bedford, Richard, ed. (1989). *Population of Vanuatu: Analysis of the 1979 Census*. Population Monograph No. 2. Noumea, New Caledonia: South Pacific Commission.

Cook, Rebecca J., and Bernard M. Dickens (1988). International development in abortion laws: 1977-88. *American Journal of Public Health* (Washington, D.C.), vol. 78, No. 10 (October), pp. 1305-1311.

International Planned Parenthood Federation (1984). Family planning in Vanuatu. IPPF Open File: a news digest of the world's largest voluntary family planning organization (two weeks ending 9 March). London. Mimeographed.

International Planned Parenthood Federation (2000). Country Profiles: Vanuatu [http://ippfnet.ippf.org/pub/IPPF_Regions/IPPF_CountryProfile.asp?ISOCode=VU]

Jarayaman, T. K. (1995). *Demographic and Socio-economic Determinants of Contraceptive Use among Urban Women in the Melanesian Countries in the South Pacific: A Case Study of Port Vila Town in Vanuatu.* EDRC Occasional Paper No. 011. Manila: Asian Development Bank, Economics and Development Resource Centre.

Song Shem, Keiasipai (1999). Statement by the Minister of Health of Vanuatu to the General Assembly at its twenty-first special session devoted to the overall review and appraisal of the implementation of the

Programme of Action of the International Conference on Population and Development. New York, 2 July1999.

United Nations Committee on the Rights of the Child (1997). *Consideration of Reports Submitted by States Parties under Article 44 of the Convention: Convention on the Rights of the Child: Initial Reports of States Parties Due in 1995.* Vanuatu. (CRC/C/28/Add.8).

United Nations Fund for Population Activities, and Harvard Law School Library (1982). *Annual Review of Population Law, 1982*, vol. 8. New York: UNFPA.

World Health Organization (1982). *International Digest of Health Legislation* (Geneva), vol. 33, No. 4, p. 720.

Venezuela

Colmenares, Maria Magdalena (1988). Case study on Venezuela. Paper prepared for the United Nations Secretariat, Expert Group Meeting on Social Support Measures for the Advancement of Women, Vienna, 14-18 November. EGM/SSMAW/1988/CS.15.

International Planned Parenthood Federation (1988). *Family Planning in Latin America and the Caribbean.* Country Fact Sheets. New York.

International Planned Parenthood Federation (2000). Country Profiles: Venezuela [http://ippfnet.ippf.org/pub/IPPF_Regions/IPPF_CountryProfile.asp?ISOCode=VE].

Pan American Health Organization (1990). *Health Conditions in the Americas: 1990 Edition*, vol. I. Scientific Publication, No. 524. Washington, D.C.

__________(1998). Country Health Data: Venezuela. [http://165.158.1.110/english/sha/prflven.html].

Singh, Susheela, and Deirdre Wulf (1996). Issues in Brief: Anoverview of clandestine abortion in Latin America. *International Family Planning Perspectives*, vol. 22, No. 4 (December 1996).

United Nations Fund for Population Activities (1979). *Survey of Laws on Fertility Control.* New York: UNFPA.

__________ (1993). *Latin America and the Caribbean.* New York: UNFPA.

Urbina, Yolanda Rojas (1999). Statement by the Vice-Minister of the Family of Venezuela to the General Assembly at it twenty-first special session devoted to the overall review and appraisal of the implementation of the Programme of Action of the International Conference on Population and Development. New York, 1 July1999.

Viel, Benjamin (1988). Latin America. In *International Handbook on Abortion*, Paul Sachdev, ed. New York; Westport, Connecticut; and London: Greenwood Press.

World Health Organization (1978). *International Digest of Health Legislation* (Geneva), vol. 29, No. 3, pp. 688-689.

Viet Nam

Can, N. (1983). Fertility regulation methods used in Viet Nam. In *Research on the Regulation of Human Fertility: Needs of Developing Countries and Priorities for the Future*, vol. 1, E. Diczfalusy and A. Diczfalusy, eds. Copenhagen, Denmark: Scriptor.

Deutsche Presse-Agentur (dpa) (1999). Condom shortage helps fuel Viet Nam's soaring abortion rate (9 July 1999).

Goodkind, Daniel, and Phan Thuc Anh (1997). Comment: reasons for rising condom use in Viet Nam. In *International Family Planning Perspectives*, vol. 23, No. 4 (December).

Henshaw, Stanley K., and Evelyn Morrow (1990). *Induced Abortion: A World Review, 1990 Supplement.* New York: The Alan Guttmacher Institute.

Henshaw, Stanley K., Susheela Singh and Taylor Haas (1999). The incidence of abortion worldwide. *International Family Planning Perspectives* (New York), vol. 25 (January), Supplement, pp. S30-S38.

__________(1999). Recent trends in abortion rates worldwide. *International Family Planning Perspectives* (New York), vol. 25 no. 1 (January), pp. 44-48.

Institute for the Protection of Mother and Newborn (1985). Maternal mortality in selected areas of Viet Nam. Paper prepared for the World Health Organization Interregional Meeting on Prevention of Maternal Mortality, Geneva, 11-15 November.

International Planned Parenthood Federation (2000). Country Profiles: Viet Nam [http://ippfnet.ippf.org/pub/IPPF_Regions/IPPF_CountryProfile.asp?ISOCode=VN].

Lâ, Thanh-Liêm (1987). La planification familiale au Viêt-Nam. *Population* (Paris), vol. 42, No. 2 (mars/avril), pp. 321-336.

Macro International Inc. (1997). *Viet Nam Demographic and Health Survey 1997.* Calverton, Maryland: Macro International.

Nam Phuong, Nguyen. Population-Vietnam: amid social change, abortion numbers soar. Inter Press Service, 17 December 1999. [http://vietsandiego.com/vietnews/archives/dec99/vg1281G.html].

Presswell, Nanette J. (1982). An approach to family planning for Indochinese refugee women. *Australian Family Physician* (Joliment, Victoria, Australia), vol. 11, No. 8, pp. 644-648.

Ross, John A., and others (1992). *Family Planning and Child Survival Programmes As Assessed in 1991.* New York: The Population Council.

Tietze, Christopher (1983). *Induced Abortion: A World Review, 1983.* New York: The Population Council.

Trung Chien, Tran Thi (1999). Statement by the Minister-Chairwoman of the National Committee for Population and Family Planning of Viet Nam to the General Assembly at its twenty-first special session devoted to the overall review and appraisal of the implementation of the Programme of Action of the International Conference on Population and Development. New York, 1 July1999.

United Nations Population Fund, and Harvard Law School Library (1989). *Annual Review of Population Law, 1986*, vol. 13. New York: UNFPA .

__________ (1990). *Annual Review of Population Law, 1987*, vol. 14. New York: UNFPA.

__________ (1992). *Annual Review of Population Law, 1989*, vol. 16. New York: UNFPA.

Yemen

Macro International Inc. (1997). *Yemen Demographic and Health Survey 1997.* Calverton, Maryland: Macro International.

United Nations Fund for Population Activities (1976). *Survey of Contraceptive Laws: Country Profiles, Checklists and Summaries.* New York: UNFPA

Yemen (1992). *National Population Strategy, 1990-2000 and Population Action Plan.* Sana'a.

Yugoslavia

Andolšek, Lidija (1988). Yugoslavia. In *International Handbook on Abortion*, Paul Sachdev, ed. New York; Westport, Connecticut; and London: Greenwood Press.

Cook, Rebecca J. (1989). Abortion laws and policies: challenges and opportunities. In "Women's health in the third world: the impact of unwanted pregnancy", A. Rosenfield and others, eds. *International Journal of Gynecology and Obstetrics* (Limerick, Ireland), Supplement No. 3, pp. 61-87.

Cook, Rebecca J., and Bernard M. Dickens (1988). International developments in abortion laws: 1977-88. *American Journal of Public Health* (Washington, D.C.), vol. 78, No. 10 (October), pp. 1305-1311.

David, Henry P., and Robert J. McIntyre (1982). *Reproductive Behavior: Central and Eastern European Experience.* New York: Springer Publishing Company.

Henshaw, Stanley K., Susheela Singh and Taylor Haas (1999). The incidence of abortion worldwide. *International Family Planning Perspectives* (New York), vol. 25 (January), Supplement, pp. S30-S38.

__________(1999). Recent trends in abortion rates worldwide. *International Family Planning Perspectives* (New York), vol. 25 no. 1 (January), pp. 44-48.

Kapor-Stanulovic, Nila (1989). Liberal approach for a patchwork population. *People* (London), vol. 16, No. 3, pp. 16-18.

Malacic, Janez (1989). Family planning population policy and declining birth rates in Yugoslavia. *Planned Parenthood in Europe* (London), vol. 18, No. 2 (September).

__________ (1990). Political changes in Yugoslavia and family planning. *Planned Parenthood in Europe* (London), vol. 19, No. 2 (September).

Royston, Erica, and Sue Armstrong, eds. (1989). *Preventing Maternal Deaths.* Geneva: World Health Organization.

United Nations Fund for Population Activities (1976). *Survey of Contraceptive Laws: Country Profiles, Checklists and Summaries.* New York: UNFPA.

United Nations Fund for Population Activities, and Harvard Law School Library (1979). *Survey of Laws on Fertility Control.* New York: UNFPA.

__________ (1980). *Annual Review of Population Law, 1979.* New York: UNFPA.

World Health Organization (1970). Comparative health legislation: abortion laws. *International Digest of Health Legislation* (Geneva), vol. 21, No. 3, pp. 437-512.

World Health Organization, Regional Office for Europe (1990). Yugoslavia. *Entre nous: The European Family Planning Magazine* (Copenhagen), No. 16 (September), pp. 11-12.

Zambia

Castle, Mary Ann, Rosemary Likwa and Maxine Whittaker (1990). Observations on abortion in Zambia. *Studies in Family Planning* (New York), vol. 21, No. 4 (July/August), pp. 231-235.

Coeytaux, Francine A. (1988). Induced abortion in sub-Saharan Africa: what we know and do not know. *Studies in Family Planning* (New York), vol. 19, No. 3 (May/June), pp. 186-190.

Cook, Rebecca J., and Bernard M. Dickens (1979). Abortion laws in Commonwealth countries. *International Digest of Health Legislation* (Geneva), vol. 30, No. 3, pp. 395-502.

Frank, Odile (1988). The demand for fertility control in sub-Saharan Africa. *Studies in Family Planning* (New York), vol. 19, No. 4 (July/August), pp. 181-121.

Goliber, Thomas J. (1989). *Africa's expanding population: old problems, new policies. Population Bulletin,* vol. 44, No. 3. Washington, D.C.: Population Reference Bureau.

Henshaw, Stanley K., Susheela Singh and Taylor Haas (1999). The incidence of abortion worldwide. *International Family Planning Perspectives* (New York), vol. 25 (January), Supplement, pp. S30-S38.

__________(1999). Recent trends in abortion rates worldwide. *International Family Planning Perspectives* (New York), vol. 25 no. 1 (January), pp. 44-48.

International Planned Parenthood Federation (2000). Country Profiles – Zambia [http://ippfnet.ippf.org/pub/IPPF_Regions/IPPF_CountryProfile.asp?ISOCode=ZM]

Likwa R.N., and M. Whittaker (1996). The characteristics of women presenting for abortion and complications of illegal abortions at the University Teaching Hospital, Lusaka, Zambia: an explorative study. *African Journal of Fertility, Sexuality and Reproductive Health,* vol. 1, No. 1, pp. 42–49.

Macro International Inc. (1996). *Zambia Demographic and Health Survey 1996.* Calverton, Maryland: Macro International.

Mhango, Chisale, Roger Rochat and Andrew Arkutu (1986). Reproductive mortality in Lusaka, Zambia, 1982-1983. *Studies in Family Planning* (New York), vol. 17, No. 5 (September/October), pp. 243-251.

Tembo, Christon S. (1999). Statement by the Vice-President of Zambia to the General Assembly at its twenty-first special session devoted to the overall review and Appraisal of the implementation of the Programme of Action of the International Conference on Population and Development. New York, 30 June 1999.

United Nations Fund for Population Activities (1979). *Survey of Laws on Fertility Control.* New York: UNFPA.

Zimbabwe

Cook, Rebecca, and Bernard M. Dickens (1979). Abortion laws in Commonwealth countries. *International Digest of Health Legislation* (Geneva), vol. 30, No. 3, pp. 395-502.

Feltoe, G., and T. J. Nyapadi (1989). *Law and Medicine in Zimbabwe.* Harare: Baobab Books and Legal Resources Foundation.

Hove, R. C. (1999). Statement by the Planning Commissioner of Zimbabwe to the General Assembly at its twenty-first special session devoted to the overall review and appraisal of the implementation of the Programme of Action of the International Conference on Population and Development. New York, 2 July 1999.

International Planned Parenthood Federation (2000). Country Profiles – Zimbabwe [http://ippfnet.ippf.org/pub/IPPF_Regions/IPPF_CountryProfile.asp?ISOCode=ZW]

MacPherson, T. A. (1981). A retrospective study of maternal deaths in the Zimbabwean Black. *Central African Medical Journal* (Harare), vol. 27, No. 4, pp. 57-60.

Macro International Inc. (1994). *Zimbabwe Demographic and Health Survey 1994.* Calverton, Maryland: Macro International.

Ncube, Welshman (1989). *Family Law in Zimbabwe.* Harare: Legal Resources Foundation.

Stewart, Julie, and others (1990). The legal situation of women in Zimbabwe. In *Legal Situation of Women in Southern Africa,* Julie Stewart and Alice Armstrong, eds. Harare: University of Zimbabwe Publications.

United Nations Fund for Population Activities, and Harvard Law School Library (1979). *Annual Review of Population Law.* New York: UNFPA.

Zimbabwe, Central Statistical Office, and Institute for Resource Development/Macro Systems, Inc. (1989). *Zimbabwe Demographic and Health Survey, 1988.* Harare, Zimbabwe: Ministry of Finance, Economic Planning and Development; and Columbia, Maryland: Institute for Resource Development.